*The authors dedicate this book to their families and
to journalists worldwide
struggling to report the news freely.*

Contents

8   *Beyond the Basics*   137

9   *Practical Exercises*   170

11   Careers   234

Preface

The style of writing in this book isn't like that in other college textbooks you've read. It's informal. It's conversational. The reason is simple: that's how you must learn to write as a broadcast or Internet news journalist. One of the first concepts we discuss is the three Cs: Clear, Concise, and Conversational. It didn't make sense to approach this book in any other way. We use the style we're attempting to teach.

The approach of this text is also decidedly nuts and bolts. Each chapter is designed to tell you what you need to know to pursue a career in broadcast or Internet journalism, from news gathering to conducting interviews to thinking ethically.

Up to this point, Internet writing has almost exclusively fallen into the realm of print (newspaper) courses, mostly by default. But the style of writing for the Internet is a unique mix of print *and* broadcast writing. And because most professional broadcasters today are called upon to write versions of their stories for the Internet, we integrate this important component into the text.

You'll have lots of opportunities to apply what you learn as you go because one of the best ways to become a good writer is through practice. The more you practice now the farther ahead you'll be when it comes to entering the ultracompetitive fields of radio, television, and Internet. Regardless of the medium, the secret to success begins and ends with good, strong writing.

Acknowledgments

A special thanks to all who generously gave permission for their work products to be reproduced, especially CBS News President Andrew Heyward, the Associated Press, CNN and Reuters. Much appreciation also to our many friends working in radio, television or the Internet who lent advice and support to this educational project. Thumbs up to the Allyn & Bacon team, especially Karen Hanson, Molly Taylor, Michael Kish, Karen Mason and Martha White Tenney who surmounted unusual challenges due to precisely formatted and styled scripts in preparing this text for publication. And finally, but not least, deep gratitude and love to our families who indulge our passion for journalism daily, and encourage us even when we come home from long days at work . . . only to sit down and write some more.

We would also like to thank the following individuals who reviewed this book and offered helpful suggestions:

Paul Adams, California State, Fresno
Jeanni Atkins, University of Mississippi
Lawrence Budner, Rhode Island College
Marian L. Huttenstine, Mississippi State University
Jeffrey McCall, DePauw University
Catherine M. Stablein, College of DuPage
L. Lee Thomas, Doane College

About the Authors

This textbook is written by Sharyl Attkisson and Don Rodney Vaughan, who have more than forty years experience between them in broadcast and Internet journalism.

Sharyl Attkisson is a writer, correspondent, and substitute anchor for Columbia Broadcasting System (CBS) News. She also writes for CBS News Radio and the CBS News Web site. She's anchored for Cable News Network (CNN), hosted the Newsweek Production of the weekly Public Broadcasting System (PBS) series HealthWeek, and worked in four local news television markets as reporter, anchor, and producer. Her favorite moment in journalism was being among the first journalists to fly on a B-52 combat mission over Kosovo.

Don Vaughan has worked in small markets as a radio and TV news writer and reporter and has taught broadcast news writing at Mississippi State University. He's pursuing a Ph.D. in Mass Communication at the University of Southern Mississippi. Vaughan was inspired to become a broadcast journalist when he was a kid listening to J. Mark Shands reporting state and local news over WKOR-AM in Starkville, Mississippi.

1

Defining and Diffusing News

Chapter Objectives

- To define "news"
- To discuss news value and judgment
- To introduce the theory of broadcast news diffusion
- To identify some barriers to clearly written stories
- To describe techniques for unmistakably clear writing

What, exactly, is news? The simple dictionary definition is *current information; reports of recent happenings*. But the practicing definition is much broader and depends on a number of subjective factors, such as who is making the determination? Who is the intended audience? What type of news program is involved? For example, a fire at a senior citizens' center in Oakland, California, might make for an interesting and important report on the local evening news, but would never see the light of day on a national network news magazine show such as *60 Minutes*, which is long form, investigative in nature, and aimed at a national audience.

In this first chapter, we'll explore news value and judgment. Then we'll address the theory of broadcast news diffusion and why it's so important that stories be written so that they can be diffused—or spread—frequently and accurately. The single most important factor in accomplishing this task is unmistakably clear writing.

Defining "News"

There are two basic types of news: *hard news* and *soft news*.

1. **Hard news** refers to stories that can't be ignored, including *breaking news, current issues* and *happenings*, and *agenda-setting news*.

- Hard news is often **breaking news,** meaning the story is developing at the same moment it's being reported. For example, in Tupelo, Mississippi, a tornado wipes out one entire neighborhood and is moving toward another. There isn't a Tupelo area newscast or Web site that wouldn't devote significant coverage to such a story of obvious local importance and interest. Many of them would choose to break into regular programming with live coverage as the story breaks.
- **Current issues and happenings** refers to current stories of a serious nature, though not necessarily breaking or developing at the moment. Examples are a criminal trial and a political race.
- **Agenda-setting news** stories are ones that you, your colleagues, or superiors decide your audience should know about, even if the audience may not realize its relevance or importance beforehand. An example is privacy on the Internet, which is something that may not be a burning issue in many people's minds, but could be reported in such a way that demonstrates how it affects them and why they should care.

2. **Soft news** refers to a broad range of stories that appeal to the audience because the stories are amusing, entertaining, informative, dramatic, weird, or otherwise compelling. Examples are a human interest story on a local beekeeper and a report on how to save money when shopping for groceries.

In the following box, determine which of the following topics are hard and which are soft. Identify whether the hard stories are breaking, current issues and happenings, or agenda setting. Our answers are provided at the end of the chapter.

Hard or Soft?

1. A television news profile of an elderly woman who's organizing an effort to chase the drug dealers out of her neighborhood
2. A radio news report on a rush-hour traffic pileup involving twenty cars
3. An Internet news exposé about underground gambling at local bars
4. A television report on preparing your garden for winter
5. A radio report on a rally for a candidate for governor

News Value and Judgment

There's an infinite supply of hard and soft news stories, but only a limited amount of space available in a given television newscast, radio broadcast, or news Web site. Choosing which stories will actually be seen and heard requires predicting which ones have the highest **news value** to your audience. Audiences tend to place the highest value on news they believe to be *newsworthy,* or important and relevant to their lives.

The media as gatekeeper

Determining what news to report is a practice known as exercising **news judgment.** Everyone who writes broadcast or Internet news exercises news judgment and is thrust into the role of **gatekeeper.**

As gatekeeper, you stand at the figurative gateway between all the information that's out there in the world, and the audience. *You* determine what gets through to the audience. . . and what doesn't. That decision should be based, in large part, on the demographics of your audience. The audience could be mostly college students, senior citizens, low income people, middle-class parents, or a mix of several prevalent groups. Each audience is different; each has its own unique ideas of what constitutes news. The questions you must ask before writing any story include will this be of value to the audience? How can I write the story in such a way as to maximize its news value to the audience?

Proximity, Timeliness, Significance, and the Medium

Proximity, timeliness, significance, and the medium are all factors that influence whether a particular audience is touched or moved by a given news story and are all factors to consider when judging news value.

Proximity: Up Close and Personal
Proximity is *the feeling of closeness to a particular news event* and, under that heading, three elements increase a story's newsworthiness to the audience: *compassion, familiarity,* and *vicariousness:*

1. The **compassion element** of proximity applies to stories that evoke feelings of empathy or sympathy for someone else, as in a tragedy ("Oh, that's terrible. I hope no one was hurt!").
2. The **familiarity element** of proximity applies to stories that involve news about someone a viewer might know, as in a school shooting ("Listen, that could be someone we know.") or a historic building being torn down ("Hey, that's where our favorite antique bookstore is!").
3. The **vicariousness element** of proximity applies to stories that cause audience members to place themselves inside the story ("Hey, I drove through that intersection just five minutes before that massive pileup occurred. I could have been one of the victims!").

Timeliness: The Time Is Ripe

The next factor, after proximity, that can help you judge a story's news value is **timeliness.**

- *Audiences are more likely to pay attention to events that are timely in the sense that they are happening or have just happened.* Two examples are the first results from an important local election and news that a neighborhood child has just been kidnapped. Note that both of the examples also have proximity working in their favor.
- *Stories are also considered timely if they coincide with events happening in the audience's real life.* A television news story detailing ways to keep your child safe from abductors might be timely if it's reported at the same time as the neighborhood kidnapping. Another example is an Internet news story giving advice on income tax preparation. It would be very timely in the weeks leading up to April 15th, but would not be particularly timely—or of high news value to your audience—if it appeared on the Web site in May after most people have already filed their income tax returns.

Significance: The Direct Effect

Significance—whether the story has a direct effect, immediate or long term, on the audience—is another factor that influences news judgment. There are countless ways in which a story may prove significant. It could be significant because it tells the audience how to save money, how to avoid getting cheated, or how to stay healthy. The story could discuss a common disease, a well-known personality, or a local weather phenomenon. Research shows that audiences tend to judge stories to be highly significant when they are about familiar people, institutions, or issues.[1]

The Medium

Finally, the **medium** plays a role in determining a story's news value. For example television stories must be visually compelling; radio stories rely on sound, rather than pictures. Therefore, a passenger jet captured on videotape making a crash landing might be a compelling television news story, but it would have a lower news value to radio listeners who obviously can't see the pictures. A radio newscast might give such a story less prominence or might not cover it at all.

Sutton Says

Many people in broadcast and Internet news have devised their own methods for determining news value and writing clear stories. One example comes from a woman named Amy Sutton, who anchored, produced, and wrote local and national television news for many years. See the box for three principles she developed for news writers that we call Sutton Says.

Broadcast News Diffusion

You've heard the sayings "the news spread like wildfire" or "good news travels fast." On occasion, bad news travels even faster, and, in the process of spreading quickly, the facts in a broadcast or Internet news story can be inadvertently misquoted and misunderstood. How many times have people passed along bits of stories they heard on the news or read online only to later discover they didn't have the whole story or didn't really understand it?

Sutton Says . . .

1. ***Don't assume the audience will find a story interesting just because you do.***
   What's fascinating to some audience members may be dull as dishwater to others. Likewise, what interests *you* may not be of interest to your audience at large. You might be enthralled by the dangerous college campus fad of car surfing, but, if your audience members skew higher than age forty, they may not care about the topic in the slightest, that is, unless you're able to determine that many of them have college-aged children.
2. ***Don't assume the audience wants or needs too many details.***
   Give newspapers and magazines rights to all the minute details. In conventional broadcasting newscasts, there's little time for anything beyond the basics that it takes to tell a story in an accurate and interesting fashion. Typical broadcast news scripts range in length from about fifteen seconds (:15) to two minutes (2:00). Composing your scripts on the computer allows you the luxury of writing and then editing out some details to trim the story to the appropriate length. The challenge, of course, is to do this, but still make the story complete and compelling.
3. ***Don't write for a highly educated audience.***
   Even if your audience members *are* well educated, keep in mind that the words in your story will go by in an instant. Unlike newspapers or even the Internet, there's no chance for viewers or listeners to re-read, contemplate, or mull over meanings. If people have to stop even for a moment to discern the meaning of a word you've used, you've lost their attention. Also, radio listeners and television viewers typically don't focus their entire attention on a given story. They might be cooking dinner while listening to a radio newscast or talking with their children at the same time they're watching the evening news. Write simple stories that are easily understood by busy, distracted people and by those with a only high school education or less.

If a story isn't written accurately and in a way that its meaning is crystal clear to the audience, it's meaningless. It can cause confusion and may raise more questions than it answers, which is certainly not a model for effective communication. What's worse is that the misunderstanding and confusion from a poorly written story only stands to be compounded when it's passed along to others.

The word *diffuse* comes from a Latin word meaning "to spread or to send out in all directions." The way broadcast and Internet news travels from one person to another is a concept that we refer to as **broadcast news diffusion.** Your goal should be to write accurate, clear stories that can then be diffused to others with frequency and precision.

Bad News Travels Fast

On March 30, 1981, President Ronald Reagan was shot by John W. Hinckley, Jr., outside a hotel in Washington, D.C. The story has been told that a businessman inside the hotel was talking on the telephone to a man in London who was watching Cable News Network (CNN). The man in London interrupted the conversation to say, "Hey, President Reagan has been shot, and he's not far from where you are!" Sure enough, the Washington businessman pulled back the curtain, looked out his hotel window, and saw the disturbance. Ironically, the man less than a block from the assassination learned about it from the man overseas minutes after it happened!

This anecdote illustrates the power of **broadcast news diffusion.** Any story you write has the potential to go far beyond the initial audience. How accurately the story is told and how well it is initially understood is critical to how it is then diffused to an even wider audience.

The Two-Step

The **two-step flow theory** can be considered an early precursor to broadcast news diffusion. Two-step flow holds that information from the media is "processed," in the sense that it is passed down from the original audience to many others. Some evidence supporting the two-step flow theory came from the 1940 Voting Study in which researchers interviewed four groups of registered voters in Erie County, Ohio (600 registered voters in each group) at regular intervals throughout the election campaign to determine which factors had the greatest influence in their decision making. The research team discovered media messages first reached opinion leaders, who then passed on what they heard or read to associates who looked to them as being influential. Part of the study involved the participants listing names of people they relied upon for advice; anyone listed by at least four participants was designated an opinion leader.[2] This two-step flow of communication appeared to have had more influence on voting decisions than did the mass media! It was a revelation that led to the phasing-out of an earlier theory that media messages were like magic bullets influencing opinion by hitting direct targets.

One wry analysis of the 1940 Voting Study debunked the magic bullet theory as follows:

> The audience, when observed closely, usually refused to fall over and play dead. It even refused to play the target. Sometimes the bullet bounced off, and at other times the audience actually seemed to be trying to catch the bullet in its hands and eat it like chocolate! Trying to explain these phenomena in the early years of intensive audience research, sociologists and advertisers began to use an approach people have called the 'category theory.' The advertisers needed some simple way of categorizing the audience so they could more easily predict responses to mass media. It was quickly discovered that highly educated people responded differently from poorly educated ones, young people from old, men from women, Chinese from British, rich from poor. As attitude measurement developed, it was found that attitude tests would also help predict responses to messages related to those attitudes. The categorical approach demonstrated that more than the mass media stimulus entered into the effect of 'propaganda.'[3]

At the end of World War II, a research team in Decatur, Illinois, discovered the tendency for news to be passed on through a *chain of influence*, rather than a dyad of influence. Their study revealed that opinion leaders had been influenced by other opinion leaders. What's more, they found that various opinion leaders were influential only at certain times and on certain topics.[4] Thus, the two-step flow gave way to the theory known as the **multistep flow.** Broadcast news diffusion and multistep flow share a concept: Social relationships play a critical role in the dissemination of news.

The Vaughan-Attkisson Model

The **Vaughan-Attkisson Model of Broadcast News Diffusion** (Figure 1.1) depicts information flowing through the communicator and medium to the audience where it may then be diffused to others. **Pure information** is designated by the "I." The public is rarely given information in its raw or pure form.

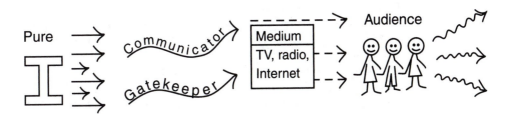

FIGURE 1.1   *Vaughan-Attkisson Model of Broadcast News Diffusion*

The **communicator,** which can include writers, anchors, and producers, filters and adds personal interpretations of the information before disseminating it as **news** to the audience. A television reporter who has a special interest in social work may tend to do stories that reflect social injustice, whether he does so knowingly or not. A Web site producer who has a special interest in business news may gravitate toward stories with some sort of business tilt. The practice of the communicator determining what information or stories to reject and which to pass along to the audience is often referred to as **gatekeeping.**

The **medium** is the method by which the communicator transmits information to its audience, whether computer, television, or radio. Each medium has its own inherent constraints that further filter and influence the **news.** For example, stories that do not have any videotape to go along with them are less likely to be used in a television newscast. Complex stories that require lengthy descriptions and explanations are more likely to be used in a newspaper or on Web sites where people can read at their own pace and reread what they don't understand.

The **audience** is made up of the receivers of the news, after it has gone through the filters of communicator and medium. The personal biases of these audience members again filter and influence the news; they simply won't pay attention to or diffuse stories that they don't care about or that they feel don't affect them. They may disagree with stories that don't reflect their values. Each audience member assigns a news value to each story and may choose to **diffuse** it to others.

 ETHICS NOTE: It's impossible for communicators to be strictly objective on all stories because subjectivity is an undeniable human trait. We all have experiences and biases that make us who we are. However, it's important for communicators working in the field of journalism to try their utmost to reflect fair and divergent opinions in stories, to examine issues from diverse views, and to excise their own biases.

Diffusion in Action

Even in the 1960s, as United States (U.S.) households became more and more saturated with television sets, people continued to get an extraordinary amount of news from diffusion instead of directly from the media. A 1964 study investigating the diffusion of news about the assassination of President John F. Kennedy questioned people in Dallas, Texas, where the tragedy occurred. Only one-fourth of those surveyed got the news from television reports. One-sixth heard it on the radio, and an amazing number—more than half of the subjects interviewed—heard about it from a nonmedia source.

There were similar findings in a study the same year far from Dallas, Texas. In San Jose, California, half of the 419 participants first heard about Kennedy's assassination from nonmedia sources![5] That's despite the fact that a full 92 percent of all homes in the United States had a television set at the time, and nearly half owned clock radios![6]

The terrorist attack on the World Trade Center twin towers and the Pentagon on September 11, 2001, is a prime example of a news story that spread quickly around the world, largely through broadcast news diffusion. Some information was accurate, but much of it was not. In the diffusion confusion that ensued, all kinds of inaccuracies were perpetuated: reports that a plane had hit the presidential retreat at Camp David (it hadn't), that a truck carrying biological agents was careening out of control in downtown Washington D.C. (there wasn't), and that a plane almost hit the Capitol building (it didn't).

Likewise, the initial reporting of the terrorist bombing in Oklahoma City, Oklahoma, on April 19, 1995, was so fraught with inaccuracies that it sparked diffusion with dire consequences. A total of 168 men, women, and children died when a vehicle loaded with explosives rammed into the federal building in Oklahoma City. In the immediate aftermath, the identity of the suspects was a mystery, but some journalists and analysts wrongly reported or speculated that the assailants appeared to be Middle Eastern. For more than a day, news reporters followed false leads, reporting on possible suspects overseas and interviewing experts on Mideast terrorists. As the news about suspects diffused, it took on a life of its own.

It wasn't long before the true bombing suspects were identified as middle Americans, not Middle Easterners, but the damage from the initial inaccurate diffusion had already been done. In a relatively short period of time, eight Muslim mosques were burned and vandalized, hundreds of hate crimes were reported against Muslims in this country . . . crimes believed to have been motivated by the diffusion of false facts in the bombing case.[7]

The repercussions weren't just felt in the United States. Palestinian officials condemned "the defamation campaign by the West against the Arab world and Islam." In Syria, the state press accused "certain Western media bodies" of racing to accuse Arabs in the explosion.[8]

The point is that the news that you write and communicate will have an impact far beyond the original intended audience. Your goal should be to write accurate stories that can be clearly understood by the primary audience and that have the best potential for distortion-free diffusion.

It should be noted that, even when a story is clearly and accurately written, broadcast news diffusion is subject to a degree of human error. Even primary audience members tend to hear what they want to hear, often inferring facts that were never implied or drawing conclusions that weren't intended. Your task is to use techniques that minimize the potential for misunderstanding, inaccuracies, and confusion.

Clear Writing: The Complex Art of Simplicity

Much of this text is devoted to explaining how to write stories that can be easily understood and accurately diffused by the audience. It's easier said than done, especially for beginners. It requires **clear, concise,** and **conversational** writing; think of them as the three Cs.

Broadcast news diffusion confusion

Oddly enough, this type of writing is much more difficult to perfect than con-voluted, lengthy, and unclear writing, which is the type that untrained writers tend to churn out. But the more you practice it means the easier it'll become. Eventually clear, concise, and conversational writing will become second nature.

Take a look at the following example of a poorly written sentence:

Example of a poorly written sentence

The perpetrator, a white male, believed to be approximately twenty-five or twenty-six years old, was chased by police officers who gave chase on foot for approximately two-point-three miles, who then eluded them and was reported to be still at large.

Now for an analysis of what's wrong:

- **Confusing jargon:** Words and phrases such as "perpetrator," "gave chase," and "at large" may be used in police reports and police press releases, but they aren't *words and phrases that ordinary people commonly use in conversation.* When selecting wording for a script, always ask, *"would I use this language in common conversation? If not, what words would I likely use in telling the story casually to someone else?"* Few of us would ever tell a friend, "Police are looking for a perpetrator who's still at large." We'd be more likely to say something like, "Police haven't caught the suspect yet."
- **Unnecessary detail:** The description of "approximately two-point-three miles" is more detail than any viewer or listener needs to know and so is the wording "approximately twenty-five or twenty-six years old." When deciding how much detail to include in a script, ask yourself *"What would be lost if I leave out this*

particular detail? Is it crucial to the story? Is there a way I can synopsize necessary details into a briefer, clearer reference?"

- **Convoluted sentence structure:** The sample sentence is anything *but simple and declarative*. It contains too many clauses and commas, making it difficult for an anchor to read aloud and even tougher for the audience to comprehend.
- **Passive sentence structure:** The sample sentence is passive. The type of writing you need to learn should generally be active, not passive. In the example, the structure reads, "The perpetrator . . . was chased by police officers . . ." A clearer, better choice would have placed those taking action—the police—first in the sentence: "Police chased the suspect . . ." Another choice would be to leave the perpetrator or suspect first in the sentence, but to reword the script so that the suspect is taking action: "The suspect ran from police . . ."

The Comparison

Now we'll take another look at the poorly written sentence, and compare it with a clear, concise, and conversational version.

Poorly written sentence	*Clearly written sentence*
The perpetrator, a white male, believed to be approximately twenty-five or twenty-six years old, was chased by police officers who gave chase on foot for approximately two-point-three miles, who then eluded them in the forestry and was reported to be still at large.	The suspect led police on a two-mile chase and then escaped by slipping into the woods.

In making the sentence clearer, we've also shortened it dramatically. Seventy syllables and forty-seven words were neatly reduced to little more than twenty syllables and seventeen words, without losing any meaning. It's no small feat. You'll often find yourself counting words and syllables as you attempt to condense your scripts into the limited time allotted for them.

☞ **TIP:** Get used to *reading all of your scripts aloud as you write them*. If a script sounds awkward or nonconversational, if the meaning doesn't seem clear when the words are spoken, or if you find yourself tripping or stumbling over words, those are all indicators that you should consider rewriting.

Poorly written story	*Clearly written story*
A Fran County man is in custody across the Kansas state line in connection with a carjacking Saturday night. According to the Fran County sheriff's office, 28-year old Roy H. Brittan of Armstrong Drive, Carter City, faces charges of kidnapping, armed carjacking and assault after he allegedly abducted 19-year old Richard Buell and Brittan's ex-wife Tammy Louise Brittan, both of Carter City. Buell and Brittan's ex-wife were together in Buell's car and entered the parking lot of a nightclub. Brittan allegedly forced Buell at gunpoint to move over, and took control of the car heading west on U-S Highway 2-0-9. About 40 miles south of the Colorado state line in the Ruth Community, Brittan allegedly threw Buell and the woman out of the car and continued westbound. Law enforcement officers stopped Brittan in the victim's car early Sunday morning. Fran County Sheriff Fred Moore says that Brittan will waive extradition. Buell and Mrs. Brittan were treated at a hospital in Walsh, Colorado, and later released.	A Carter City couple got the scare of their lives Saturday night. 19-year old Richard Buell and 27-year-old Tammy Brittan were in the parking lot of a local nightclub when Brittan's ex-husband allegedly forced his way into the driver's seat of their car and kidnapped them. Police say Roy Brittan drove the couple for miles and then pushed them out of the moving car. Neither was seriously hurt. Police arrested Roy Brittan early this morning and charged him with kidnapping, armed carjacking, and assault.

Now, read the following two sample stories aloud. It should quickly become obvious which one is clearer.

Story Structure and Content

When you're first starting out, it's hard to know how to begin writing a diffusible story of high news value that has all the desirable elements: clarity, conciseness, and accuracy. It's a tall order, and success depends on issues of basic **story structure** and **content.**

Unless writing for a national audience, you should typically **localize** your story. This simply means capturing the audience's interest by pointing out, preferably in the first sentence, that the story affects people in the local area where the story is appearing. Remember, **proximity** is a key factor in determining the news value that an audience member places on a given story, as seen in the following example:

A nonlocalized story	The same story localized for a Sarasota, Florida, audience
Twenty U.S. soldiers were injured today in Saudi Arabia. Officials say the Army troops were hurt when a live grenade accidentally exploded too close during a training exercise. A Sarasota man, Lieutenant John Foster, is among the injured, but Army officials say no one was seriously hurt. They're investigating how the accident happened.	A Sarasota Army Lieutenant is among twenty soldiers injured in Saudi Arabia today. Officials say John Foster was hurt in a training exercise when a live grenade accidentally exploded too close. Army officials say none of the injured were seriously hurt. Foster's parents, who also live in Sarasota, say his left leg is broken and he'll be allowed to return home briefly to recover.

The first sentence, referred to as the "lead" sentence, should not only make a **local** reference when possible, but should also include two Ws: **where** and **what**. Together we call the elements that should be in a typical lead sentence **L2W**.

The previous example puts L2W to practice. The *local* factor is the injury of a soldier from Sarasota where the story is airing. The *where* is Saudi Arabia. The *what* is soldiers being injured.

After the lead sentence, the body of your stories should include **cause,** *how and why it happened,* as well as **effect,** a statement that reveals *the impact or the result of what happened* and why the audience should care. Think of it as a **completed circle.** Broadcast and Internet news stories should always complete the circle to satisfy the audience's psychological need for a sense of completion.

Back to the previous example, the *cause* is a grenade exploding too close during a training accident. The *effect* is Lt. Foster coming home to recover. There's often no single right or wrong answer when you're determining *effect* in a given story. You should simply try to make sure some sort of effect *is* described.

Notice the cause and effect or completed circle in the next example:

Example of clear, completed circle writing

Police are searching for the hit-and-run driver who killed a Milton City man [where, what]. Earlier this evening, a car ran down 62-year-old Randolph Baxter as he walked across the street in front of his Honeysuckle Road home [cause]. The car didn't stop. It's the latest in a string of accidents along a two-mile stretch of road. Worried residents say it adds fuel to their push for a lower speed limit in the area [effect].

A story written in the completed circle fashion is much easier for an audience member to remember.

TIP: To make sure your stories *complete the circle*, including *cause and effect*, include *what happened, why it happened, and what the result was.*

Note the previous example about the Milton City hit-and-run also follows the L2W principle. The lead sentence includes "Milton City" (local and where) and that the subject was killed by a hit-and-run driver (what).

Contrast that with the following example of a poorly written story that leaves the audience hanging because it doesn't complete the circle and fails to follow other guidelines we've established for clear, concise writing and accurate diffusion potential.

Example of a poorly written story

A hit-and-run perpetrator is being searched for by police authorities. Honeysuckle Road has been the scene of a number of accidents in recent memory. The victim was run down by a vehicle as he walked across the street near his home. The driver of the vehicle apparently did not stop when the accident occurred.

This story breaks almost every rule for clear writing. The lead sentence makes no reference to where the event happened, and nowhere does the story tell who the victim is. Furthermore, one can only assume by the way it's written that the accident happened on a "Honeysuckle Road," but it's not clearly stated. There is also no clearly stated effect in this script. In short, it fails to complete the circle and raises more questions than it answers, leaving the audience hanging. You may also notice that the story uses jargon, such as "vehicle" instead of "car" and "perpetrator" instead of "suspect" and is written in passive, rather than active, tense. Finally, unlike the clearer version, it fails to make the story of interest to a broad audience by mentioning the neighborhood's movement to lower the speed limit.

Barriers to Clear Writing and Accurate Diffusion

Now that you've read several examples, we'll tell you how to lift five typical **barriers to clear writing and accurate diffusion:** *word fat, passive writing, poor attribution, dependent clauses,* and *appositions.*

1. Word Fat

When you're searching for simple, declarative, and conversational language, think of cutting the **word fat:** eliminating most everything but the meat of the story you're trying to tell. As mentioned in the previous example of a poorly written sentence, cutting out the word fat means avoiding complicated words, phrases, or jargon when short, simple, and conversational wording will suffice. Here are some examples of word fat, followed by leaner or better wording.

Word Fat	*Word Lean*
incarcerated	locked up/jailed
evidenced	proved
demonstrated	showed
released	let go
perpetrator	suspect
conflagration	fire
procure	get
obtain	get
male	man/boy
encounter	meet
modify	change
mollify	smooth over
initiate	start/begin
objective	goal
altercation	fight

2. *Passive versus Active Writing*

In a previous example, we mentioned passive sentence structure. It's another barrier to clear writing. Your goal is **active writing.** It won't always be possible to achieve, and there are times when you'll need to use passive wording. However, typically, you should tell stories in an active voice. The best way to explain the difference between passive and active writing is through the following example:

Passive Writing	*Active Writing*
The bill was written by Republican senators.	Republican senators wrote the bill.
Four people were killed by the tornado.	The tornado killed four people.
The meeting was called by county leaders, who wanted to find answers to the garbage problem.	County leaders called the meeting to find answers to the garbage problem.
The dangerous intersection was marked by signs posted by victims' families.	Signs posted by victims' families mark the dangerous intersection.

Note that the active forms of the previous sentences eliminate words such as "was," "were," and "wanted." Such past tense and passive wording can make a story sound dated or old. The goal is to make each story sound timely so that the audience will be more likely to pay attention and to diffuse it to others accurately.

3. *Poor Attribution:* Who Says?

Attribution is the practice of stating the source of information. It's essential when broadcast and Internet news stories use information that's not commonly known or held. It's also necessary when reporting information or opinions that may be in dispute. And it's required in stories that contain accusations or charges against a person or entity. In short, you must tell the audience *who* is providing the information, opinion, or accusations. Typically, you should include attribution in the *first* part of the applicable sentence. When it's placed *last* in a sentence, it's called a *dangling attribution*—something we typically work to avoid.

Dangling attributions are usually barriers to clear writing because they require the audience to "think back" to the initial statement after they hear the attribution and then to rescore mentally the value they place on the statement. It's easily done in print, but, if television viewers or radio listeners go through that exercise, you've probably lost their attention for the rest of the story. Read the following examples aloud.

Dangling Attribution	*Proper Attribution*
The suspect had a history of irresponsible behavior, including failing to pay child support, and a pattern of alcohol and drug abuse, according to his ex-wife.	The suspect's ex-wife told police he had a history of irresponsible behavior, including failing to pay child support, and a pattern of alcohol and drug abuse.

Proper attribution can also remove the abstractness from stories, add credibility, and give the audience the chance to consider the source of the information. In the following example, poor attribution might lead the audience to ask, *"Says who?"*

Poor Attribution	*Proper Attribution*
A large deficit in the city's budget could mean a hike in personal taxes in the next six months.	Spearville's mayor says a large deficit in the city's budget could mean a hike in personal taxes.

There are two types of attribution: **primary** and **secondary**. *Primary attribution* refers to the first time you state the source of facts or opinions. It typically includes the source's full name and title (or title only). You'll often need to make secondary reference to the same source within the story to remind the audience where the information is coming from. In *secondary attribution* you can use the source's last name only, title only, or a version of the title used earlier.

The following are examples of appropriate primary and secondary attribution:

Primary Attribution	*Secondary Attribution used later in the story*
Chelsea Mayor Lennon Taylor announced big changes in the budget . . .	The Mayor insists the cuts are needed to avoid tax hikes . . . or Taylor insists the cuts are needed to avoid tax hikes . . .

Primary Attribution	*Secondary Attribution used later in the story*
The director of the Naval Institute for Oceanic Studies says millions of dollars is missing . . .	The director notified police last night . . . or The Institute's director notified police last night . . .

Primary Attribution	*Secondary Attribution later in the story*
The head of the National Weather Service John Foster says get ready for the big chill . . .	The top weatherman predicts more sleet and snow than the last four years combined . . . or Foster predicts more sleet and snow than the last four years combined . . .

Primary Attribution	*Secondary Attribution later in the story*
Marshall Schroeder . . . the ousted Chairman of the School Board . . . is calling the election a fraud . . .	Schroeder accuses ballot-counters of rigging the vote . . . or Chairman Schroeder accuses ballot-counters of rigging the vote . . . or The Chairman accuses ballot-counters of rigging the vote . . .

Don't make the mistake of including attributions where none are needed, as in the following example. When considering whether to attribute, ask *am I quoting someone directly?* (If so, you must attribute.) Is the information controversial, or does it fall under the category of opinion? (If so, you must attribute.) Do I need to use attribution to lend credibility to the information? Would anything be lost if I drop the attribution?

Example of unnecessary attribution

Herndon police are cracking down on picnickers who bring alcohol into city parks. Police Chief Bob McKewon says the city outlawed alcohol in its parks four years ago.

In the previous example, it's clearly not necessary to attribute the fact that alcohol was outlawed four years ago to the police chief; this is an easily checked fact.

Here's one more set of examples:

Lack of Necessary Attribution	*Proper Attribution*
An elderly Chantilly man is hospitalized after he was attacked by a neighbor's pitbull. The dog crossed onto the victim's property unprovoked as he returned from a friend's house last night. What's worse, the dog's owner encouraged the wild animal to make the vicious attack.	An elderly Chantilly man is hospitalized after he was attacked by a neighbor's pitbull. **Police say** the dog crossed onto the victim's property unprovoked as he returned from a friend's house last night. **Authorities are investigating witnesses' claims that** the dog's owner encouraged the wild animal to make the vicious attack.

4. Dependent/Subordinate Clauses:

A **dependent** or **subordinate clause** has a subject and verb, but doesn't make a complete sentence. It may read just fine on paper, or even on the Internet, but it can cause much confusion when read aloud on television or the radio, making stories more complex and difficult to understand. At times, you will intentionally use dependent or subordinate clauses, but, generally, their use in broadcast stories should be very limited.

 TIP: When you find yourself writing a sentence with lots of commas and clauses, consider breaking it up into two shorter, simpler sentences.

The following shows examples of poorly used and properly used dependent clauses:

Poor Writing with Dependent Clauses	*Clearer Writing*
Mayor Linda Argent, appearing exhausted from the mayors' conference in Kansas City, Missouri, says that the meeting, which lasted five days, was well worth her time and River Town's money.	Appearing exhausted from the week-long mayors' conference in Kansas City, Missouri, Mayor Linda Argent says the meeting was well worth her time and River Town's money.

Now on your own, try making the clear version in the previous example even better: divide it into two shorter sentences. Later, compare what you write with our version in the Answers section at the end of the chapter.

5. Appositions

An **apposition** is a word or set of words that rename(s) a noun. Frequently found in print writing, appositions should usually be avoided in broadcast news because they are barriers to clarity.

Poor Writing with Too Many Appositions	*Clearer Writing with Fewer Appositions*
A Washington D.C. woman saved her own child's life, catching **the young boy** as he jumped from the second floor of a house that was on fire. **The worried mother,** Allyson Johnson, had herself escaped from the **burning building** and then stood outside the window encouraging **her distraught child** to make the leap. **The brave woman** caught **the four year old** in her arms, using a blanket to help soften the impact. The **frightened youngster** is reported to be a little shaken up, but otherwise fine. Officials don't know what started the fire.	A Washington D.C. mother saved her own four year old's life, catching him as he jumped from the second floor of their burning house. Allyson Johnson had herself escaped and then stood outside below the window encouraging her son to make the leap. When he did, she caught him in her arms using a blanket to help soften the impact. The boy is reported to be a little shaken up, but otherwise fine. Officials don't know what started the fire.

In Short . . .

Tips for writing clear stories that can be easily understood and diffused:
- Highlight elements that will cause the audience to judge the story to be of high news value.
- Eliminate unnecessary detail.
- Use normal, conversational language. Avoid jargon.
- Write simple, declarative, and active sentences.
- Use concise, "lean" wording.
- Include *where and what* in the lead sentence.
- Make sure each story *completes the circle* by including *cause and effect*.
- Check your work by reading it aloud.

Answers

1. A television news profile of an elderly woman who's organizing an effort to chase the drug dealers out of her neighborhood. **Soft news**

2. A radio news report on a rush-hour traffic pileup involving 20 cars. **Hard news:** *breaking or current issues and happenings*

3. An Internet news exposé about underground gambling at local bars. **Hard news:** *agenda setting or current issues and happenings*

4. A television report on preparing your garden for winter. **Soft news**

5. A radio report on a rally for a candidate for governor. **Hard news:** *current issues and happenings*

6. Clearer version broken up into two sentences: River Town Mayor Linda Argent appeared exhausted from the week-long mayors' conference in Kansas City, Missouri. But she says it was well worth her time—and River Town's money.

Web sites

For more information, check out the following Web sites.

www.poynter.org/dj/051700.htm
Tips on clear, strong writing from the Poynter Institute of Media Studies

www.newswriting.com/groaners.htm
A humorous look at news writing clichés

Quick Review of Terms

- **Active wording:** Preferred wording that has a subject acting upon, rather than being acted upon. For example, *The ball was caught by the pitcher* is passive. *The pitcher caught the ball* is active.
- **Attribution:** The practice of telling the source when including controversial information or opinions in a story. Also used to add credibility to information in a story.
- **Broadcast news diffusion:** The concept of broadcast and Internet news traveling from one person to another by means other than the originating medium.
- **Cause and effect or completed circle:** The concept of including in a story *how and why* an event happened, as well as the impact or result.
- **L2W:** The recommended practice of localizing a news story for a particular audience and including where and what in the lead sentence.
- **News value:** The importance and relevance assigned to a particular story. Influenced by factors, such as proximity, timeliness, significance, and medium.
- **The Vaughan-Attkisson Model of Broadcast News Diffusion:** Diagram illustrating how pure information is filtered and shaped before it is received and diffused by listeners and viewers.
- **Word fat:** Unnecessary jargon or needlessly lengthy words and phrases. Concise wording is preferred.

Review Questions

1. Why is clarity so important to effective broadcast and Internet news writing?

2. What are some factors that are likely to cause the audience to consider a story to be of high news value?

3. What elements are likely to increase or decrease the chances any given script will be easily understood and accurately diffused?

4. What are some of the hallmarks of poorly written, unclear stories?

Summary

This chapter has demonstrated the importance of writing crystal clear scripts and explained ways to lift barriers to clear writing and effective diffusion. It described how poorly written stories impact broadcast news diffusion. First and foremost, stories should be written in such a way that the primary audience can easily understand its meaning. Poorly written stories with word fat, jargon, passive language, and too much detail stand little chance of being clearly understood and accurately diffused. The chapter included tips on how to write stories that have the most potential for audience comprehension and accurate diffusion, such as ensuring that a given story has news value and then writing it in clear, simple terms. Students following the guidelines in this chapter will be equipped with the building blocks necessary to begin writing clear scripts for broadcast or Internet news.

Notes

1. Berkowitz, D. "Refining the Gate Keeping Metaphor for Local Television News." *Journal of Broadcasting and Electronic Media 34*, no. 1(1990): 59.

2. Severin, W.J. and J.W. Tankard. *Communication Theories: Origins, Methods, and Uses in the Mass Media*, 3rd ed. (New York and London: Longman, 1992), 193.

3. Schramm, W. *Men, Messages, and Media-A Look at Human Communication.* (New York: Harper & Row, 1971), 243, 244.

4. Severin and Tankard, 199.

5. Severin and Tankard, 201.

6. *Statistical Abstract of the United States*, 87th ed. (1966), 754.

7. Shaheen, Jack "Stereotypes on Screen; Movie Unfair to Arabs, Muslims," *The Record*, Monday, June 16, 1997, Sec. A, p. 13.

8. Monday, Mark, "Tangled Up in Who; Wrong Conclusions by Terrorist Experts on the Perpetuators of the Oklahoma City Bombing," *The Quill*, July 18, 1995, no. 6, vol. 83, p. 24.

2

Broadcast News Writing Style

Chapter Objectives

- To demonstrate the contrasts between print and broadcast news writing
- To provide a basic broadcast style guide
- To introduce the concept of *pronouncers*
- To describe the process of camel squeezing

You might assume that writing for radio or television news is much like writing for newspapers, but there are significant differences. Furthermore, writing for the Internet is yet again another style, which will be discussed in Chapter Five. In this chapter, we'll demonstrate the contrasts between traditional newspaper (print) writing and radio and television (broadcast) writing. This chapter also includes a basic style guide that explains the specifics of numbers, punctuation, prounouncers, and more in broadcast news scripts. And we'll explore ways to make your writing clear, concise, and conversational.

Print versus Broadcast

The following table outlines some of the differences between writing for newspaper and writing for radio and television:

Newspaper	*Radio and TV News*
Longer sentences, more words	Shorter sentences, fewer words
More details	Fewer details
Not as conversational (rarely would contractions be used and never sentence fragments)	More conversational (contractions used and sometimes sentence fragments)
Gives precise numbers	Rounds off numbers
Attributes sources more often, more detailed	Less attribution, less detail
Uses parenthetical phrases	Avoids parenthetical phrases
Uses appositions	Avoids appositions
May use inverted pyramid (most important information presented first, least important presented last)	Often uses completed circle (has a beginning, middle, and end)
Uses colons, semicolons, quotation marks	Uses dashes, three dots; uses fewer colons, semicolons, quotation marks
Frequently uses direct quotes	Rarely uses direct quotes (uses actual interviews instead)

Probably the best way for you to get practical knowledge of how print and broadcast news writing styles differ is by reading examples.

Let's begin with some basic facts from a story about egg-laying turtles:

Story location: Smathers Beach in Key West, Florida

Details: The city of Key West has invested $1.5 million buying tons of special sand and moving it to Smathers Beach to try to create a habitat that encourages Key West's giant, rare turtles to lay their eggs. The special sand is made up of grains that are bigger than ordinary sand and lighter in color and are believed to be conducive to turtle nesting. The sand-moving job started a week ago and is to be finished today, just a week before the turtle's nesting season begins. City maintenance workers are doing the work. The adult turtles weigh up to 300-pounds each. There are fewer than a half dozen left, but the city is hoping the beach project will encourage a comeback.

Quotes: Joe Roundtree, manager of Engineering Services for Key West stated: "The turtles just weren't interested in the regular sand, but they're said to be attracted to the color and texture of the specially shipped sand."

Here's how those facts could be written into a newspaper story:

KEY WEST—The city has invested $1.5 million in a giant project at Smathers Beach to encourage a comeback of Key West's giant 200 to 300-pound turtles.

The money went to buy special sand that's lighter in color and larger grained than ordinary Smathers Beach sand.

The reason: scientists believe the special sand is more conducive to egg-laying.

Key West City workers began moving the sand in a week ago, and should have the project completed tomorrow, before the start of nesting seasons.

Joe Roundtree, manager of engineering services for Key West, says "The turtles just weren't interested in the regular sand, but they're said to be attracted to the color and texture of specially-shipped sand."

Key West's turtles—which number less than half a dozen—could soon die out altogether if authorities are unable to devise a way to increase their number.

Now here's how the same story might be written for broadcast news:

(ANCHOR)

Key West is investing big bucks in a project to try to bring back the population of its rare, giant turtles.

(VO)

The city is spending one-and-a-half million dollars to cart in tons of special sand that has lighter, larger grains. The reason? The 300-pound turtles are said to find it more inviting.

(SOUND BITE/INTERVIEW: JOE ROUNDTREE, PROJECT MANAGER)
"THE TURTLES JUST WEREN'T INTERESTED IN THE REGULAR SAND, BUT THEY'RE SAID TO BE ATTRACTED TO THE COLOR AND TEXTURE OF SPECIALLY SHIPPED SAND."

(VO)

There are fewer than a half dozen of the giant Key West turtles left. With a little luck . . . there will be more after the coming nesting season.

(XXX)

You can see contrasts between the two stories right off the bat. The obvious differences in format—the way the two stories appear on the written page—are discussed in the next chapters. But there are also differences in style, such as the way numbers are written, the way abbreviations are spelled out, and the type of punctuation used.

Style Guide

Broadcast news style is largely determined by two factors: that the written words will be *read aloud* by an anchor and *heard* by the audience. Therefore, stories must be written in a way that reduces the risk of misreads by the anchor and minimizes the possibility of confusion in what the audience hears. Here are the basic guidelines:

1. Numbers and Money

    a. *Spell out the numbers "one" through "eleven";* they're easiest to read that way. It also reduces the risk that an anchor will mistake the number "1" for the letter "l" or "I", and the digital number "11" can look like the Roman numeral two.

    b. *Translate other amounts into digits and words.* You would never write "$12,000,000.00" because it would require the anchor to stop, count zeroes, and hunt for the decimal point. Instead, it's "12-million dollars."

    c. *Avoid dollar and cents signs and decimal points.* In the newspaper version of the previous turtle egg story, "$1.5 million" was used. But for broadcasting, it's either "one-point-five-million dollars" or, more simply, "one-and-a-half million dollars."

    d. *Round out complex numbers* so that they take less time to say and are easier for the audience to absorb as they go by in a flash. A report on "a $7,998,457.02 budget" would be written as "a seven-point-nine million dollar budget" or "a budget of almost eight million dollars."

    e. *For dates prior to the twenty-first century or far in the future, hyphenate the year.* For example, "1937" would be "19-37." This reduces the risk that 1937 could be read as "one thousand nine hundred and thirty-seven." The year "2027" should be written as "20-27."

    f. *More contemporary year dates are usually understood in their normal form.* For example, the year "2003" need *not* be written as "two thousand three" or "20-oh-three."

Here are examples of the wrong and right uses of money and numbers:

Wrong	*Right*
5 yr. old girl	five-year old girl
$14,000.47	14-thousand dollars
11 children	eleven children
7,000 people	seven thousand people
27,000,000 telephones	27-million telephones
.39	about forty cents
$7.29	more than seven dollars

Translate the following numbers into broadcast style. Answers for this and other exercises appear at the end of the chapter.

> $142.37
>
> 2,000,000,064
>
> 3 yr. old
>
> thirty-four
>
> .05

2. Punctuation

   a. *Avoid using colons, semicolons, and quotation marks;* they can be difficult for the anchor to read.

   b. *Use three dots (. . .) or dashes (—) to indicate where the anchor should pause.*

   c. *Use hyphens to indicate words or letters that are connected* and should be read without pausing.

   d. *Use hyphens to separate "non-anti-co-semi" prefixes,* for example, non-factor, anti-war demonstrations, co-worker, semi-conscious. This is the **non-anti-co-semi rule.**

   e. *Do not use hyphens to divide a word* at the end of a line and continue it on the next. In broadcasting, words are *never* divided from line-to-line; if there's not enough room for the whole word, move it to the next line.

Translate the following story into a version with appropriate broadcast punctuation:

A new vaccine that protects mice from West Nile virus could one day help people: that's according to researchers at Yale University. The deadly virus, carried by mosquitoes that feed off infected birds, first appeared in the U.S. in New York in 1999. The new vaccine developed by the Yale team uses a protein from the virus and, say researchers, shows "promise" for use in humans. West Nile virus was first identified in Uganda in 1937 and is nonharmful to most people, but can cause a "flu like" infection in the weak and elderly, leading to crippling, even fatal, brain inflammation.
(XXX)

3. Abbreviations

   a. *Don't abbreviate unless you want the word, phrase, or name read in abbreviated form.* If the anchor is to say "American Telephone and Telegraph," don't write "A-T-and-T."

   b. *Only use abbreviations that are widely known to the audience.* Examples include N-F-L, A-M, P-M, U-S, G-O-P, F-B-I, C-I-A, P-S, F-D-A, and P-O-BOX.

Assume most abbreviations are not widely known, such as A-B-A (American Bar Association) and SCOTUS (Supreme Court of the United States).

  c. *Abbreviations that are not widely known may be used in second references,* for example, "The treasurer of the Area River Rescue Fund has been charged with embezzling money from the charity . . . the A-R-R-F was founded in 19-84."

Here are examples of right and wrong uses of punctuation and abbreviations.

Wrong	*Right*
AAA	Triple-A
codefendant	co-defendant
N-A-S-A	NASA
NAACP	N-DOUBLE-A-C-P
N-A-T-O	NATO
African American	African-American
aol.com	a-o-l-dot-com
U.S. Highway 1	U-S Highway One
Sat.	Saturday
The UN	The U-N
7:00 pm	seven p-m
911	nine-one-one
semicircle	semi-circle
52 year old	52-year old
7.3 million gallons	seven-point-three million gallons
Pineberry St.	Pineberry Street

Translate the following story into a version with appropriate broadcast abbreviations and punctuation:

> Federal Bureau of Investigation agents are looking for a man suspected of mailing 3 letter bombs to a coworker. Fifty seven year old Larry Beisler, Jr., has been on the run since Tues. when he first heard that the letters had been traced to him in Ore. through fingerprints.
> (XXX)

4. Contractions

Use contractions when they would be used in ordinary speech. Your goal is conversational writing, so "The Mayor says *he's* pleased with the clean-up," sounds better than "The Mayor says *he is* pleased with the clean-up."

5. Direct Quotes

a. *Use actual interviews rather than direct quotes.* Notice that, in the turtle egg example, the broadcast version did not use a written quote from the Key West worker; instead, it included videotape of an actual interview with the worker. The selected piece of an interview is called a "sound bite" in television and an "actuality" in radio and is preferred over written quotes.

b. *Use direct quotes occasionally for impact.* Direct quotes *can* be used when they're pointed or dramatic and when no better sound bite or actuality is available. An example is "When the jury announced the guilty verdict . . . the suspect shouted—quote—you'll die for this!"

c. *Consider paraphrasing.* Instead of using a direct quote, consider paraphrasing it in concise, clear language. For example instead of: "The mother-to-be said—quote—I will never be able to find a way to possibly tell the police officer how much I truly appreciate the things that he did and thank him for helping me so much," you could write: "The mother-to-be said she doesn't know how to thank the police officer who helped her."

6. Names and Titles

a. *Only use names in the lead sentence of a story when they're widely known* by the audience. Examples of names likely to be widely known are prominent community activists, the mayor, a governor, or a celebrity. Keep in mind that names that are familiar to you may be unfamiliar to your audience. Someone who is very well known in one town may be an unknown in the next.

b. *Always give a title or context when using lesser-known names.* In the following example, the name is not used in the lead sentence because it's not widely known. Instead, the lead sentence gives the title and context for Molly Gladbrook (Girl Scout leader who saved lives), who's then mentioned by name in the next sentence:

An Aspen Girl Scout leader is credited with saving the lives of her troop this afternoon. 29-year old Molly Gladbrook was leading the scouts on a hike some 30 miles northeast of Aspen when she felt the telltale vibrations that precede an avalanche. Gladbrook thought fast and shouted for the 17 girls to run in the direction she was pointing. Deadly snow and other heavy debris fell less than a minute later in the exact spot where they'd been hiking.
(XXX)

c. *Use no name at all if it's not important to the story.* In the previous example, you want to mention Molly Gladbrook by name because she's the hero of the story. But in many cases, specific names won't matter to a story and shouldn't be used. Read the next example aloud:

Starting tonight, it'll be easier for homeless people to find a place to sleep. Mayor Grant Pemberton says the city is beginning its new plan to turn two government buildings into night shelters between the hours of eight p-m and six a-m. Social services coordinator Jackie Montober says there have been more people in need . . . than beds. But now Montober says 80 new beds will be provided. Frances Gould, head of the Inter-Faith Charitable Services, and Ron Shivone, chairman of Advocates for the Homeless, say the city needs to work to reduce homelessness, not just find more beds.
(XXX)

What if we excised all the names? Read the following version. It's clearer, more concise, and nothing important to the story has been lost:

Starting tonight, it'll be easier for homeless people to find a place to sleep. The city begins its new plan to turn two government buildings into night shelters between the hours of eight p-m and six a-m. Officials say there have been more people in need . . . than beds. But now 80 new beds will be provided. Charity groups say the city needs to work to reduce homelessness, not just find more beds.
(XXX)

d. *Generally, do not use Mr., Mrs., or Miss* when mentioning names in stories. Leaders of nations are exceptions. They *always* get a "Mr. or Mrs." in front of their last names when their leadership titles aren't used. For example, "President Bush" can be called "Mr. Bush," but is never simply "Bush."

e. *Use the title "doctor" when mentioning someone who has a medical degree.* A person with a doctorate (Ph.D.) is *not* called "doctor," but may be referred to as "professor."

f. *Use appropriate titles for clergy.* Roman Catholic clergy should be referred to as "The Reverend" and in each subsequent reference as "Father." For Jewish members of the clergy, the title is "Rabbi." Protestant members of the clergy are called "The Reverend."

g. *Generally, refer to adults by last name only on second references.* Soft news features can be exceptions; they may refer to adults by first name only. Clergy and national leaders should have a title before their last name on second reference.

h. *Generally, refer to children by first name only on second references.*

i. *Generally, do not use middle initials, names, and Jr. or Sr.* unless you're trying to distinguish a common name. For example, when William Kennedy Smith was tried (and acquitted) on sexual assault charges in the early 1990s, reporters always used his middle name. Doing so distinguished him from the thousands of other William Smiths and served to remind the audience that he's related to the famous Kennedy family, which is why the case received national attention. When reporting on crimes or controversies, a middle name or initial may be used to distinguish the subject of the story from innocent people who have the same first and last names. It's also acceptable to use a middle name, initial, or Jr. or Sr. if it's an integral part of the name. Examples are former Federal Bureau of Investigation (FBI) Director J. Edgar Hoover, President John F. Kennedy, and John F. Kennedy, Jr.

7. Age

a. *Avoid using a person's age unless it's relevant, satisfies curiosity, or distinguishes.* For example, age would be "relevant" in a story about a lady beating up a robber if the lady is 85 years old and the robber is 30. Giving the age of a young child who managed to call 9-1-1 when his house caught fire would "satisfy the curiosity" of audience members who wonder *how* young he is. Giving a person's age can also serve to "distinguish" between people with common names.

b. *When using age, make it conversational.* Years ago, the rule was always to put age before a person's, name as in "The victim was identified as 28-year old Heather Morrison." But there's a new trend, particularly at news networks. It's more conversational to say "The victim was identified as Heather Morrison, who was 28 years old." You can also choose to work the age into the story another way, such as "Jane Roxford refused to open the door. At age 67. . . she'd learned to be suspicious when strangers approached after dark."

 ETHICS NOTE: News writers have a responsibility to avoid embarrassing or stigmatizing the innocent. Try to distinguish people in your stories who have common names by using further identifiers, such as title or age. Instead of reporting that "Jeremy Williams is charged with selling crack cocaine," you could write that "28-year old Jeremy Williams is charged . . ." so that the suspect is less likely to be confused with innocent Jeremy Williams' in the area. Other alternatives would be "Jeremy Williams of Annview Lane is charged . . ." or "Jeremy Williams, a local stockbroker, is charged . . ."

8. Pronouncers

a. Use **pronouncers** for words written in television or radio news stories that may be mispronounced. Pronouncers are phonetic spellings broken down into syllables, telling an anchor or reporter reading the script aloud how to pronounce the word(s). Here's a pronouncer for Loxahatchee: (lox-uh-HATCH'-ee).

b. Enclose pronouncers with parentheses.

c. Separate syllables in a pronouncer with dashes.

d. Indicate which syllable of the pronouncer has the accent by capitalizing that syllable only and/or putting an apostrophe after it.

e. Radio pronouncers should be written next to the word itself, as in the following example:

> Campus police are investigating an overnight explosion at Cochrane (KOCK'-run) Hall.

f. Where television pronouncers are placed depends on the preference of the anchor or reporter who will be reading the story aloud. Television pronouncers can appear next to the word *or* on the left-hand side of the script, which is divided in two columns, as in the following example:

(DEE'-zen-berg's)	THE SCHOOL BOARD HAS VOTED TO STAND BEHIND SUPERINTENDENT KEITH DEZENBERG'S DECISION ALLOWING CORPORAL PUNISHMENT IN COUNTY SCHOOLS.

Read the following pronouncers aloud:

United Arab Emirates	United Arab Emirates (EM'-ih-rits)
pronouncer	(pro-NOUNTS'-er)
Chechnya	(CHECH'-nyah)
Rezulin	(REZ'-uh-lin)
Shimon Peres	(shee-MOHN' PEHR'-es)
Clarinex	(CLAIR'-ih-nex)
Vladimir Putin	(VLAH'-duh-meer POO'-tihn)

Practice writing pronouncers for the following words. For this exercise, we're using common words that ordinarily need no pronouncers to see how well you grasp the concept. Our answers are at the end of the chapter:

Mississippi

interim

announcement

bacon

Oklahoma

regional

void

disposition

An abbreviated version of the previous broadcast style guide is provided in Appendix A.

Keep It Simple

One of the cardinal rules of good broadcast writing is **keep it simple.** A television or radio audience is more likely to understand a story if it's written in clear, concise, and conversational language that eliminates unnecessary wording and detail. Remember that, unlike print, broadcast information is presented just *once* and the audience has no chance to reread the story to sift through detail or to sort out meaning.

Get used to the concept *"think listeners not readers."* It's a great piece of advice from Mervin Block, who once taught at Columbia's graduate school of journalism and wrote for veteran network television anchors Dan Rather, Tom Brokaw, Mike Wallace, and Walter Cronkite. "Think listeners not readers" means to always keep in mind somebody will be *hearing* your story rather than *reading* it.

Condensing an extraordinary number of details into a short, crisp broadcast style script that's easy to listen to is one of most difficult things for beginners to learn, but it's a skill that broadcast and Internet writers must call on daily. We call it **camel squeezing.** In ancient Israel, camel riders were often faced with the difficult chore of squeezing a tall, broad camel through "the eye of a needle" with the "needle" being the entrance of a city. With a lot of practice, camel squeezing will begin to come naturally.

First, read the following facts:

Police from Chicago and four suburbs along with federal officials are looking for a man who impersonated a police officer, an F-B-I agent, and a census taker to get into homes to assault female residents. Police believe all five break-ins were by the same perpetrator. Four of the victims were Asian women, leading police to believe the attacks were not done at random. Police said sexual assaults have taken place twice and were attempted in the other cases. Des Plaines police are talking with investigators to see if there is a link between these and the November 30th, 1999, slashing death of a Korean flight attendant, Young Kavila, in her Des Plaines apartment. Police advise residents not to open their doors unless they're absolutely sure who their visitors are.

(XXX)

Camel squeezing

This story is approximately 129 words long and would take approximately 40 seconds to read aloud. In the next example, Let's camel squeeze it down to 30 seconds while working to make it clear, concise, and conversational. A lot of facts and details can condensed or omitted entirely without compromising the point of the story.

The hunt is on for a man who impersonated an F-B-I agent, a policeman, and a census taker to get into homes and assault women. Authorities believe the same man is responsible for five separate break-ins. He may be targeting Asian-American women . . . because four of the five victims are Asian-American. Two were sexually assaulted. Officials want to know whether the cases are linked to the murder of a Korean woman in her Des Plaines apartment last year.
(XXX)

Some serious camel squeezing has reduced the story from 129 words to about 77. The length is now 25 seconds. Read it aloud; it's clear, concise, and conversational.

Believe it or not, if you were writing this story for a radio news brief, you'd want it to be even shorter. Try camel squeezing it even further to about 15 seconds. You'll have to lose some facts and detail, but retain the main point of the story. Compare your version to ours at the end of the chapter.

Now here's our next camel squeezing exercise:

Halloween Murder

A Florida man is charged with murder after a Halloween night that turned violent and deadly. Sheriff's deputies in Broward County say **that** someone had showered the home of Richard Day with eggs, and **had also** sprayed it with shaving cream **on Halloween night.** When **Richard** Day discovered the vandalism, **Broward County sheriff's** deputies say he became enraged. **They say Richard Day** got a carton of eggs **and then** ordered his twelve-year-old son to get into the family pickup. Then, **Day** sped off. His first stop was allegedly a house just a few blocks up the road where police say he **then** got out of the truck and threw eggs **at the house.** Then, deputies say **Richard** Day went to another house, **one** where a family his children knew lived, and threw eggs at that house. Investigators say a man who lived there ran out to confront **Richard** Day and that Day hit him with his truck and dragged him one hundred feet. As neighbors tried to help the man, they say **Richard** Day shouted **out the window of his truck,** "He got what he deserved." **Broward County sheriff's deputies arrested Day at his home. He is charged with murder** and is being held without bond.
(XXX)

First, we'll cut out unnecessary repetition. For example, it's not necessary to say "Broward County sheriff's deputies" again and again after the venue is already established. Richard Day should be referred to by his last name only after the first reference. The story said Day was charged with murder in the first sentence, so you shouldn't say it again in the last sentence.

Next, we'll cut unnecessary detail. We don't really need to know in chronological order details of how Day grabbed the eggs, got in the truck, and made each stop. Think of a way to summarize the events.

Last, we'll remove other unnecessary wording (highlighted in the previous example). Here's the first camel squeezed version:

Halloween Murder

A Florida man is charged with murder after a Halloween night that turned violent and deadly. Sheriff's deputies in Broward County say someone showered the home of Richard Day with eggs and sprayed it with shaving cream. When Day discovered the vandalism, deputies say he became enraged, got a carton of eggs, and sped off in his pickup along with his twelve-year-old son. Deputies say Day stopped at two

(Continued)

houses and threw eggs. At the second house, a man ran out to confront Day. Investigators say Day hit the man with his truck and dragged him one hundred feet. As neighbors tried to help the man, they say Day shouted, "He got what he deserved." Day is being held without bond.
(XXX)

Not bad. We've shaved the 208-word story down to about 123 words. But we can tighten it up even more. For example, it's *obvious* that the Halloween night turned "violent and deadly" because "the Florida man is charged with murder," as the lead sentence says. So instead of saying it turned "violent and deadly," we'll use that lead sentence to give a clearer overview of the entire story: "A Florida man is charged with murder after allegedly retaliating for Halloween night vandalism."

Here's our final camel squeezed version (also now using appropriate broadcast style):

Halloween Murder

A Florida man is charged with murder. . .after allegedly retaliating for Halloween night vandalism. Broward County sheriff's deputies say Richard Day's home was pelted with eggs and shaving cream. He saw the mess—deputies say—and retaliated by throwing eggs at two other houses. When a man ran out of the second house . . . investigators say Day hit him with his truck and dragged him a hundred feet—killing him. Witnesses quote Day as saying the man got what he deserved.
(XXX)

This camel squeezed version is 80 words instead of the original 208 and takes less than 30 seconds to read aloud. It's also a lot clearer and easier to follow when read aloud.

When camel squeezing a story, keep these minds in mind:

- Keep focused on the nucleus of the story.
- Narrow it down to the key point or points.
- Don't attempt to say too much or to cover every angle.
- Condense or omit unnecessary repetition, wording, and detail.

Answers

1. Money and Number translations:

   $142.37:   about 142-dollars

   2,000,000,064:   two billion

3 yr. old: three-year-old

thirty-four: 34

.05:   a nickel or five cents

2. Punctuation Correction:

> A new vaccine that protects mice from West Nile virus could one day help people. That's according to researchers at Yale University. The deadly virus . . . carried by mosquitoes that feed off infected birds . . . first appeared in the U-S in New York in 19-99. The new vaccine developed by the Yale team uses a protein from the virus and—say researchers—shows promise for use in humans. West Nile virus was first identified in Uganda in 19-37 and is non-harmful *[or harmless]* to most people . . . but can cause a flu-like infection in the weak and elderly . . . leading to crippling—even fatal—brain inflammation. (XXX)

3. Punctuation and Abbreviation Corrections:

> F-B-I agents are looking for a man suspected of mailing three letter bombs to a co-worker. 57-year old Larry Beisler has been on the run since Tuesday when he first heard that the letters had been traced to him in Oregon through fingerprints. (XXX)

4. Pronouncers (various answers are possible):

Mississippi (miss-ih-SIP'-ee)

interim (IN'-ter-um)

announcement (uh-NOUNTS'-ment)

bacon (BAY'-kin)

Oklahoma (oak-luh-HOME'-uh)

regional (REE'-juh-nul)

void (VOYD)

disposition (dis-puh-ZIH'-shun)

5. 15-second Camel Squeezed Story:

> The hunt is on for a man who got into the homes of five women by impersonating police or other officials. Most of the victims are Asian-American; two were sexually assaulted. The case could be linked to the murder of a Des Plaines woman last year. (XXX)

Web sites

For more information, check out the following Web sites.

www.poynter.org/special/poynterreport/broadcast/broadcast1.htm
A primer on writing for broadcasting

www.poynter.org/dj/062800.htm
Tools of a writer, from the Poynter Institute

Quick Review of Terms

- **Camel Squeezing:** condensing an extraordinary number of details into a short, crisp broadcast-style script that's easy to listen to by omitting or condensing unnecessary repetition, wording, and details.
- **The non-anti-co-semi rule:** a rule stating that words beginning with the prefixes "non," "anti," "co," or "semi" should be hyphenated.
- **Pronouncers:** phonetic spellings of words broken down into syllables, instructing an anchor or reporter reading the script aloud how to pronounce the word(s).

Review Questions

1. What are some of the basic differences between writing for print and writing for broadcast news?
2. What are the reasons behind those differences?
3. When and why are pronouncers used?
4. What are some things to consider when camel squeezing?

Summary

Broadcast news writing is styled to reduce the risk of mistakes or "misreads" by the anchor or reporter who *reads* the script aloud to the audience. At the same time, the writing must leave little chance for misinterpretation by the audience who will *hear* the words. Unlike print, broadcast stories are presented orally, and the audience has just one chance to get the point. There's no opportunity to mull over the meaning of a confusing sentence or to reread it. Punctuation, abbreviation, and numbers are all written in ways to make the words simple and clear on the written page and easy to digest by the audience hearing them. Pronouncers should be used to guide anchors through difficult or unfamiliar names and phrases. Camel squeezing is one way to systematically whittle down too much information into a clear, concise, and conversational script that the audience can easily understand.

3

Page Format for Radio News

Chapter Objectives _____

- To give students a practical working format for radio news writing
- To define basic script terms
- To explain commonly used technical and audio script references
- To demonstrate the purpose and effectiveness of "actualities"

This is the first of two chapters in which we attempt to give you a guide—a sort of format—for how broadcast scripts should look on the physical page. Our first focus is on radio news scripts.

There's a tremendous amount of variation as far as what's accepted and what's expected in radio news scripts. We'll demonstrate a format that incorporates common elements found in radio news scripts at many different companies.

Paper versus Computer

It might be hard to imagine in this age of computers, but, not too long ago, all radio news scripts were typed onto paper using a manual typewriter. Today, of course, the vast majority of scripts are composed on computers, either written in the newsroom on desktops or filed from the field on laptops. Often, the finished product is printed on paper for anchors to read on the air. But in a growing number of news radio operations, paper has become passé altogether. The anchors read stories live on the air straight from the computer screen without a single sheet of paper in sight.

Within a radio newscast, different types of **sound** are used. A story may call for the anchor to pause his reading at a specific point so that a short piece of a relevant interview can be played for the audience. That piece of an interview is called an **actuality.** Sometimes, the anchor introduces a **wrap,** where the reporter is heard reading a story, often in the field where the action is happening.

Wraps and actualities used to be prerecorded on tape in bulky cassettes called **carts.** A technician following along on the scripts played each cart at the appropriate time in the newscast. Now, actualities and wraps are more often recorded digitally and stored in computers. The process is so streamlined that the news anchor can double as technician, playing his own actualities and wraps during his live newscasts with a click of the mouse or the stroke of a key.

We'll discuss wraps and actualities in greater detail in a few moments.

Longtime radio anchor Jim Johnson tells how it works at the nationally known news radio station WLS in Chicago:

> For the most part, I read right off the screen. I rewrite the wires and other stories we've covered here in Chicago or the network has fed. My actualities are put inside my script and I read the whole thing off the screen, hopefully clicking [the mouse in] the right places. My actualities are fired off by a click. I do keep my weather and sports copy pasted up on paper in front of me at my anchor desk. Don't ask me why – I guess I just like the cluttered look. Since I started reading off the screen with no paper I have had a couple of times where my computer froze and I ad-libbed the rest of the newscast sounding like a fool!

One benefit of all-computer operations is that the computer automatically handles many script-formatting issues. However, your first radio news job may be in a small- to medium-sized city where the news department may be less digitally advanced. The basic "page format" we're setting forth can be easily adapted to such operations.

The Basics

First, when using paper, it should be **standard-sized paper** (8-1/2 by 11 inches) for radio news scripts. Scraps of paper and half-sheets mixed in with standard-sized paper are difficult to manage. A story written on a strip of paper could easily fall out of the stack as you make your way to the microphone.

Radio news scripts can be written in **upper** and **lower-case type** or **ALL CAPITAL LETTERS LIKE THIS.** What you end up doing will depend largely on the policy at the radio station or on a particular anchor's personal preference. **Twelve-point Times New Roman** is a font style and size that's usually easy to read and that minimizes misreads or mistakes on the air. Radio news scripts may be **single-spaced** or **double-spaced,** again depending largely on the preferences of whoever will be reading the script aloud on the air. However, in any event, there should be **one-inch margins** on each side of the page.

Following these specific guidelines makes it easy to time a story; that is, to figure out precisely how much time it will take an anchor to read it aloud. It's a critical calculation because of the material for a newscast must be carefully timed in advance to make sure it all adds up to the total time allowed. For example, a three-minute newscast must include *exactly* three minutes of news material; no more and no less. If an anchor is mistakenly given scripts that add up to three minutes *and twenty seconds* instead of three minutes, it won't all fit in the newscast. On the

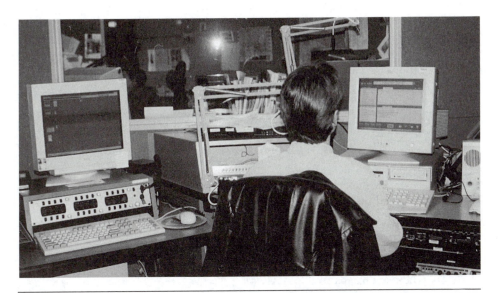

FIGURE 3.1   *Radio news journalist at work in the studio*

other had, if he's handed scripts that add up to *less* than three minutes, he won't have enough material to fill the time allotted for the newscast. The general rule of **line timing** is that each line of a radio script typed in the recommended format takes about four seconds for an anchor to read aloud (one line of copy equals four seconds).

Many radio stations now use computer software that automatically times the length of a script based on what you've typed and displays the figure at the top of the computer screen.

The Slug

Each story is assigned a brief title called a **slug.** The slug is usually just a word or two and is part of each radio news page. It should be typed in the upper-left corner of the page, followed by the date and time that the story was written and the last name of the newswriter. The following is an example of a slug:

House Fire
May 20, 2003 - 3 p.m.
Vaughan

How is the term "slug" used in a sentence? An anchor might ask a producer, "What's the slug of the story you're beginning the nine o'clock newscast with?"

If a story runs onto a second page, you should type the word "more" at the end of the first page. On the next page, repeat the slug and add the page number in the upper-left corner. Never break up a sentence from page one to page two. If there isn't room for an entire sentence at the end of the first page, carry the entire sentence to the second page as in the following:

Page 2, House Fire

At the end of each story, use a triple X (XXX) to tell the newscaster that he's reached the end of the script.

Now, let's take a look at a news story in proper radio news format. It's a copy story, which means there's no sound included.

House Fire / Copy
May 20, 2003 - 3 p.m.
Vaughan
Leesburg Police are trying to find out whether a fire that killed two
toddlers was intentionally set. The fire broke out early this
morning at a home on West Main Street. It's been the site of
several recent crack cocaine busts. The children—ages two
and three—were sleeping on the second floor and died of smoke
inhalation before rescuers could reach them. Arson investigators
combed the charred rubble of the house and say they found
"suspicious signs"... but aren't giving details.
(XXX)

Use the line timing rule to estimate the total time it will take an anchor to read the story in the previous example. Then see how accurate your guess is by having someone time it from start to finish with a clock or watch as you read it aloud. Refer to the Answer section at the end of the chapter to see if your calculations match up.

Actually, What's an Actuality?

As we've mentioned, many radio stories make use of bits of audio from interviews, segments of speeches, or other "sound." These selected bits are referred to as **actualities (act-you-AL'-iht-ees).** An actuality could be a seven-second long segment of the President's speech inserted into a radio news story. It could be a ten-second long portion of an interview with the survivor of a boating accident. Or it might be a four-second long comment from a bystander in a colorful parade. How is the term, "actuality," used in a sentence? A producer might tell an anchor, "We'll use two actualities in the next hourly newscast: one goes with the bomb threat story, and the second goes with the last story about the dog show."

Here's the first example again, but with an actuality added:

House Fire / Actuality
May 20, 2003 - 3 p.m.
Vaughan
Leesburg Police are trying to find out whether a fire that killed two
toddlers was intentionally set. The fire broke out early this
morning at a home on West Main Street. It's been the site of
several recent crack cocaine busts. The children...ages two and
three...were sleeping on the second floor. Officer Larry Brown says
they died of smoke inhalation before rescuers could reach them.
START: BROWN
OUT CUE: "...THE FRONT DOOR."
TIME: 14
Arson investigators combed the charred rubble of the house and
say they found "suspicious signs" but would not be more specific.
(XXX)

In the preceding script, we've indicated there's an actuality by using **script signals.** Script signals are like road signs that tell what's ahead. The word "START" in all capital letters indicates the place in the script where the anchor should stop reading and the actuality should start. A technician or the anchor will physically push the button or click the mouse to play the actuality on the air.

Following START is a one-word name given to the particular actuality. In the example, the actuality is a bit of an interview with Officer Larry Brown, so the actuality is titled BROWN.

The next script signal is the OUTCUE. An outcue is the last few words of the actuality. Suppose that, in the actuality in our example, Officer Brown says: "There were four firefighters on the scene desperately trying to get inside the building, because we knew from neighbors that two kids were inside. But there was just no use...the whole thing was engulfed in flames before they could even get through **the front door.**" The OUTCUE is "the front door."

Last, the time—the length or duration of the actuality—should be noted. In our example, Officer Brown's actuality lasts fourteen seconds (:14).

There shouldn't be a long, silent pause after the actuality ends and before the anchor realizes it's over and begins reading aloud again. With information such as the OUTCUE and length of the actuality, the anchor is positioned to be ready to resume reading aloud the moment that the actuality ends.

Practice your timing skills by calculating the total time of the House Fire actuality script. Remember, each full line is four seconds. Don't forget to add the length of the actuality itself. The answer is provided at the end of the chapter.

That's a Wrap!

Sometimes an anchor introduces an entire story that's been prerecorded by a reporter. It's more than an actuality; it's called a **wrap.** A wrap may include several actualities, but, when it's played in the newscast, it's all self-contained in a single tape or computer file. How is the term, "wrap," used in a sentence? A producer might instruct a reporter in the field, "Give us a wrap of the news conference for the 10:15 newscast." Here's our house fire story again, only this time written as a wrap:

House Fire / Wrap

May 20, 2003 - 3 p.m.

Vaughan

Leesburg Police are trying to find out whether a fire that killed two

toddlers was intentionally set. Reporter Heather Martin has the

latest from the scene:

START: MARTIN

OUTCUE: "W-B-V-X NEWS."

TIME: 40

(XXX)

As you can see in this wrap, it's not the anchor who reads the details of the story. Instead, he reads a few lines to introduce or "toss" to a story prerecorded by a reporter named Heather Martin. The script signal that indicates when the wrap begins is the word START followed by the word MARTIN. Suppose in her wrap, Martin gives a few details about the fire, includes a short piece of an interview with Officer Brown, and then ends with the word "in Leesburg, I'm Heather Martin, **W-B-V-X News.**" In that case, the OUTCUE is W-B-V-X NEWS.

Each radio station has its own trademark or **standard outcue** that all its reporters are to use when doing wraps. Standard outcues usually include the location of the report, the reporter's name, and the station's "call letters" or identity, such as "in Leesburg, I'm Heather Martin, W-B-V-X News." Often, instead of writing out a literal outcue for a wrap that ends with a standard outcue, it's okay to simply write STANDARD. Sometimes standard outcue is also abbreviated as "SOC" or "S-O-C."

What's the total length of the House Fire wrap script? Be sure to include the anchor's introduction in your calculations.

Live

Instead of tossing to a prerecorded wrap, an anchor sometimes introduces a reporter who's *live* in the field with a report. This can be indicated on the script simply by typing the words LIVE REPORT instead of START. There should still be an OUTCUE noted, with the last three or four words that the reporter *plans* to say. That, of course, is something that will have to be decided on and discussed before the newscast begins. Here's our example modified to indicate a *live* wrap instead of a *prerecorded* wrap:

House Fire / Live Wrap
May 20, 2003 - 3 p.m.
Vaughan

Leesburg Police are investigating whether a fire that killed two
toddlers was intentionally set. Reporter Heather Martin is live on
the scene with more. Heather?

LIVE REPORT
OUT CUE: STANDARD

(XXX)

Variety

Some stories will have no actualities at all; others will have more than one. You can adapt the basic script format to fit all of the possibilities. Check out the next example:

Take a few moments now to calculate the total length of the turtle story on page 46. You'll have to count four seconds per line of written script and then add in the actualities. The answer is provided at the end of the chapter.

Why Use Actualities?

What's the purpose of actualities? Experts have found that actualities can be very valuable because they may "add variety, interest, pace, drama, excitement, and credibility to a newscast."[1] They also cause "audience members to participate vicariously in news events by taking them to the scenes of such events and allowing them to hear the actual voices of the newsmakers."[2] Such powerful effects may enhance the audience's understanding of a story and increase the likelihood of accurate broadcast diffusion.

Turtles / Actualities
May 20 - 3 p.m.
Vaughan

It's become a little more turtle-friendly at Smathers Beach in Key West, Florida. Special sand has been brought in...to the tune of one-and-a-half million dollars. Project Manager Ann Lachner says the new sand should be better for the rare, 300-pound Key West turtles to lay their eggs in.

START: LACHNER
OUT CUE: "...MEANS MORE FEMALES."
TIME: 08

Turtle expert Tina Brown says the giant turtles leave their birthplace and tour the world for 20 years...then amazingly find their way back to Key West when it's time to lay their eggs.

START: BROWN
OUT CUE: "...LOVE THESE TURTLES!"
TIME: 12

Turtle nesting season begins April first.
(XXX)

However, actualities should not be included merely for the sake of having them. If they aren't interesting, if they don't enhance the story, or if there are too many of them, the audience may view them as distractions or interruptions. Repeatedly going from the anchor's voice to an actuality and then back to the anchor again can be jarring for listeners. Remember, in radio—unlike television—the audience has no visuals to help make the story clear. In radio—unlike print—the audience can't go at its own pace and reread something that was confusing.

When you *do* use an actuality, the script should clearly introduce or "set up" the actuality so that the audience is clear as to whose voice they're about to hear. In our earlier example of the House Fire actuality, the script "set up" the actuality by stating "Officer Larry Brown says they died of smoke inhalation . . ." That simple sentence prepared the audience for the voice they were about to hear next so that it didn't come out of the blue, leaving them guessing as to the voice's identity.

Review each of this chapter's actuality and wrap examples and identify how each one is "set up" so that the audience is clear as to who's speaking.

Network Radio Page Format

We've already mentioned that the format of radio scripts will look different from station to station. But they're all variations of the same basic principles included in this chapter. Here's a look at the actual news scripts from an hourly newscast at a technically sophisticated, computerized network news operation: CBS Radio.

(GURU/WRAP)
CBS NEWS, I'M CAMI MCCORMICK.
A FORMER ANTI-WAR ACTIVIST AND COUNTER-CULTURE GURU...IS ON A PLANE BOUND FOR THE U-S...TO FACE CHARGES HE MURDERED HIS GIRLFRIEND MORE THAN 20 YEARS AGO. CBS NEWS CORRESPONDENT ELAINE COBBE WITH THE STORY.
[TAKE STUDIO
NAME: COBBE
OUTCUE: SOUTHWESTERN FRANCE
DURATION:0´35´´]
(XXX)

(FIRE/ACTUALITY)
FIREFIGHTERS IN BALTIMORE ARE STILL TRYING TO PUT OUT A FIRE FROM A TRAIN DERAILMENT IN A DOWNTOWN TUNNEL. FIRE CHIEF HECTER TORRES:
[TAKE STUDIO
NAME: TORRES
OUTCUE: ACCOMPLISH EXTINGUISHMENT
DURATION:0´13´´]
THE FIRE HAS BURNED FIBER OPTIC CABLES...WHICH HAS SLOWED INTERNET SERVICE NATIONWIDE. IT'S ALSO SHUT DOWN THE ORIOLES' BALLPARK.

(XXX)

(HURRICANE/ACTUALITY)
WHAT'S THE HURRICANE FORECAST OVER THE NEXT SEVERAL YEARS?
HERE'S GOVERNMENT METEOROLOGIST STAN GOLDENBERG:
[TAKE STUDIO
NAME: GOLDENBERG
OUTCUE: ANYTHING YET
DURATION:0´01´´]
GOLDENBERG SAYS ATLANTIC WARMING OVER THE PAST FEW YEARS IS
ACTING LIKE JET FUEL FOR DEVELOPING STORMS. AND THE TREND
COULD CONTINUE FOR AS LONG AS 30 OR 40 YEARS.
(XXX)

(CAT/ACTUALITIES)
A GRAY AND WHITE CAT NAMED MUFFY FORCED THE CANCELLATION
OF A CONTINENTAL AIRLINES FLIGHT OUT OF PROVIDENCE TODAY. SHE
BROKE OUT OF HER CAGE IN AN AIRLINE BAGGAGE AREA, DARTED
DOWN THE TARMAC, AND HID IN A SECTION OF THE PLANE.
[TAKE STUDIO
NAME: KING
OUTCUE: DIDN'T WORK
DURATION:0´08´´]
CONTINENTAL SPOKESWOMAN JULIE KING SAYS NOTHING COULD
CONVINCE MUFFY TO BUDGE. DRASTIC MEASURES WERE CALLED FOR...
[TAKE STUDIO
NAME: KING
OUTCUE: SEVEN HOURS
DURATION:0´11´´]
THE MORE THAN 80 PASSENGERS WERE PUT ON ANOTHER FLIGHT...AND
MUFFY WAS REUNITED WITH HER FAMILY.
(XXX)
MORE...AFTER THIS.
Commercial

(IMMIGRANTS/WRAP)
THE ATTORNEY GENERAL IS CRITICIZING A RECENT SUPREME COURT
DECISION ON ILLEGAL IMMIGRANTS. CBS NEWS REPORTER LEE FRANK
WITH MORE FROM DENVER.
[TAKE STUDIO
NAME: FRANK
OUTCUE: SOC
DURATION:0´29´´]
(XXX)

(G-M/COPY)
SPORTS STADIUMS ARE OFTEN NAMED AFTER COMPANIES...NOW THE
SMITHSONIAN INSTITUTION IS CLOSE TO NAMING AN EXHIBITION
HALL FOR GENERAL MOTORS...IN RETURN FOR A REPORTED 10 MILLION
DOLLAR DONATION. IT'S NOT A FIRST FOR THE SMITHSONIAN
THOUGH...IT RE-NAMED A NATURAL HISTORY INSECT ZOO...AFTER
ORKIN PEST CONTROL MADE A DONATION.
I'M CAMI MCCORMICK. CBS NEWS.
(XXX)

In the CBS Radio scripts, the basic formatting is similar to what we described in the beginning of this chapter, but different terminology is used. The start of an actuality or wrap is indicated by the script signal "Take Studio" instead of START, but it means the exact same thing. Likewise, the length of actualities and wraps is indicated by the word "Duration" instead of "Time," but the meaning is the same. Also, the single-word title of the actuality or wrap follows the word "Name." These CBS Radio scripts are single-spaced and written in all capital letters. The margins are not an issue because CBS Radio has software that automatically times the lines of the script and even adds up the length of the actualities and wraps.

One divergence from our recommended style is in the previous script with the slug "CAT/ACTUALITIES." The first actuality in the Cat story is from Continental spokeswoman Julie King. Yet you'll notice there's no mention of King before the actuality. In other words, her actuality is not "set up" in advance to prepare the audience for the voice they're about to hear. Instead, King's name and title are given *afterward*. Disclosing the identity of someone speaking in an actuality *after the fact* rather than *beforehand* can confuse listeners because first, they're left wondering whose voice they're hearing. Then, when they're finally told, they're required to "think back" to what the person said to put the information in context. Requiring listeners to perform that mental process can be a barrier to clarity and accurate diffusion. We recommend you use this technique sparingly, if at all.

Answers

1. The House Fire *copy* script times out to thirty seconds (:30). Explanation: 8 *full* lines of copy at :04 per line would equal :32. However, the example is only seven and a half lines long, so the last line is approximately :02 instead of :04 long.

2. The House Fire *actuality* script times out to forty-six seconds (:46). Explanation: There's eight full lines at :04 per line, which equals :32. Add the :14 actuality, and the total time is :46.

3. The House Fire *wrap* script totals :50. Explanation: two and a half lines of copy at :04 per *full* line equals :10. Add the :40 wrap for a total length of :50.

4. The Turtles *actualities* script (repeated for your reference) is :54 long. Explanation: There are approximately eight and a half full lines of copy in the script, which adds up to :34. Add in the two actualities (:12 + :08) for a grand total of :54.

Turtles / Actualities

May 20 - 3 p.m.

Vaughan

It's become a little more turtle-friendly at Smathers Beach in Key West, Florida. Special sand has been brought in to the tune of one-and-a-half million dollars. Project Manager Ann Lachner says the new sand should be better for the rare, 300-pound Key West turtles to lay their eggs in.

START: LACHNER

OUT CUE: "...MEANS MORE FEMALES."

TIME: 08

Turtle expert Tina Brown says the giant turtles leave their birthplace and tour the world for 20 years...then amazingly find their way back to Key West when it's time to lay their eggs.

START: BROWN

OUT CUE: "...LOVE THESE TURTLES!"

TIME: 12

Turtle nesting season begins April first.

(XXX)

Web sites

For more information, check out the following Web sites.

www.newscript.com/index.html
Writing for radio site (including use of natural sound)

www.npr.org/
National Public Radio

www.bbc.co.uk/radio/
British Broadcasting Corporation (BBC) Radio

Quick Review of Terms

- **Actuality:** a bit of audio from an interview, segment of a speech, or other "sound."
- **Line timing:** the process of determining the length of a script by counting approximately four seconds per line of script (one line of copy equals four seconds).
- **Live:** Not prerecorded; taking place in real time.
- **Outcue:** the last few words of an actuality or wrap.
- **Script signals:** the "road signs" of radio scripts that tell what's ahead, including the "outcue," and "time" or length/duration of an actuality or wrap.
- **Standard outcue:** a reporter's last few words in a taped or live wrap; usually includes the reporter's name, location (city), and the radio station's call letters (identity).
- **Wrap:** an entire self-contained story that's introduced by the anchor and prerecorded or delivered "live" by a reporter; may contain actualities.

Review Questions

1. What are some of the format basics for radio news scripts?
2. What's the purpose of an actuality?
3. What's the difference between an actuality and a wrap?
4. What's the purpose of script signals?
5. How is the length of a given radio news script calculated?

Summary

This chapter defined and demonstrated some commonly used terms and formats in radio news writing. Some of the basics include one-inch margins and script signals that indicate the technical details about actualities and wraps. The formats used at individual radio stations and network radio operations are variations of the same basic ideas. Formats are dictated in part by the personal preferences of the anchor who will be reading the scripts aloud on the air and by whether or not the newsroom is computerized.

Notes

1. Wulfemeyer, Tim K. and Lori L. McFadden. "Effects of Actualities in Radio Newscasts." *Journal of Broadcasting and Electronic Media* 29, no. 2, (1985): 189.
2. Wulfemeyer and McFadden, 189.

4

Page Format for Television News

Chapter Objectives _____

- To give students a practical working format for television news writing
- To define basic script terms
- To explain commonly used technical and video script references
- To introduce the concept and functions of a rundown

Now, we'll give you a guide for how your television news scripts should look on the physical page. As in radio, there's no standard accepted format for television news scripts. However, we've identified some common "looks" and typical language and terms widely used in the industry. There's a lot to absorb, but after you begin writing and using the jargon, it'll quickly become second nature.

Sharyl's Story

I found the lack of a universal format very frustrating when just starting out in the professional world and desperately searching for a sense of order. Like other young beginners, I wanted to do things right; I wanted my scripts to be correct and understandable. But nobody at my first television news job could point to any standard or even a recommended format. I ended up grabbing old scripts out of the trash can after the news and simply tried to copy what I saw others do. Because there were many variations, I incorporated the pieces that made the most sense to me and that, I hoped, would make my script instructions clearly understood and interpreted by the people responsible for putting them on the air. Today, there's still nothing close to a universal television news script format. The "trash can approach" still seems to be one of the best ways to become familiar with what writers at a particular television station are doing.

Left versus Right

In writing television news stories, the first thing you have to get used to is how different the scripts *look* from a normal written page in a report, a book, or even the radio scripts you've already studied. The following examples show that there are two distinct elements: the editorial story content itself, which is called **copy,** and the technical video references and instructions.

> USUALLY, THE **COPY** IS WRITTEN ENTIRELY ON THE RIGHT HALF OF THE PAGE, LIKE THIS. THE WORDS "COPY" AND **"SCRIPT"** ARE OFTEN USED INTERCHANGEABLY.
>
> THE LEFT SIDE OF THE PAGE, OVER HERE, IS RESERVED FOR VIDEO REFERENCES AND OTHER TECHNICAL INSTRUCTIONS.

The following are definitions and examples of the various formats used in television news stories. Try to become familiar with the terms, but don't become fixated on exactly why they're called what they're called. Suffice it to say that these are the terms that caught on after being informally coined when video was emerging as a broadcast medium. These are commonly used terms, but don't be surprised if you end up working at places that use different ones.

Readers: No Video

A **reader** is a television story that includes absolutely no video, so is "read" entirely by the anchor appearing on camera. It's also called a **copy story.** When we refer to anchors "reading" a story or script, it means they're "reading" it *aloud* on camera. How is the term, "reader," used in a sentence? A producer might tell a writer, "Write me a twenty-second reader on the car crash that just happened downtown."

All stories should end with XXXs in parentheses. It helps separate the stories for the anchors, who read the right half of the script from a studio camera Teleprompter.

Often, television anchor copy is typed in ALL CAPITAL LETTERS, which many anchors find easier to read from the Teleprompter. However, some anchors prefer normal upper and lower case type. What you end up doing in the workplace may vary from job-to-job and even from anchor-to-anchor. The box on the next page shows an example of a reader:

```
CAR CRASH READER
ANCHOR/ON CAMERA                    (ANCHOR)
                                   IN THE NEWS TONIGHT...
                                   FOUR PEOPLE ARE
                                   HOSPITALIZED AND
                                   TWO MEN ARE IN JAIL
                                   AFTER A DESTRUCTIVE
                                   CAR CHASE THROUGH
                                   SARASOTA'S DOWNTOWN
                                   DISTRICT. 24-YEAR OLD
                                   STEVE BROWN AND
                                   30-YEAR OLD JOHN REDMOND
                                   ALLEGEDLY LED POLICE
                                   ON A HIGH-SPEED CHASE
                                   DOWN MAIN STREET AT
                                   MORE THAN 60 MILES AN
                                   HOUR. FOUR ELDERLY
                                   PEOPLE WERE INJURED
                                   AS THEY TRIED TO JUMP
                                   OUT OF THE WAY. THE
                                   VICTIMS' NAMES AND
                                   CONDITIONS HAVEN'T
                                   BEEN MADE PUBLIC...
                                   BUT OFFICIALS SAY ONE
                                   OF THEM WAS CRITICALLY
                                   INJURED.
                                   (XXX)
```

A typical reader can be anywhere from fifteen seconds (:15) to thirty seconds (:30) in length when read aloud. Generally, you can estimate the length or time of a television news script by counting one second per line of copy.

Readers are not the favorite type of story among television broadcasters, and it's easy to understand why: there's simply nothing visual about them. They could easily be written in the newspaper or for radio. But television, after all, is a *visual* medium. Television news producers, who create newscasts and choose which stories will be in them, search for visually compelling stories . . . stories that utilize video to enhance, explain, and illustrate them. So for the most part, readers are used sparingly in television news, generally reserved for reporting on breaking stories in which video news photographers haven't yet arrived on the scene, or haven't been able to get their video back to the television station.

Picture This: Voice Overs

A type of story that is much more up television's alley is a reader with something extra: videotape. It's called a **voice over** or **VO** (pronounced "vee-oh"). In a typical VO, the anchor begins reading the story on camera, just like a reader. But after a sentence or two, videotape is started ("rolled"). That means while the anchor continues reading the story, the viewer sees videotape. It could be video of an accident scene, a day care center, or whatever is relevant to the story.

How is the term, "VO," used in a sentence? A writer might ask an assignment editor, "Is the photographer back with the video of the car crash, yet? I need to see it before I write my VO so that I know what pictures we have available." Here's how that VO script might look on paper:

CAR CRASH VO	
ANCHOR/ON CAMERA	(ANCHOR)
	IN THE NEWS TONIGHT...
	FOUR PEOPLE ARE
	HOSPITALIZED AND
	TWO MEN ARE IN
	JAIL AFTER A
	DESTRUCTIVE CAR
	CHASE THROUGH
	SARASOTA'S DOWNTOWN
	DISTRICT.
(VO)	(VO)
Font: Sarasota	THIS IS THE MESS
	LEFT BEHIND AFTER
	POLICE SAY 24-YEAR
	OLD STEVE BROWN
	AND 30-YEAR OLD
	JOHN REDMOND
	BARRELED DOWN MAIN
	STREET AT MORE THAN
	60 MILES AN HOUR
	WITH POLICE CLOSE

(Continued)

BEHIND. FOUR ELDERLY
PEOPLE WERE INJURED
AS THEY TRIED TO JUMP
OFF THE STREET AND
GET OUT OF THE WAY.
THEIR NAMES AND
CONDITIONS HAVEN'T
BEEN MADE PUBLIC...
BUT OFFICIALS SAY ONE
OF THEM WAS CRITICALLY
INJURED.
(XXX)

Notice the wording of the VO is basically the same as the reader. However, keeping in mind that viewers will be seeing video of the aftermath of the car chase, we've added this reference: "This is the mess left behind . . ." Such specific references to video aren't always necessary, but can be helpful, especially when viewers might otherwise have trouble figuring out exactly what they're seeing in the video. In our example, the video may be of a bent, toppled-over street sign, broken glass on the street, and people standing around and looking.

As far as the way a VO looks on the physical page, the anchor reading the script on the air is primarily concerned with the *right* side of the page where the written "copy" appears. (The written words in a script are referred to as "copy" even when the stories aren't readers or copy stories.)

The behind-the-scenes players, such as the producers and directors of newscasts, are the ones who pay closest attention to the *left* side of the page. Writers must be adept at navigating back and forth between the two sides; comfortable in both the editorial job of writing the copy *and* the technical job of providing necessary video references and instructions. In the preceding example, you see the VO indicated on both the right side where the anchor reads and on the left side. A typical VO can last or "run" twenty seconds (:20) to thirty seconds (:30) in length when read aloud.

This is a good place to address the important function of parentheses in broadcast news scripts. Parentheses isolate words or phrases in the anchor copy that are *not to be read aloud on the air*. Examples of notations that should appear in parentheses on the anchor's right side of the page include the letters "VO" indicating where the video begins. Naturally, we don't want the anchor literally to say **"VO, this is the mess left behind after police . . . ,"** so parentheses separate the letters "VO" from the rest of the copy that *is* to be read aloud. The XXXs signaling the end of the story also belong in parentheses.

Of course, anchors are only human, and they *have* been known accidentally to read parenthetical notations on the air with embarrassing results! This phenomenon was humorized in the classic broadcast news situation comedy, *The Mary Tyler Moore Show*. It's election night and producer Murray Slaughter is looking over some copy in which hapless anchorman Ted Baxter has made some parenthetical notations of his own. The script reads:

> STAY WITH W-J-M'S CONTINUOUS ELECTION NIGHT COVERAGE. REMEMBER, WE'LL STAY ON THE AIR UNTIL A WINNER IS DECLARED (TAKE OFF GLASSES AND LOOK CONCERNED).

"Take that out of the script," the producer snaps, referring to the part that anchorman Ted Baxter has added about the glasses.

Ted responds, "Oh, come on Murray, let's leave it in there. That's the way I remember my motivation!"

"I don't mind you remembering your motivation," producer Murray responds, "but it frosts me when you read it over the air like you did last night. 'Mississippi River rises. . .thousands flee homes. . .take off glasses and look sad!'"

As a general rule, true life anchors are pretty good at distinguishing between what *is* and what *is not* to be read aloud, with the help of those precious parentheses.

Back to the car crash VO. You'll notice in the example, there's a **"font"** instruction on the left side to indicate where the videotape was shot: Sarasota. Fonts are not read aloud, but instead appear in writing on the television screen along with the video as the viewer watches. It's a visual assistance—a sort of label—used to tell viewers more about the video they're watching. Fonts are also called other names: "CGs" for the "character generator" that physically creates the fonts; "Chyron's" the brand name of one widely used character generator; or "lower-thirds" because many fonts appear on the lower-third portion of the television screen.

How would the word, "font," be used in a sentence? A writer might say, "I need to know where this videotape was shot so I can write the font on the script."

Fonts are not only used to describe locations. They're also used on screen to give the name and title of a person being interviewed in a news report. An example of such a font is Morgan Jones, Sarasota Co. Police Dept.

Add a Little "Bite": VO-SOTs

A selected piece of an interview with somebody for a television news story is called a **sound bite.** Some people use the term **"sound"** or **"bite"** for short. It can also be called a **SOT** (pronounced "saht" or "ess-oh-tee"), which stands for "sound on tape."

Bites can range from just a few seconds in length to twenty seconds or more, depending on the type of story being told and the type of newscast in which they will appear. They're typically used along with videotape to form what's called a **VO-SOT** (pronounced "voh-saht" or "vee-oh-saht"), or also called a **VO-BITE** (pronounced "vee-oh-bite"). How would such a term be used in a sentence? A writer might ask a reporter, "Who did you get 'sound' from for the car crash story? I need to write a VO-BITE." Here's an example of a VO-BITE:

CAR CRASH VO-SOT	
ANCHOR/ON CAMERA	(ANCHOR)
	IN THE NEWS TONIGHT...
	FOUR PEOPLE ARE
	HOSPITALIZED AND TWO
	MEN ARE IN JAIL AFTER
	LEADING POLICE ON A
	DESTRUCTIVE CAR CHASE
	THROUGH SARASOTA'S
	DOWNTOWN DISTRICT.
(VO)	(VO)
Font: Sarasota	THIS IS THE MESS LEFT
	BEHIND AFTER POLICE
	SAY 24-YEAR-OLD STEVE
	BROWN AND 30-YEAR
	OLD JOHN REDMOND
	BARRELED DOWN MAIN
	STREET AT MORE THAN
	60 MILES AN HOUR.
	FOUR ELDERLY PEOPLE
	WERE INJURED AS THEY
	TRIED TO GET OUT OF
	THE WAY.
(SOT)	(SOT)
Font: Morgan Jones, Sarasota Police Dept.	IN: "THE VICTIMS WERE TRYING..."
	OUT: "...DIDN'T MAKE IT."
(VO)	RUNS: 14
	(VO)
	THE NAMES AND
	CONDITIONS OF THE
	INJURED HAVEN'T BEEN
	MADE PUBLIC, BUT
	OFFICIALS SAY ONE
	OF THEM WAS CRITICALLY
	HURT.
	(XXX)

You'll see in the preceding example that the name and organization of the person who was interviewed, Morgan Jones, is typed on the left side of the scripts so the technical folks know to font it on the television screen as viewers see and hear Jones' bite.

In VO-SOTs, we usually don't type out every word an interview subject says in a sound bite. Instead, type the first few words and the last few words of the bite and indicate the total length of the bite in seconds. Here's the sound bite portion of the script:

(SOT)	(SOT)
Font: Morgan Jones,	IN: "THE VICTIMS WERE TRYING..."
Sarasota Police Dept.	OUT: "...DIDN'T MAKE IT."
	RUNS: 14

The first words of the sound bite, called the **incue,** are typed beside the abbreviation "IN," and the last words of the sound bite, called the **outcue,** are typed beside the abbreviation "OUT." The length of the bite, which is its **run time,** is typed next to the abbreviation "RUNS." Therefore, the incue of the Morgan Jones sound bite is "The victims were trying . . ." (The triple period is sort of like saying etcetera, indicating the sound bite continues even though all the words aren't written out in full.) The outcue is ". . . didn't make it." The bite runs a total of fourteen seconds, indicated by a colon and the number fourteen in parentheses (:14). This is all important technical information that's critical to your partners in the newscast, from the videotape editors and technical director to the producers and anchors.

In our example, after the sound bite, more videotape is shown. The way you know this by the VO written on both sides of the script in parentheses after the sound bite.

A typical VO-BITE (the same thing as a VO-SOT) can run anywhere from twenty-five seconds (:25) to a minute (1:00) in length when read aloud, including the length of the sound bite.

In the real world, it really doesn't matter much whether you remember to put quote marks around the incues and outcues or whether you use a colon after the word "Font" on a script, so don't get hung up on minutia. However, it *is* important that the incues and outcues, as well as the *length* of the bite and the *spelling* of the particular font, be *accurate.*

In our previous discussion of radio, we showed how the length of stories and actualities is designated. It works much the same way in television news. In the VO-SOT example, you see the sound bite is fourteen seconds long. Here are examples of how other times should be written in scripts:

- :14 designates a length of fourteen seconds.
- 1:14 designates a length of one minute and fourteen seconds.
- 2:01:14 designates a length of two hours, one minute, and fourteen seconds.

Introducing . . . Lead-ins

A **lead-in** is the script that the anchor reads to introduce a reporter's live shot or pre-recorded story. A producer could tell a writer, "Write me a ten second lead-in to the car crash story; Shannon Page is the reporter." The resulting lead-in could look something like this:

CAR CRASH INTRO
ANCHOR/ON CAMERA

                                    (ANCHOR)
                                    TWO SARASOTA MEN
                                    ARE IN JAIL TONIGHT
                                    AFTER LEADING POLICE
                                    ON A WILD AND
                                    DESTRUCTIVE CHASE
                                    THROUGH THE DOWNTOWN
                                    AREA. SHANNON PAGE
                                    REPORTS FOUR ELDERLY
                                    BYSTANDERS WERE HURT
                                    IN THE CHAOS.
(PKG)   (PKG)

Anchor lead-ins are typically ten seconds (:10) to twenty seconds (:20) in length when read aloud. The previous example is ten lines long, so it times out to approximately ten seconds.

The Whole Package

A **package** is the name given to a reporter's prerecorded story. The anchor usually introduces the package with a lead-in, and then the reporter takes over the storytelling. In the previous lead-in example, Shannon Page is the reporter. The viewer will actually hear her voice and will probably see her appear on camera somewhere in her report.

The common script abbreviation used to indicate a package is "PKG," as in the example. Here's how the word "package" might be used in a sentence. A producer could tell a reporter, "Be sure your package is no longer than a minute and a half. We don't have time for anything longer."

The script that the reporter writes for the package itself looks entirely different than the anchor copy we've examined so far. To learn about the format of package scripts, you should learn one more set of terms.

First, when a reporter appears on camera within the story, that segment of video is called a **STANDUP** or an **ON CAMERA**. Reporters often use standups at the end of their packages: a **STANDUP CLOSE**. It's rare that reporters do a standup at the very *beginning* of a package, but that would be called a **STANDUP OPEN.** A standup anywhere in between is referred to as a **BRIDGE.**

How would the word, "standup," be used in a sentence? A reporter on location might tell his supervisors back in the newsroom, "We're all done with interviews, but I still have to shoot my standup before I head back to the studio."

The package script is not written in the left hand/right hand Teleprompter style because the anchor won't be reading it; the reporter will. How should the package script look? Individual reporters tend to develop their own formats. You may work someplace that requires a certain format. If so, it'll be easy to adapt what you're learning here.

At first, reading a package script might seem like reading Greek. However, as you begin to write for yourself and actually use the format, it'll make sense. In the meantime, keep the following example nearby to refer to. It's a package script written in a format that could be clearly understood at most television stations.

ATTKISSON CAR CRASH PACKAGE

(VO/SARASOTA ambulance & victims)
All four victims are in their eighties...their names aren't released. Police say they were crossing Main Street after attending the Sarasota Food Festival...when a green truck barreled toward them at more than 60 miles an hour.

(SOT-MORGAN JONES, SARASOTA CO. POLICE DEPT.)
THE VICTIMS WERE TRYING TO GET TO THE PARKING LOT, THEY HAD JUST FINISHED EATING AT THE FISH MARKET AND WERE IN A LEGAL CROSSWALK AND HAD THE RIGHT OF WAY. THEY SAW THE TRUCK COMING TOWARD THEM AND RAN TOWARD THE SIDEWALK, BUT OBVIOUSLY THEY DIDN'T MAKE IT. (:14)

(VO/hospital and street scenes)
Witnesses say the victims were two men and two women. As ambulances rushed them to the hospital...a police officer on site chased after the truck in his patrol car. The chase went on for eight miles before the men in the truck finally stopped. Sam Popkin witnessed the arrests.

(SOT-SAM POPKIN, WITNESS)
THE DRIVER JUST GOT OUT AND PUT HIS HANDS BEHIND HIS HEAD BEFORE THE COP EVEN HAD TO ASK HIM TO. THEN THE PASSENGER JUMPED OUT AND DIDN'T COOPERATE, I MEAN THE COP WAS REALLY YELLING AT HIM TO PUT HIS HANDS UP. GUY WHO WAS DRIVING SEEMED DISORIENTED. HE WAS REALLY STAGGERING AROUND. (:12)

(Continued)

(VO/suspects walk into jail)

Police won't say whether the driver, Steve Brown, was drinking...but they do say felony charges are pending against him. Passenger John Redmond is charged with disorderly conduct and resisting arrest. Both men are from Bradenton.

(ATTKISSON STANDUP)

AS FOR THE ELDERLY VICTIMS, THREE OF THE FOUR ARE REPORTED IN GOOD CONDITION AT THIS HOUR, BUT ONE IS CRITICALLY INJURED...SO MORE CHARGES COULD BE FILED. MEANTIME, FESTIVAL ORGANIZERS SAY EXTRA SAFETY PATROLS WILL BE ON DUTY NEXT WEEKEND TO HELP PROTECT PEOPLE CROSSING MAIN STREET. SHARYL ATTKISSON, WXXX-TV, SARASOTA.

The package script contains two distinct components. One is the reporter's **narration,** also referred to as **track,** which is shown in regular upper and lower case type. It comprises all the sentences the reporter records in his own voice to tell the story. In our example, there are three sections of narration (track): the paragraphs beginning with "All four victims . . .," "Witnesses say . . .," and "Police won't say . . ."

The other major component is the **field elements,** which are designated by all capital letters. This includes all of the elements gathered on location, such as the sound bites (from interviews conducted in the field) and the standup (which is video-taped in the field). In our example, the field elements include the sound bite with Officer Morgan James, the sound bite with witness Sam Popkin, and the Attkisson standup close.

Using upper and lower case for the narration (track) and all capital letters for the field elements makes it easy for anyone reading the script to distinguish the narration from the bites and standup. It's important for everyone from the supervisor reviewing your script for quality and accuracy, to the videotape editor who uses the script as a guide to compile the final story.

Other formatting features you'll notice in the example include sound bites marked by SOT in parentheses, followed by the name of the person interviewed for the bite. Then, *the entire text of the sound bite is typed out verbatim* in all capital letters. (This is in contrast to *VO-BITES* where only the incue and outcue are noted.) Last, the length of that bite is noted in parentheses. The policeman's bite runs fourteen seconds (:14); the eyewitness bite runs twelve seconds (:12).

The beginning of each track (narration segment) is marked with VO in parentheses, noting the type of video that will be shown over that particular track (such as "suspects walk into jail"). This helps the supervisor reviewing the script visualize the way the story may look. It also guides the videotape editor to the pictures (video) you had in mind when writing each track.

There's no formula for how many tracks and how many sound bites belong in a package or what pattern they should follow. Fledgling reporters often want to know,

"Should I write a track, bite, track, bite, standup?" Actually, the possibilities are endless. Packages can be done with no sound bites at all or with several sound bites from the same person. Sound bites from the same or different people can be "butted" back-to-back in a story, meaning linked together with no track in between. Occasionally, an entire package can be done without any narration at all by stringing together sound bites and so-called **natural sound,** such as laughter, gunshots, wind blowing, or birds singing. Your only limit is your own creative ability.

In regular newscasts, packages can range in length from a minute (1:00) to three minutes (3:00) in total length. A minute and thirty seconds (1:30) is probably average. For magazine-type shows, packages may run much longer, ten minutes (10:00) or more.

Decisions, Decisions . . .

Who, exactly, determines whether a story should be told using a full-fledged reporter package or using a shorter and simpler VO-BITE? Who decides whether a package should be a minute long (1:00) or two minutes and fifteen seconds (2:15)? Generally, such decisions are left to a newscast's *producer,* with input and guidance from lots of people including news directors, reporters, and assignment editors. The discussion usually begins in a morning meeting, but the status of a given story could change several times throughout the day as other news develops or fails to develop. If there aren't enough interesting elements, a story that begins the day as a package could turn into a VO-BITE. On the other hand, a VO or VO-BITE could be expanded into a package if a reporter gets to the scene of the story and finds there's more to show or more to tell.

Look A-Live

A staple of almost every local newscast in America is the **live shot**. A live shot is when the reporter is actually reporting on location, in the field, *during* the newscast. The anchor usually reads a lead-in introducing the reporter. Then the reporter begins telling the story and may introduce the package.

How is the phrase, "live shot," used in a sentence? A producer could tell a writer, "I've changed Shannon Page's package to a live shot, so you'll have to rewrite the lead-in to reflect that." Here's how the resulting script might look:

CAR CRASH LIVE INTRO	
ANCHOR/ON CAMERA	(ANCHOR)
	TWO SARASOTA MEN
	ARE IN JAIL TONIGHT
	AFTER LEADING POLICE
	ON A WILD AND
	DESTRUCTIVE CHASE
	THROUGH THE DOWNTOWN
	AREA. SHANNON PAGE
	IS LIVE DOWNTOWN
	TONIGHT WITH THE
	LATEST ON THIS
	DEVELOPING STORY. SHANNON?
(LIVE SHOT)	(LIVE SHOT)

Notice that the live shot lead-in is very similar to the package lead-in. The difference is in the last sentence in which the anchor actually "tosses" to Shannon in the field.

The Lowdown on Rundowns

Now that you know the important terms used in the industry, it's time to show you the format used to organize all of these types of scripts into an actual newscast.

It's the job of the newscast or show producer to assign the stories that must be written, determine the format of each story, designate how long it should be, and time the total newscast with such precision that it is neither one single second longer nor one second shorter than it's supposed to be. To do this, producers use something commonly referred to as a **rundown** or a line-up. A rundown or line-up is an outline of the newscast, organized and timed on paper. Every newscast of the day has its own separate rundown. Even a brief, five-minute-long newscast has its own rundown.

Typically, putting together rundowns is *not* the writer's job. However, you need to know about them because they serve as the writers' assignment sheet, telling which writers will write which stories, which anchors will read them, what the slugs and formats are, and what total time is allotted. It's also important to understand rundowns because writers often end up producing shows, and producers often end up writing.

How could the word, "rundown," be used in a sentence? A producer might tell a writer, "You'll see on the rundown that I've assigned you to write the first four stories. If you don't think you have enough time to write them all, let me know and I'll give one of them to another writer."

As with script formats, rundowns have many possible formats, but they share some common elements. At first glance, rundowns are even more confusing to read

FIGURE 4.1   *The first segment of a CBS Evening News rundown*

than packages. But broken down line by line, they aren't as confusing as they might seem.

The following is a *very* simplified, introductory version of a rundown to give you an idea of how one might look, followed by an explanation.

Page	*ANCHOR*	*SLUG*	*FORMAT*	*TIME*	*WRITER*	*BACKTIME*
0	Two-Shot	Headlines	VO	:20	John	
1	Two-Shot	Hello	COPY	:10	John	
2	Paul	Tornado	VOBITE	1:00	Ted	
3	Ann	Car Crash	LEAD-IN	:15	Ted	
4		Car Live	LIVESHOT	2:00	John	
5	Two-Shot	Tease	VO	:20		
COMMR.1				*2:10*		
20	Ann	WeathToss	AD LIB	:15		
21	Malcolm	Weather		4:00		
22	Three-Shot	Tease	VO	:15		
COMMR.2				*1:30*		
30	Three-Shot	SportsToss	AD LIB	:10		
31	Holly	Sports		4:30		
32	Three-Shot	Tease	VO	:10		
COMMR.3				*2:10*		
40	Paul	FlyingTurtle	VO	:30	Ted	
41	Four-Shot	Goodbye	COPY	:10	John	
COMMR.4				*1:30*		

Our example is a half-hour newscast divided into four news blocks. The blocks are simply the chunks of news separated by commercial breaks. The first block in our example consists of the following stories slugged: "Headlines," "Hello," "Tornado," "Car Crash lead-in," "Car Crash Live Shot," and "Tease." The second block includes "Weather Toss," "Weather," and "Tease." The third block is "Sports Toss," "Sports," and "Tease," The fourth block is "Flying Turtle" and "Goodbye."

A producer might tell a writer, "The Flying Turtle story goes in the fourth block. It's not a hard-hitting story, so try to make it humorous." The word "section" is interchangeable with the word "block." A producer might say, "The tornado story will lead off the first section of the newscast."

The far-left column shows the page number assigned to each story. Take a look at the sample rundown and see if you can figure out the page numbering system used. Use a little logical thinking. You'll discover the scripts in the first block begin with page number zero and continue in consecutive order from there. But, suddenly, in the second block, the numbers skip up to twenty. The third block script pages start with thirty and the fourth block with forty. Are you noticing the pattern? This is a common numbering system that helps organize and order the newscast on paper.

Next to the page number, the producer lists the name of the anchor assigned to read that particular story on camera. Sometimes both anchors are seen on the television screen at the same time in what's called a "two-shot." In our sample rundown, "Headlines," "Hello," and some "Teases" are two-shots. That means the writer must divvy up copy in a single script so that each anchor has some copy to read.

Here's an example of how the script for page zero, the "Headlines" in the example, might be written. Note that the anchor assigned to read the copy is noted in parentheses at the beginning of the script on the right-hand side. The left side includes the page number (0), the slug (Headlines), the shot (two-shot of Paul and Ann), and where video (VO) is seen.

```
0. HEADLINES
PAUL / ANN 2-SHOT                    (TWO-SHOT / PAUL)
                                     IN THE NEWS TONIGHT...
(VO / TORNADO)                       (VO)
                                     A TORNADO RIPS THROUGH
                                     A POLK COUNTY MOBILE
                                     HOME PARK. TWO PEOPLE
(VO / CAR CRASH)                     ARE MISSING.
                                     (VO / ANN)
                                     AND A WILD CHASE
                                     THROUGH DOWNTOWN
                                     SARASOTA LANDS FOUR
                                     ELDERLY PEOPLE IN THE
                                     HOSPITAL.
                                     (XXX)
```

In this example, both anchors, Paul and Ann, are *seen* at the beginning of the story, but it's Paul who's designated to *read* first. Then Ann takes over with the words, "And a wild chase . . ."

Now refer back to the rundown. Following the page number and the name of the anchor is the story's title, or slug; then the format; the time allotted for the story; and the name of the person assigned to write it. Last, there's a column for the producer's **backtiming** notes. Backtiming is the process of precisely calculating each component of the newscast to make sure it all adds up to exactly one half-hour, or whatever the designated length of the newscast is.

The "Hello" of a newscast is where the anchors first greet, or "say hello," to the viewers. Here's how a "hello" could look on paper:

```
1. HELLO
PAUL/ANN 2-SHOT                    (TWO-SHOT/ANN)
                                   GOOD EVENING, I'M ANN WEAVER.
                                   (TWO-SHOT/PAUL)
                                   AND I'M PAUL REASON.
                                   (XXX)
```

In this "Hello," the two anchors are seen together, but Ann begins reading first, introducing herself. Then Paul gives his name.

"Teases" are scripts that tell what's coming up in the newscast. They "tease" viewers by giving them a bit of tantalizing information about an upcoming story hopefully to keep viewers tuned in through the commercial break. Here's how the script for our "page five" tease might look:

```
5. TEASE
PAUL/ANN 2-SHOT                    (TWO-SHOT/ANN)
                                   AFTER THE BREAK...
                                   FIND OUT WHAT WEATHER
                                   RECORD WAS SET TODAY.
(VO)                               THE FORECAST AHEAD.
                                   (VO/PAUL)
                                   AND LATER...A TURTLE THAT
                                   REALLY CAN FLY.
                                   YOU WON'T BELIEVE THIS ONE!
                                   (XXX)
```

You can see the tease, page five, begins with both anchors on camera in a two-shot. Ann speaks first, teasing the weather forecast. Then videotape of the flying turtle rolls while Paul reads the tease for that story. There are countless ways to divide up copy between the anchors, to write teases, and to begin or end a newscast . . . again limited only by the creativity of the producers and writers involved.

The last story in a newscast before the "Goodbye" is referred to as the "kicker." It's often funny or light in nature. Certainly it doesn't *have* to be, but teasing humorous kickers throughout the newscast can help keep people tuned in until the end of the show. After an entire newscast of serious—sometimes disturbing—stories, kickers help end things on an upbeat note.

FIGURE 4.2 *Behind the scene, a reporter (seated at right) prepares to give a live report from the newsroom. The teleprompter operator is seated behind him.*

Speaking of ending things, this is a good time to draw this chapter to a close.

Use the format examples in this chapter to guide you as you put the concepts into practice writing your own readers, VOs, VO-SOTs, and packages. Before long, you'll commit the terms and formats to memory.

Web sites

For more information, check out the following Web sites.

www.ryakuga.org/tutorials/broadcast.html
Tips for shooting and writing a basic news story

www.newswriting.com/r_soundbites.htm
A suggested guide to using sound bites

www.tvrundown.com/voice.html
Advice on writing VO's from "TV Rundown" Web site

www.rtnda.org/trades/writing.shtml#feature
Tips on writing good teases

www.newswriting.com/r_californiaman.htm
Discussion on why to keep ages and addresses out of your stories

Quick Review of Terms

- **Field elements:** Package components gathered in the field, including bites and standups.
- **Font:** On-screen words indicating the location where video was shot or a sound bite's name and title or organization.
- **Incue:** The first few words of a sound bite, designated by "IN."
- **Lead-in:** The anchor's introduction to a reporter's live shot or prerecorded package.
- **Live shot:** Reporter's on-location report; *not* prerecorded on tape.
- **Narration:** The sentences in a package script that the reporter reads aloud; also referred to as *track*.
- **Outcue:** The last few words of a sound bite, designated by "OUT."
- **Package:** Reporter's prerecorded story.
- **Reader:** Anchor copy with no video.
- **Rundown:** An outline of the entire newscast organized and timed "on paper."
- **Run time:** Total length of a sound bite, designated by "RUNS."
- **Sound Bite or SOT:** A selected piece of an interview with a person.
- **Standup:** The part of a package in which the reporter appears on camera in the field.
- **Voice over/VO:** Anchor copy with video.
- **VO-SOT or VO-BITE:** Anchor copy with video and a sound bite.

Review Questions

1. What's the reason for the right side/left side page format for television news scripts?
2. What type of information generally appears on each side of the page? Be specific.
3. What are the terms used for the various types of stories that can be written using video and/or sound bites?
4. What's the purpose of a font?
5. What type of information is fonted?
6. What's the purpose of parentheses?
7. What are the purposes of a rundown?

Summary

This chapter has defined and demonstrated widely used terms, phrases, and formats in television news writing. There is no universal industry standard, but there are many common format basics, such as writing copy on the right side of the page and reserving the left side for video instructions and references. Students who attain a working knowledge of the information in this chapter will be equipped with the physical script building blocks they need in a real work environment.

5

Online News

- To give an overview of writing online
- To contrast and compare radio, television, print, and online writing
- To provide a basic Internet style guide
- To explain the organization of a typical Web site newsroom
- To explore the Internet as a research tool

"The rules are different." "It's breaking all the rules." "There *are* no rules." Each of these things has been said about the Internet, and, to some degree, each of them is true. We want you to become familiar with this fast-paced, developing medium that is the source of so many job opportunities and is becoming increasingly important in our everyday lives.

Some of you may land jobs exclusively in the online domain. But even if you end up working in radio or television news, expect your job to have some overlap with cyberspace. Chances are, at a minimum, that you'll be required to adapt versions of your broadcasting stories for your company's Web site. So you should have a basic working knowledge of this relatively new arena.

Each company has its own standards and ideas for Web writing. What's encouraged, expected, or accepted on any given Web site is as varied as the sites themselves.

Brief History

Today's teenagers and young adults don't remember a time when the Internet was not a fact of life. But in the context of media history, the Internet is a relative newcomer.

Many people consider the origin of the Internet to be a system that was set up in the 1960s: it was a "government-financed linkup of supercomputers intended to keep vital communications open in the event of a war." Government scientists and academics were allowed to hook in, using the limited, but still amazing, innovation as a research tool. It connected Advanced Research Projects Agency Network (ARPANET), the network used by the Defense Advanced Research Projects Agency, to a thousand independent electronic networks at universities; the National Science Foundation's 700 research and education networks; the National Aeronautics and Space Administration (NASA) Science Network; and the Energy Sciences Network.[1]

In the 1980s, thousands of commercial entities, libraries, and educational institutions around the world joined the Internet. Last to hop on board the information superhighway were ordinary citizens with desktop computers. However, after the public did go online, there was no stopping the popularity explosion. The Internet "quickly established itself as an exhiliratingly anarchic free-form" medium.[2]

By the late 1980s, there were an estimated 500,000 Internet users, but something was lacking. They still had no easy way of doing what we now take for granted: sending electronic mail to people who are using *other* systems. That capability came when two academic hackers devised their own gateway connection between Internet users and the half-million-plus users on CompuServe. CompuServe is an Internet provider, meaning it provides the technical means to get people with no direct link on to the Internet. That big news was reported in relatively understated fashion in November 1989:

> Karl Kleinpaste and George Jones of Ohio State University's computer science department automated a dial-up through Hayes 1200-baud modems for checking and transferring mail from one system to the other. Internet uses the Simple Mail Transfer Protocol (SMTP), while CompuServe uses its own Message Interchange Format (MIF). Once the gateway became popular with some users, CompuServe offered to help support the link. Delivery time varies based on the route messages take through the Internet system. CompuServe users pay regular connect-time charges but Internet users can send or receive messages at no charge.[3]

By late 1992, nearly a million estimated hosts were on the Internet, with a thousand new hosts a day joining in. When you consider that the ARPANET component was comprised of a mere *four* nodes in 1969, you get an idea of the galactic pace of expansion.[4]

With no one organizing or regulating the Internet, Internet journalism followed no single path as it evolved into its trademark freewheeling form . . . with no plan, set of rules, or guidelines.

Newsrooms Go Online

Just a few years ago, reporters and writers relied largely on whatever archives they could assemble on their own when researching a story, such as files of newspaper clippings. If there was time, we could occasionally make a trip to the library or search records in a public building, such as a county courthouse. If we needed to find out about a group or organization, we had to make phone calls and wait for faxed responses.

That was a problem.

Broadcasters, especially in local news, seldom have the luxury of spending minutes—let alone hours—digging for background or turning up data before a tight deadline. The reality was that it was often simply not possible to get information that could prove helpful or even critical to a story.

Newsrooms lucky enough to have the money employed their own librarians who could quickly research stories and develop original newspaper clipping and research files.

In the late 1980s, more newsrooms retired typewriters and became computerized. This allowed for an important transition in wire service delivery. Wire copy used to be delivered through special machines that printed the stories on rolls of paper that were then ripped into sections and saved, discarded, or distributed. It was a highly inefficient way to receive information.

With computers in newsrooms, wire services finally became widely available on each computer terminal. Some newsrooms bought software that allowed users to search through an archive of wire copy that had crossed (been sent) hours or even days before. Some newsrooms also subscribed to computerized research services, such as Lexis-Nexis, giving a way to access and search public files, as well as magazine and newspaper archives going back years.

Yet these advances were *nothing* compared to the capabilities that would be offered in just a few years on the Internet at the click of a mouse: instant access to public data, opinions, newspaper, and articles; background on organizations; addresses and phone numbers; maps; home pages of political candidates; and real-time communications with sources worldwide, to name just a few.

Defining Internet, Web, and Online

The **Internet,** also called the Net, simply refers to the entire system of the international network of computers linked together to form the single largest source of information on the planet. The World Wide Web, also called the **Web,** is the most user-friendly portion of the Internet where most of us do our surfing, researching, shopping, and business. Because the majority of people using the Internet are actually on the Web portion of the network, the two terms have become nearly synonymous and are often used interchangeably, which may gall purists, but is just the reality of the situation. When you are in the act of using or being on the Internet, you are **online.**

Printcast

With that brief background and definition of basic terms, it's time to look at the art of writing news online. We've coined the term **"printcast"** to make the point that online writing is often a combination of print and broadcast styles. The following table shows what traits online writing uses.

Online Combines . . .

Newspaper Traits	Broadcasting Traits	Added Dimensions
Headlines, captions	Immediacy, live capability	Links to related pages
Still images, graphics	Audio, video	More physical space
Complex writing	Conversational writing	Interactivity

The preceding table demonstrates the fact that Internet writing doesn't neatly fit into either a print or broadcasting mold. There are similarities and also profound differences among the three mediums:

- Like newspapers, Web sites have headlines and make use of still images and graphics.
- Like broadcasting, Web sites have the capability to report news instantaneously as it happens.
- Web sites can use real-time audio and video, like in live radio and television.
- Web sites alone can make important links to related pages.
- Online writers often have the luxury of more time and space than is possible in traditional broadcasting mediums.
- It's acceptable for online writing to be somewhat more complex than broadcast writing because people can reread complicated sentences on their computer terminal if necessary, much as readers can reread newspaper articles if they don't understand a point the first time around.
- At the same time, online writing can lend itself to a more casual and conversational style than traditional newspaper writing.
- The online world stands alone in its unique interactive relationship with viewers, listeners, and readers: "users."

Staying Current

Web sites that report news are constantly challenged to stay as current as possible. After all, who wants to visit a newspaper's Web site only to find the same stories that were printed in the morning edition of the paper hours before? What Internet user would be satisfied to visit a television station's Web site only to find a rehash of the previous evening's news?

News grows stale at a faster rate on the Internet than it does anywhere else, largely because of the expectations of the audience, which demands fresh and current events by the moment, preferably twenty-four hours a day and seven days a week. Successful news Web sites must provide something different and better than traditional sources, whether it's more depth and detail, a different perspective, or links to related information.

Organizing the Story

Print journalists were traditionally taught to write news in a style called *inverted pyramid*. Picture an upside-down triangle pointing down. The most important information, represented by the wide base of the upside-down triangle, is presented first in the story. The least important information, represented by the pointy tip at the bottom, is given last. Those less important details—the pointy tip—can be easily chopped off the bottom of the story if it turns out to be too long.

Broadcast writers, on the other hand, often use the *completed circle* style of writing described earlier. Often, the information given at the end of a broadcast story is *not* the least important; in fact, it can be integral.

Considering these divergent styles, what's the best way to write news for the Internet audience, applying *printcast* concepts?

Some expert advice for this text comes from Ellen Crean of the CBS News Web site: CBSNews.com. Her title is producer, but like other Internet producers, she's also very much a writer.

"When writing news for the Internet, write tight," Crean advises. "But forget about the full-blown (print-style) pyramid. It's better to think about a knish or an eggroll: Lots of stuff packed tightly into a small space."

"Put yourself in the surfer's shoes. What do they want to see on a Web site that is dedicated to news? You may be certain that they expect something different from other media. So if you write a news story for the Web as if you are writing analysis for a magazine, or even a standard newspaper article, don't be surprised if your Web content is less than compelling."

Crean gives the following example of a news story as it might appear in print and then presents her own Internet version of the same report:

A man in Smalltown, USA, returned from his tropical vacation to find that his house had turned into a zoo. John Jones had no sooner unlocked the door at his Elm Street home than he was greeted by a cacophony of animal noises—and a very distinctive odor. It turned out that he had mistakenly left a kitchen window open, which certain local wildlife had taken as an invitation to come in and have a party. A phone call from a panicked Jones brought an animal rescue team to break up the festivities.

Taken into custody, and later released in the nearby woods, were seven squirrels, three raccoons, a family of moles, and several wild birds. As for Jones, he is still assessing the damage, which so far includes yards of ruined carpeting, fourteen broken Hummel figurines, three pieces of formerly upholstered furniture, and a dining room table which he describes as "pretty scratched up." Adds Jones, "Just tell everyone to make sure all their windows are shut before they leave the house."

Following is the same story as it might be written in *printcast* for the Internet:

SMALLTOWN, USA—

Take John Jones' advice: Don't leave the house without shutting all your windows. When he came back from a tropical vacation recently, he was greeted by a few new tenants:

- Seven squirrels
- Three raccoons
- A family of moles
- Several wild birds

While the wildlife was soon dispatched to their native habitat by an animal rescue team, Jones was left to inventory the damage, including:

- 14 broken Hummel figurines
- Three pieces of formerly upholstered furniture
- Yards of ruined carpeting
- A "pretty scratched up" dining room table

Printcast news stories make liberal use of what is sometimes termed *bullets*, simply meaning a list of short words or phrases, usually offset by some sort of graphic device. The preceding story includes bullets describing the so-called new tenants and the damage done to the house.

It may be left up to you, as writer, to figure out ways to enhance your Internet stories. In the previous example, that could mean including:

- Links to Web sites about home repair, dealing with wildlife, medical advice on contact with wild animals, animal help organizations, and possibly hints on how to remove pet stains from carpet.
- Photographs of the damaged house.
- Streamed video.
- A poll. In this case, it's an offbeat story that might lend itself to an offbeat question. For example:

Which of the following wild animals would be most welcome in your home? (a) squirrels (b) moles (c) raccoons (d) foxes (e) the World Wrestling Foundation.

Perhaps more than in any other medium, a writer of Internet news must always be thinking in multimedia terms: considering the print elements of the script; the graphic look of the page; video and audio possibilities; still photos; suggested links; and interactivity, such as polls.

Translating Broadcasting Scripts

What constitutes effective storytelling in radio or television doesn't always work in printcast. When attempting to turn broadcasting scripts into good Internet stories, Chris Hawke, a CBSNews.com producer tells us one particular technique doesn't translate well.

"Using quotes from nonexperts, which on television is an effective way to give the viewer the 'everyman' perspective, does not work as text online. Often, television scripts have to be completely reordered, because the visual logic that holds them together no longer applies," says Hawke.

For example, in a television package about the Vietnam Wall, a writer may choose to begin with touching scenes of people leaving mementos at the monument. The decision to start the story in this way dictates, in part, how the rest of it is written. But the same story on the Internet would have to be rethought completely because the audience reads the script without seeing visual images simultaneously.

Also remember when translating a script that the Internet version can include much more detail, depth, and analysis than a typical radio or television news report. So try to find out if there are additional facts that didn't make it the broadcast version and work them into your Internet story.

When producer Hawke translates television news scripts into Internet stories at CBSNews.com, he says the "assertions of the correspondents (reporters) can be bolstered using wire copy, links to source documents, and, ideally, more of the correspondent's original reporting that was not used because of time constraints. An ideal would be for an online news story on, say, drug prices to become a take-off point for a public policy debate, with links to think tanks, relevant legislation, policy papers, and forums for the public to speak out."

Figure 5.1 is a CBS News television script. Figure 5.2 is the printcast version of the same story, which was translated by a writer and producer for the CBS News Web site.

(ATTKISSON/ROSS-TAYLOR/RADOVSKY/FIRESTONE 7/19/01)
TRT: 1:55

(VO)
The federal investigation into Firestone tires reached critical mass today—Firestone rejected the government's request to recall millions more tires. That pushes Firestone and the National Highway Traffic Safety Administration, NHTSA, closer to a nasty confrontation...a FORCED recall.

Some observers say that could be the kiss of death for the financially-troubled tiremaker, which employs 45-thousand people (in the Americas). But NHTSA is said to be determined to take action, under pressure from Congress to prove itself in the high-profile investigation that's dragged on for more than a year.

Late today, Firestone didn't budge on the company's longstanding position:

(SOT-JOHN LAMPE, FIRESTONE CEO)
"OUR TIRES AND OUR WILDERNESS A-T TIRES SPECIFICALLY ARE SAFE." (05)

(VO)
But sources say behind the scenes, Firestone was seriously discussing removing more tires. The negotiations with NHTSA reached an impasse over wording: Firestone wanted to call it a "product improvement program", NHTSA insisted on a formal "recall".

(GRAPHIC #1 POSSIBLE NEW RECALL)
The tires involved are: ALL 15 and 16-inch Wilderness AT tires except ones made at the company's Aiken, South Carolina plant.

(GRAPHIC #2 AUGUST 2000 RECALL)
Last year Firestone agreed to recall only ATX tires and 15-inch Wilderness tires made in Decatur, Illinois.

(VO/Mechanics replacing)
Ford is already replacing 13 million of the non-recalled tires on its own. But that still leaves 27 million Wilderness tires that were sold for use on other vehicles.

(VO/Rodriguez)
Hundreds of lawsuits are pending against Firestone. Set for trial next month is the case of Marisa Rodriguez, mother of 3, now brain-damaged after a Ford Explorer rollover on Firestone tires last year. Her husband says their family is forever changed.

(SOT-JOEL RODRIGUEZ)-first portion of bite covered
(10:41:14) JOEL THE THREE YEAR OLD CHILD, HE WAS ALREADY TOILET TRAINED AND HE WAS SLEEPING IN HIS OWN ROOM. AND RIGHT NOW HE HAS TO GO TO SLEEP WITH US AND I HAVE TO GIVE HIM MY HAND SO HE CAN GO TO SLEEP. (:15)

(ATTKISSON/LIVE STANDUP)
BY REJECTING ANOTHER RECALL, FIRESTONE HAS PUT THE BALL SQUARELY IN NHTSA'S COURT. NHTSA IS NOW CONSIDERING TAKING THE NEXT LEGAL STEP IN THE LENGTHY PROCESS REQUIRED TO FORCE A RECALL, AND THAT'S ANNOUNCING AN "INITIAL FINDING OF A SAFETY DEFECT."

FIGURE 5.1   *CBS News broadcast news story*

Source: Reprinted with permission from CBS.

Here's the Web site version:

Firestone: No More Recalls

- *Tire-Maker Says It Will Not Issue A Broader Recall*
- *Says NHTSA Failed To Show Other Firestone Tires Were Dangerous*
- *Agency Close To Completing Major Investigation*

WASHINGTON, July 19, 2001

(CBS) Bridgestone/Firestone Inc. will not issue a broader recall of Firestone tires, saying Thursday the federal government has failed to show that other tires made by the company pose a danger to motorists. That, reports **CBS News Correspondent Sharyl Attkisson,** pushes Firestone and the National Highway Traffic Safety Administration (NHTSA), closer to a nasty confrontation—a forced recall.

The tire maker recalled 6.5 million tires last August after determining they had a high rate of failure. Since then, federal safety officials have been reviewing the safety of millions of other Firestone tires.

Some observers say that a forced recall could be the kiss of death for the financially troubled tire maker, which employs 45,000 people in the Americas. But NHTSA is said to be determined to take action, under pressure from Congress to prove itself in the high-profile investigation that's dragged on for more than a year.

But sources say behind the scenes, Firestone was seriously discussing removing more tires. The negotiations with NHTSA reached an impasse over wording—Firestone wanted to call it a "product improvement program", NHTSA insisted on a formal "recall."

The tires involved are all 15 and 16-inch Wilderness AT tires except ones made at the company's Aiken, South Carolina plant.

"If one of our tires might jeopardize that safety, then we'll take it off the road. We've done it before and, if it becomes necessary, we'll do it again. But that is simply not the case here," Bridgestone/Firestone CEO John Lampe said in a statement.

NHTSA had not publicly called for a broader recall, but Firestone spokeswoman Jill Bratina said at a meeting Thursday agency officials pressed the tire maker to voluntarily do so. Bratina said the company refused and the talks ended.

The agency can order a broader recall, but Bratina said the tire maker would challenge such a move in court.

NHTSA spokesman Rae Tyson had no immediate comment.

Meanwhile, federal officials are expected to tell members of Congress this week that the tires Ford Motor Co. is using to replace 13 million Firestone tires show no significant safety problems.

Last month, House Energy and Commerce Chairman W.J. "Billy" Tauzin, R-La., said his staff had uncovered questionable safety records involving several of Ford's replacement tire brands. Tauzin's staff said claims data showed that up to seven tire product lines generated worse performance records than the Firestone Wilderness AT tires being replaced in Ford's $3-billion recall.

Tauzin drew criticism for raising safety questions based on raw data in the midst of a recall. Safety advocates complained that such action could only confuse consumers, making it less likely that they would remove the Firestone tires.

(continued)

According to a story Thursday in The Detroit News, the NHTSA's findings vindicate Ford, which insisted that the replacement tires were safe.

When the tire replacement campaign was announced in May, Firestone severed all business ties with Ford.

The automaker blames the tire scandal, which has been linked to 203 deaths and more than 700 injuries, on bad tires. Firestone claims the design of the Ford Explorer is a contributing factor in the accidents.

Many involved rollovers of the highly popular Ford Explorer, which used the tires as standard equipment.

Because of accident reports, Firestone recalled 6.5 million ATX, ATX II and Wilderness AT tires. Ford said in May it would replace an additional 13 million Wilderness AT tires because of safety concerns.

Firestone has acknowledged problems with the recalled tires, but says the Explorer design is partly responsible for the accidents.

"We now know this to be a fact: You can take every Firestone tire off every Explorer and the rollovers and fatal accidents will continue," Lampe said.

That claim, strongly rejected by Ford officials, prompted the automaker to end a centurylong relationship with Firestone.

**Tire Tussle:
Complete Coverage**

The following are investigative stories by **CBS News Correspondent Sharyl Attkisson** that peer into the Firestone tire recall:

- Firestone: An Insider's View
- New Worries For Firestone
- Call For Explorer Ban
- Firestone In Tire Talks
- The Casualty Count
- Courting Firestone
- Tire Victim: Apology Seemed Sincere
- Holding Firestone, Ford Accountable
- Firestone And Ford Place Blame
- Yet Another Recall For Firestone
- Why Are Feds So Slow With Recalls?

FIGURE 5.2 *Printcast version of Figure 5.1*

Source: Reprinted with permission from CBS.

Take a moment to identify the differences between the television news script and the online version.

Mr. Potato Head

When trying to remember and apply the concepts we've been discussing, it might be helpful for you to think of Mr. Potato Head. In case you've never heard of the children's game, it begins with a plain potato. Players eventually add all the necessary features—eyes, mouth, nose, ears, hat, and other characteristics—to transform the plain potato into Mr. Potato Head.

Producer Crean of CBSNews.com applies the Mr. Potato Head concept to her Internet writing:

What does the Internet have that a newspaper, magazine, or television doesn't have? Basic answer: Interactivity. When writing a news story for the Internet, you could do worse than remember Mr. Potato Head. The prose represents the basic potato, a plain brown plastic thing with holes in it. This does NOT mean that your story is unimportant. It is the base of the article. It is the thing upon which all else hangs. The trick is to fill all those little holes. So give Mr. Potato Head some eyes. Streamed video or a live Webcast can grow out of most stories, whether it's breaking news or softer features. Stick a nose on the plastic potato. Give the story a dramatic photo or an eye-catching graphic. You can even animate it if you want. And don't forget the mouth. Invite the Internet surfer to get involved in the story by building a quiz, a poll, or even a game for soft features. You might want to give Mr. Potato Head some feet. That is, link your story to other Web sites that will offer expanded information on the subject at hand. This is a neat way to give your story depth without making it into a two-mile scroll. Stick some ears on the tater. Audio files may include bites from interviews, sounds from the scene of an event, or even quotes from the subject of an interview or obituary. If you want to get fancy, give the potato a mustache for substance. Set up a bulletin board where the readers get together and discuss the story. If it's a hot potato, so much the better. It will keep people interested and, sometimes, give them food for thought. And the capper (the hat) might be a chat session with a prominent figure involved in the story — or perhaps a well-known common tater.

Breaking News

During a **breaking news** situation, the same basic online writing guidelines apply. Writers and producers move quickly to pool and post information from every possible reliable source. For example, a writer for a broadcast news Web site will pull quotes from experts appearing on the company's television or radio counterparts and from reporters themselves who are reporting on the scene. As always, the online writer should also be on the lookout for pictures, potential links, bullets, and videotape; the writing should be clear and concise.

Arguably, the biggest breaking news story since wide use of the Web happened on September 11, 2001: the violent, orchestrated terrorist attacks on American targets. Within minutes, major news Web sites had replaced their normal home pages with special breaking news pages, such as the one that appeared on the CBS News Web site shown in Figure 5.3. See how the writers have worked to compile information and quotations from various sources to give a cohesive, clear description of the developing events.

CBS News September 11, 2001 Day of Infamy

In a horrific sequence of destruction, terrorists crashed two planes into the World Trade Center in New York City Tuesday morning. The twin 110-story towers then completely collapsed about an hour later. Explosions also rocked the Pentagon and the State Department and spread fear across the nation.

Hijacked commercial jetliners were aimed for the landmark twin towers and for the Pentagon in Washington, D.C.

President Bush, in Florida at the time of the attack, canceled plans to return to Washington and was flown aboard Air Force One to the safety of a military installation at Barksdale Air Force Base in Louisiana.

The nerve center of the nation's military burst into flames and a portion of one side of the five-sided structure collapsed when the plane struck in midmorning. Secondary explosions were reported in the aftermath of the attack and great billows of smoke drifted skyward toward the Potomac River and the city beyond.

Throughout the nation, airports shut down, the Sears Tower in Chicago was evacuated and other major train transport hubs were closed. Planes already in flight were ordered to immediately land at the closest airport. In New York, The United Nations was evacuated, and the stock markets closed. Major League baseball cancelled all games scheduled for Tuesday night. The U.S. Secret Service will not confirm President Bush's location. Every federal building in Washington D.C. was closed.

But major attacks in the nation's capital crippled the U.S. government. The West Wing of the White House, the Capitol building, the Justice Department and other government buildings in the nation's capital have been evacuated and closed down amid concerns over terrorist threats.

"This is the second Pearl Harbor. I don't think that I overstate it," said Sen. Chuck Hagel, R-Neb.

The date of the attack may have significance: On September 11, 1978, the first historic Camp David accords were signed. In June, a U.S. judge had set this Wednesday as the sentencing date for a bin Laden associate for his role in the bombing of a U.S. embassy in Tanzania that killed 213 people. The sentencing had been set for the federal courthouse near the World Trade Center. No one from the U.S. attorney's office could be reached Tuesday to comment on whether the sentencing was still on.

CBS Correspondent James Stewart reported that a United Airlines plane crashed into the vicinity of Camp David, the Presidential retreat in Maryland. The House and Senate in Washington, D.C., has also been evacuated.

(continued)

FIGURE 5.3 *Breaking news printcast on CBSNews.com*

Source: Reprinted with permission from CBS.

Here's what happened Tuesday:

Two hijacked jets slammed into the top floors of the twin World Trade Center towers on Tuesday morning, smashing gaping holes into the side of the 110-story buildings. Large fiery holes in the buildings poured thick black clouds of smoke across south Manhattan, Brooklyn and the Hudson River as debris rained to the street below the twin towers.

The first plane — reported as a Boeing 767, American Airlines' Flight 11 from Boston - bored into the westernmost of the two towers about 8:40 a.m. The second, apparently Flight 93, which was from Newark en route to San Francisco, hit about two-thirds of the way up the second tower, leading to another large explosion.

At 11:30 a.m. ET, American Airlines told the Associated Press that Flight 77 from Dulles to Los Angeles, a Boeing 757 with 58 passengers, four flight attendants and two pilots, is one of two aircraft American says it's "lost." American Airlines says it has "lost" another aircraft, which was carrying 92 people.

"I heard something like a boom sound, something like an earthquake sound," an eyewitness described the apparent accident to **CBS News' The Early Show.** "The next thing I know I saw a big ball of fire on the building."

The planes blasted fiery, gaping holes in the upper floors of the twin towers. A witness said he saw bodies falling and people jumping out. About an hour later, the southern tower collapsed with a roar and a huge cloud of smoke; the other tower fell about a half-hour after that. Firefighters trapped in the rubble radioed for help.

WCBS-TV, citing an FBI agent, said five or six people jumped out of the windows. Witnesses on the street screamed every time another person leaped. Another witness said he saw bodies falling from the 110-story towers.

"It's like a war zone. There are many injured," said New York City fire marshal Mike Smith.

About 45 minutes later, a massive explosion outside the Pentagon sent roiling clouds of smoke into the sky after another plane crashed into the building. An Associated Press reporter saw the tail-end of a large airliner plunge into the building. He says smoke is billowing out of the building. It is believed a helicopter filled with explosives also crashed into the government building.

A large plane crashed just north of the Somerset County Airport, about 80 miles southeast of Pittsburgh, airport officials said. The plane, believed to be a Boeing 767, crashed about 10 a.m. about 8 miles east of Jennerstown, according to county 911 dispatchers, WPXI-TV in Pittsburgh reported. There were no other immediate details on the Pennsylvania crash and it was not clear whether the crash was related to the others.

President Bush, speaking during a visit to promote his education agenda in Florida, said, "This is a difficult moment for America... Today we have had a national tragedy, an apparent terrorist attack on our country."

"I have ordered that the full resources of the federal government go to help the victims and their families and to conduct a full-scale investigation to hunt down and to find those folks who committed this act," the president said. "Terrorism against our nation will not stand."

He canceled his day's planned events and was returning immediately to Washington.

At around 11:30 a.m., New York Mayor Rudolph Giuliani ordered an evacuation of the lower part of Manhattan. "I have a sense it's a horrendous number of lives lost," Giuliani said. CBS News reported that there were major gas leaks in area of Wall Street, and that emergency crews were trying to make the area "sterile."

An estimated 10,000 emergency workers were at the scene or headed to the scene of the World Trade Center collapse.

FIGURE 5.3 *Breaking news printcast on CBSNews.com (continued)*

Source: Reprinted with permission from CBS.

Now here's a look at how the same breaking story was covered on the CNN Web site (Figure 5.4):

BREAKING NEWS

Photo of America
Under Attack

AMERICA UNDER ATTACK

At 8:45 a.m. EDT, the first of two airliners crashed into the World Trade Center, opening a horrifying and apparently coordinated terrorist attack on the United States, which saw the collapse of the two 110-story towers into surrounding Manhattan streets and a later attack on the Pentagon.

DEVELOPING STORY »

COMPLETE COVERAGE:

- Chronology of terror
- President Bush: U.S. will "hunt down and punish those responsible"
- World Trade Centers collapse after planes hit, 10,000 emergency workers head to scene
- Plane hits Pentagon, part of the Pentagon collapses
- American, United both confirm losing two planes each. The American planes alone held about 150 people.
- Federal buildings, United Nations evacuated
- FAA grounds all U.S. flights, sends trans-Atlantic flights to Canada
- Sen. John McCain calls attacks "act of war"
- Israel evacuates embassies
- Non-essential NATO employees asked to leave Brussels HQ
- Taliban issues statement to tell U.S. "Afghanistan feels your pain"
- Kennedy Space Center, LAX, Disney Florida parks closed
- World shock over U.S. attacks

1:35p September 11, 2001

FIGURE 5.4 *Breaking news printcast on CNN.com*

Source: Reprinted with permission from CNN.

CBS News and CNN are worldwide news entities, but Web sites for *local* television and radio stations also must know how to respond to breaking stories. Here's how the Web site for KCBS, the local CBS affiliate in Los Angeles, California, appeared the day of September, 11, 2001 attacks (Figure 5.5)

Terrorists Attack United States; Death Toll Rising

A state of emergency has been declared in the District of Columbia after a plane crashed into the Pentagon, collapsing part of the building. There have likely been hundreds of casualties resulting from the plane crash at the Pentagon. American Airlines passenger planes have crashed into the twin towers of the World Trade Center. The airline said at least 164 passengers and crew members were killed. Both WTC towers have collapsed. President Bush said the crashes were apparent terrorist attacks. There were reports of several planes crashing throughout the country. **More Details**

- CNN Reports On New York, Pentagon
- LIVE VIDEO 56K
- LIVE VIDEO 100K
- LIVE VIDEO 300K
- World Trade Center
- Second Plane Hits World Trade Center
- Dramatic Photos: WTC — Independent Photographer

Photo of World
Trade Center
Attack

U.S., World React To Attack: The Latest

Airports have closed around the country and beyond, while the world reacts to the terrorist attack on the World Trade Center, the Pentagon and the White House. **More Details**

- 757 Plane Crashes In Pennsylvania

Photo of Los
Angeles Airport

LAX Closed; Los Angeles On High Alert

In reaction to the reported terrorist attacks on the East Coast Tuesday, the City of Los Angeles has been put on tactical alert. LAX and all federal buildings and landmarks have been closed. **More Details**

- Two Of Hijacked, Crashed Jets Were Bound For L.A

FIGURE 5.5 *Breaking news printcast on local news Web site*

Source: KCBS Los Angeles Channel 2 News Web site 1:35p September 11, 2001.

The Internet Newsroom

Now we'll look inside the newsroom of one prominent news Web site, CBSNews.com. It's organized into several key sections:

- Hard News, which is devoted to the daily coverage of hard news.
- Campaign and Special Events, which is devoted to national election campaigns and special events, such as the anniversary of the fall of Saigon, for which a special section was created.
- CBS News Broadcasts, which is devoted to updating the individual CBS News broadcast sites, such as The CBS Evening News, 60 Minutes, and 48 Hours.

Most of the staff, about two-thirds, is editorial rather than technical and is responsible for actual content. The remaining one-third work in design (art) or development (computer code).

We asked Michael Sims, Director of News and Operations for CBSNews.com to describe his organization for this text. He calls it "very much like a television newsroom: assignment editors, copy editors, assistant and associate producers, and producers."

Sims says his assistant producers and associate producers are the less-experienced workers who mainly work on the technical aspects of the job, such as live Webcast and the recording and streaming of audio and video clips on the site. "As we assess their skill and development, they begin to do some writing," says Sims.

As is the trend in the budget-conscious worlds of broadcast *and* Internet news, the CBSNews Web site doesn't have specific "writers" per se. Sims says his producers are the key to putting together Web site pieces, much as a local television producer might organize and produce a newscast. "The producer first acts as reporter, gathering the facts from all sources, including net TV, net radio, local TV, and the wires. They then will site down to write the piece. Next, they search, choose, and process any still photos for the story. They'll work with the assistant and associate producers to determine what audio and video clips are available and add the appropriate ones. They'll search the site for related stories and the Internet for related links. Finally, they'll write a headline and bullet points. Once finished, the piece will be copy edited by someone else."

Dick Meyer, editorial director for CBSNews.com, further describes the function of Web site producers this way:

> The producer puts his story into a "publishing tool"—a fairly simple, template-like computer program that essentially translates the story into an Internet-accessible format. This requires some knowledge of specialized programming language, but not much. It does require a great deal of fluency with our publishing tool and a high degree of computer literacy. Updates, edits, and corrections on a story are generally made after it is put in the tool.
>
> The producer is responsible for the graphic look of the story. In most cases, this simply means the producer will select the picture or image or graphic that goes with the story. This is also done by using the same publishing tool as mentioned above.
>
> The producer also adds the multimedia elements to his story. These may include links to other stories or features on CBSNews.com, links to other relevant Web sites, attached video (such as stories from CBS News broadcasts, live events, or taped

events), attached audio-only elements, embedded graphics, and embedded 'boxes' within the story ('explainers,' side-bars, resources lists, background information). This is the phase of production that is unique to the Internet and calls on a unique kind of creativity from the producer. The producer has to write well, think visually, and have a deep knowledge of the story in order to utilize material from other media and venues.

The producer is also responsible for giving the story a headline and a summary 'short story' that might appear on the News front page, Section front pages, or elsewhere on the site besides the story page itself. These are extremely important functions that are crucial to alerting and tempting the reader to the story.

Lastly, with ongoing stories, the producer is generally responsible for keeping the story updated throughout the day.

At CBSNews.com, the assignment editor typically decides what stories are to be covered and determines who will cover them. That person also dictates how those stories are ranked in order of importance on the site.

Style Guide

The following Internet news style guidelines are taken from the CBSNews.com.

1. Overall

Make sure your headline, photo, and short story work together clearly. If there's a mug shot [photograph of a person], be sure the subject is identified in the headline or short story.

2. Short Story Tease on Index (Primary) Page

These should be short, ideally about 25 words. Always give credit to a CBS News correspondent if the story is taken from a particular CBS News program. An anchor doesn't have to be credited as long as the news program is.

3. Teases

In general, try to keep a consistent tense within a story.

  a. In *features*, use the present tense for attributions (that is, he says, she notes, he adds). A feature story can be written with "said" in past tense if the action requires.
  b. In *news stories*, use the past tense (that is, he said, he noted, he added).

4. Story Length

News stories should be about 500 words. Features can be longer.

5. *Translating Broadcast Scripts*

a. Often key information in the broadcast version is reported by use of the video-tape or in the fonts or chyrons. When translating a broadcast story for the Web, watch the video to make sure you're not missing crucial information. Add any such information to the Web version.

b. Try to avoid using language such as: "Madonna appears on *The Early Show*," which sounds too much like a broadcast script. It's better to say something such as "Madonna shares her parenting advice with *The Early Show*."

6. *Punctuation*

a. *We (CBSNews.com) do not use the serial comma.* That means there is no comma before the "and" in the following: "I am having ice cream, cake and frozen yogurt on my birthday."

b. *Write in complete sentences as much as possible.*

c. *Punctuate run-on sentences within quotes.*

d. *Put periods after complete sentences in captions, but no period if it's a fragment.*

e. *Italicize a comma or a period if it's next to an italicized word.*

7. *Quotes*

a. *Inside articles, quoted matter should not be altered.* Words within the quote marks should remain exactly how the speaker said it, except for dialects, such as use of "gonna" and "gotta," which should always be "cleaned up" to "going to" and "got to." Other questions of dialect inside quotes should be handled on a case-by-case basis.

b. *The producer of a piece is responsible to replay any video attached to be sure that the corresponding quotes match the sound bites in the video.* Close captioning and scripts are **not** reliable sources.

c. *There's no need to capitalize the first letter of the job description of a person quoted* (i.e., coal miner Joe Jones) unless that title is usually capitalized (i.e., President Bush).

d. *Use bold face for all quotes.*

8. *Word Usage*

a. *Acronyms:* If an acronym is four or more letters, capitalize the first letter and lower case the rest.

b. *Names:* Children under age 18 should be referred to by their first names on second reference. Adults should be called by their last names on second reference. The only exception is for celebrities known by one name only (i.e., Madonna or Cher).When there's more than one family member in a story, use first and last names for *both* people on second reference to avoid confusion. Better yet, "write around it" when possible to avoid the scenario in the first place.

c. *Black Americans are to be referred to as "blacks."* African American is acceptable on second reference. Please note, however, there can be a difference between "blacks" and "African Americans"; not all blacks are African Americans.

9. Dates

a. *Always use the day of the week*, not "today" or "yesterday."
b. *The style for writing a date is* (note the comma afterward): "Nov. 5, 1999," or "Nov. 1997."
c. *Spell out the month when used alone.*

10. Time

Spell *"a.m." and "p.m." in lower case letters with periods.* Use "ET/PT" when referring to the times of a broadcast. Avoid a time reference in the short story.

11. Dateline

Spell out the city and then use a comma and the name of the state all spelled out.

12. Web-Specific Terms

- Online: one word, no hyphen
- Offline: one word, no hyphen
- Email: one word, no hyphen
- Logon: one word as an adjective
- Home page: two words
- Voice mail: two words
- Web site: two words
- 'Net is the appropriate way to abbreviate the "Internet." Both 'Net and Internet are capitalized.

13. Headlines and Subheadlines (Subheads)

a. Capitalize the first letter of headlines at the top of the story and subheads at the top. If a headline appears within the story's text, such as for a book title, capitalize only the initials of major words, but not article or prepositions less than four letters.
b. Typical headline style involves a subject and verb combination. It's more powerful if the headline and the subheads all work together as one unit. The main headline should have a subject and a verb, and the subheads should play off of that. Either the subheads should include another subject with a verb or should assume the same subject, but carry a different verb.

c. Headlines can also be label style, just describing a "thing" with no verb. Often, these are playful.

14. Captions

a. Captions should accompany all photos.

b. No caption is needed for illustrations or graphics.

c. A short sentence (one, two, or three lines) gets a period. Sentence fragments get no period at the end. Avoid using words such as "file photo" or indicating from which broadcast a snapshot was pulled unless this somehow figures into the news.

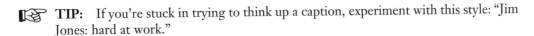 **TIP:** If you're stuck in trying to think up a caption, experiment with this style: "Jim Jones: hard at work."

15. Links

a. *We (CBSNews.com) do not link to a Web site at every proper name in the story*, only when it's relevant and useful for the reader.

b. *Do not link to any competitor's news site.*

c. *Be wary of linking to advocacy or partisan political sites.* Be sure they're relevant to the context of your story. Find an additional site with another viewpoint.

d. *When adding a link, use your discretion if it should appear on the first reference* (remember that may drive the reader away from your story to another Web site) or as a note at the bottom of the story. (For example, For more information on parents who skydive, read "Those Who Dared.")

e. *If you have a lot of suggestions at the bottom of the story for related stories and sites, use a horizontal line to set them off* or a box to highlight selections.

f. *If mentioning another Web site, it's ideal to give the name and the Uniform Resource Locator (URL) if they are different.* Write the URL in all lower case type.

The previous broadcast style guide is also included in Appendix B.

Rumor Has It . . .

What else is different about printcast besides its style and multidimensional aspects?

You may have discovered on your own that some writing on the Internet is more rumor driven and opinionated than is traditional journalism, even on the news Web sites. Here's where a journalist must be careful not to make the mistake of crossing into editorializing on controversial subjects or reporting and perpetuating unsubstantiated rumor and innuendo.

Also when you turn to the Internet as a source for stories, remember not to believe everything you read, see, and hear, no matter how official the material appears or how professionally it's put together. You must find ways to independently verify the authenticity of the information.

As *Christian Science Monitor* columnist John Hughes puts it: "Anybody can get on [the Internet], pretend to be a journalist, and publish a scurrilous rumor. I like *The New Yorker* magazine cartoon that shows a dog tapping away at a computer keyboard and saying to the dog on the floor beside him: 'Once you're on the Internet, they don't know you're a dog.'"

"It's a funny story," Hughes continues, "but it makes a serious point. The Internet is often an anonymous medium. We need to test the credibility of those who tell us things on it."[5]

Credibility Gap

The Internet's credibility problem is of no surprise to most working journalists, yet the Internet is an undeniably indispensable research tool.

A recent national study asked journalists about their use of cyberspace and the reporting of online rumors, among other topics.[6]

A majority of journalists responding said they find Web sites lacking in credibility, yet sixty percent said they would consider reporting Internet rumors and using information found on the Net for stories *as long as they had additional confirmation from an independent source.*

"While it is good that reporters' use of the Internet continues to expand, questionable ethical practices are also expanding," says one author of the study, Associate Professor Steven S. Ross of the Columbia University Graduate School of Journalism.

Professor Ross continues, "Media Web sites freely link to advertisers and to previously published articles, often failing to credit other publications' work. Many respondents also admitted to publishing rumors, often with little or no substantiation, and to using online sources whose credibility had not been adequately established.

Obviously, publishing unsubstantiated rumors or using sources with credibility that has not been established should be strictly off-limits to you as an Internet journalist.

Here's a summary of other key findings in the study regarding journalist's use of the Internet:

- Nearly three-fourths of respondents said they go online daily. They spend on average 4.7 hours per week online at home and 8.7 hours per week at the office.
- The most popular use of the Internet is "article research," which displaces email, the previous year's most popular use. The study's authors say the change clearly shows that reporters are using the Internet to add "depth and breadth to stories."
- However, email has become more popular for communicating with known sources as well as readers.

- Journalists consider responding to readers using email part of the job. More than half of the respondents say they participate in dialogues with readers through email, at least occasionally.
- Half of the respondents said they use the Internet to develop story ideas and pitches. ("Pitches" are the written or verbal summaries reporters give to their superiors to win approval to work on a story idea.)
- New technologies are also surging in popularity. One-fourth of respondents report they use instant messaging.
- When ranking Web site credibility, trade association sites were the only sites rated "more credible" than "not credible." Message boards and chat groups were ranked "least credible."
- Lack of credibility doesn't keep most journalists from using Web postings, especially if the information is confirmed elsewhere.

The Lesson?

What are the lessons in all of this? For one, it's perfectly legitimate, in fact it's becoming increasingly necessary, for journalists to go online for information and story ideas. *However, you must always be mindful of the source, understanding that just because something appears on a Web site doesn't make it true.* Web sites created by organizations with official-sounding titles may be front groups for advocates on controversial issues.

Here's an eye-opening cautionary tale recounted by a business owner explaining why he felt it was necessary for him to monitor and/or block his employees' computer access to some Web sites.

Many surfers looking for official information from the White House type in what would seem to be the obvious address, whitehouse.com, hoping to get connected to the official White House Web site. Instead, they reach a pornographic site! The real White House web site has a similar, but different address, whitehouse.gov (the letters after the period are different). Another similar address has also led some surfers astray: whitehouse.net. The home page looks nearly identical to the real White House home page, only whitehouse.net belongs to a commercial Web development firm.

A person accessing the porn site rather than the White House would immediately realize the mistake. But what if—instead of scantily clad women—the folks at whitehouse.com had created a lookalike White House Web page with official-looking, but bogus information about presidential goings-on? Many people could be fooled.

This example shows how easy it is for somebody to incorporate a well-known name in a Web site address, disguise their true identity, and create official-looking pages with false information. Never assume you're immune to such a ruse.

So when a Web site expresses a viewpoint, or even *appears* to be giving fair and unbiased facts, always ask yourself these questions: Do I know who created the Web site? Do I know who funds that person or organization? What stake does that party have in this issue? How can I confirm this information through another source?

Even when you can't confirm Internet information is truly legitimate, you'll find that it can still be helpful in giving you ideas, deciding what questions to ask in interviews, or leading you to more credible sources. Sometimes those sources will be able to confirm the Internet information.

Legitimate Opinion?

Earlier we cautioned against improperly editorializing on stories. But there *are* legitimate ways in which online writers can recount personal experiences, give humorous insight, or use other nontraditional styles in their stories.

Sharyl's Story

In 1999, as a correspondent for CBS News, I went in for military training to be among the first journalists allowed on a B-52 combat mission in the North Atlantic Treaty Organization (NATO) air campaign in the war on Kosovo.

Naturally, I filed my report for the CBS Evening News on the mission itself. But plenty of fodder was also available for me to write a behind-the-scenes story for the CBS News Web site, which follows. Notice the casual *printcast* style and personal tone of the following Web site article.

CORRESPONDENT IN COMBAT

The training to fly aboard a B-52 military plane on an actual combat mission was fairly brief but intense, and probably the most intimidating part of the whole experience.

First, I had to pass a physical. A cinch. Then, there was a four hour classroom session that covered everything from the ABC's of high altitude oxygen deprivation (hypoxia), to the right kind of diet to follow if you're about to fly. Pilots, I was taught, should take great care to eat healthfully, avoiding caffeine, sweets and high fat foods. It didn't escape my notice that the only food available all day in the classroom at Andrews Air Force Base where the session was taught—and where aspiring pilots are taught—was fast food from a candy machine (high fat, sweet), and hot chocolate or coffee (caffeinated, sweet). I held myself back from pointing out the inconsistency to my instructor.

Next, the whole bunch of us, eight journalists, including photographers and correspondents from competing networks and Newsweek Magazine, had to withstand high altitude exposure in the dreaded Altitude Chamber. Here's where the

(continued)

Air Force guys really tried to freak us all out. "People have been known to lose their minds, bleed from the ears, even *die* in these chambers!" we were warned.

Fortunately, nobody died in the Chamber that day. We removed our masks at a very high simulated altitude and got a range of hypoxic reactions from silly and forgetful, to panicky. Put the masks back on and, within a minute or two we were all back to normal.

Once we all flew out to Fairford Royal Air Force Base outside of London, England, there was more safety training. I can tell you that trying to absorb in just a few days what airmen and women had taken months to learn and practice was daunting, especially attempting to remember how to strap in correctly, how to work the oxygen regulator, what to do if the plane loses cabin pressure, how to eject (or more importantly how *not* to accidentally eject!), how to determine whether you've ejected at a high or low altitude (each has its own parachute cord to pull and mixing them up would be a fatal move), what to do if the cords tangle (pray), and—if you survive all that—how to work the rescue transmitter, safely shoot the flares, inflate the raft, and what to do if you're taken prisoner of war.

After the training, I had six false starts where I was awakened and suited up, ready to board the mighty B-52, only to have NATO cancel the planned targets. Mission aborted. (NATO stands for the North Atlantic Treaty Organization, which was calling the shots in the war.)

Finally, on my eleventh day in England, one of my flights actually flew. I was on an actual combat sortie headed toward Kosovo to fire cruise missiles at secret targets.

On the way, I awkwardly lumbered about the tiny cabin in my oversized men's size 44 flight suit, parachute, survival gear, helmet and oxygen mask—yes, carrying a small video camera and microphone to shoot video and interviews. My first question to each of the crew members was, "Have you ever done this before?"

I quickly discovered, to my chagrin, that nobody in the entire crew had ever flown a combat mission before.

The crew ultimately fired three cruise missiles at their targets. There was no way for me to know whether they hit the right spots; the details of the targets and accuracy were kept secret. But the most important outcome, from my viewpoint, was there was no need to practice my ejection skills, or see whether my parachute really worked.

A Web site producer "enhanced" the previous story by linking it to actual streamed video of my CBS Evening News report, as well as linking it to the written script of that report (translated into Internet style, of course).

Writing for the Web site was a fun way to get extra mileage out of a truly unusual experience in a way that would not have been appropriate on the traditional Evening News. Writing online requires you—*allows* you—to think "outside the box."

Web sites

Here's a list of some Web sites that we find particularly intriguing, helpful, or cool, relating to the field of broadcast and Internet journalism. Check 'em out!

www.assignmenteditor.com
Resources for writers who need to find stories and do research on the Internet

www.wtop.com
Washington, D.C.'s all news radio station

www.wire.ap.com
Associated Press

www.lib.umd.edu/UMCP/LAB
Broadcast Pioneers Library of American Broadcasting

www.broadcast.com
Yahoo broadcast audio and video clips

www.cbsnews.com
CBS News

www.rtnda.org
Radio and Television News Directors Association

www.rcfp.org
Reporters Committee for Freedom of the Press

www.wlsam.com
890 WLS News Radio in Chicago, Illinois

www.poynter.org
Poynter Institute for Media Studies (resource for research on many newsroom issues)

www.npc.press.org
National Press Club

www.npr.org
National Public Radio (provides audio of news archives)

www.pbs.org
Public Broadcasting

www.ajr.org
American Journalism Review

www.cjr.org
Columbia Journalism Review

www.whas.com
84 WHAS News Radio in Louisville, Kentucky

www.reporter.umd.edu
A Journalist's Guide to the Internet

www.google.com
Search engine that can be used to find definitions for online and computer terms

www.tvspy.com/shoptalk.htm
Don Fitzpatrick's Shoptalk Industry Newsletter

writetools.com
Write Tools, a compilation of Web-based references for professional writers and editors

www.writenews.com
The Write News, resources for media and publishing professionals and also job listings, including jobs on the Internet

www.Journalismjobs.com
Journalism Jobs, job board for media professionals

www.newsblues.com
News Blues opinions from people working in TV newsrooms about working conditions

www.missouri.edu/~jourvs/sals90s.html
Missouri School of Journalism Report on broadcast news salaries in the 1990s

whitehouse.gov/news
The White House news home page

www.pointer.org/dj/052600.htm
Tips from the Poynter Institute on how to get online information fast

www.members.aol.cm/crich13/poynter6.html
The Poynter Institute's unscientific study regarding effectiveness of broadcast vs. print style of writing online

www.rtnda.org/trades/writing2/shtml
Analysis of newswriting after September 11

We close this chapter with a fascinating glimpse into the not-too-distant future, courtesy of David S. Awbrey, a writer for the *The Kansas City Star:*

> This is news gathering, circa 2010 or earlier:
> A reporter, equipped with a laptop computer and other gadgets, arrives at the scene of a plane crash. The place is in chaos, making for great video. The journalist grabs a multitask camera and through his wireless laptop files both live action and still pictures of the tragedy to a news Web site.
> Then, he sends an audio report to the Web site. Finally, after things settle down and facts have accumulated, the reporter writes a lengthy account for the next day's newspaper, which might or might not be made of newsprint. In academia, it's called convergence, the integration of various forms of media—television, radio, print—centered on the Internet.
> From the caves of Lascaux to cyberspace, it all comes down to reporting events of importance to the reader/viewer/listener. Journalism is connecting people with the story of their own time. It's a narrative written at a rush, digested quickly and recycled constantly, but it eventually helps form the consciousness of the age, what the 19th-century Germans called the Zeitgeist.[7]

Quick Review of Terms

- **Internet:** The international network of computer systems
- **Online:** The term used to indicate you're actively reading, surfing or otherwise using the Internet
- **Printcast:** The style of writing on the Internet; a combination of print and broadcast writing with some original elements

- **World Wide Web:** The user-friendly part of the Internet where most people spend most of their time

Review Questions

1. What are some of the similarities and differences among Internet, broadcast, and print writing?

2. What components are unique to Internet writing?

3. How can you enhance a typical Web site story to take advantage of the Internet's multimedia characteristics?

4. What are the advantages and pitfalls of using the Internet as sources of information?

Summary

This chapter has defined some commonly used Internet terms and explained the unique style of Internet writing, which is a combination of print and broadcast, or *printcast*. The Internet writer must constantly think in multimedia terms, coming up with ideas for video, photographs, interactive polls, and Web site links. We explained how to translate broadcast scripts into Internet form and provided a basic Internet style guide. We also explored the advantages and pitfalls of using research from Internet sources. It's easy for Internet users to be fooled into thinking that information on Web sites is correct or legitimate, when its true source may be in doubt. Internet information is best used when the source can be confirmed or when the information can be confirmed through other means.

Notes

1. *Database Searcher*, 5, no. 10 (1989): 31.

2. *Earth Island Journal*, 15, no. 2 (2000): 30.

3. *Database Searcher*, 5, no. 10 (1989): 31.

4. *Database Searcher*, 5, no. 10 (1989): 31.

5. Hughes, John, "How Do We Find What's True?". *The Christian Science Monitor*, May 17, 2000, Opinion, p.11.

6. Poll conducted by: Associate Professor Steven S. Ross of the Columbia University Graduate School of Journalism and Don Middleberg, founder and CEO of the communications firm of Middleberg & Associates. March 2, 2000 the Sixth Annual Middleberg/Ross Media in Cyberspace Study.

7. Awbrey, David S, "Technology Changes; News Is Same," *The Kansas City Star*, Tuesday, May 9, 2000, Sec. B, p.7.

6

Sources

Chapter Objectives

- To describe various sources of news information and their proper use
- To demonstrate ways to recognize the potential of a given source
- To discuss the pitfalls of improperly using sources

A **news source** is, quite simply, a provider of information. Sources are essential to any news operation. Every single story you write will have at least one source; sometimes there will be dozens. It's critical that you learn to recognize the potential of any given source, how to find and use credible sources, and how to distill the information you receive into solid news stories.

We've coined the term **sourcery** to refer to *the practice of obtaining information from various reliable sources.* The first step toward mastering sorcery is learning who and what are possible sources of information.

A Source by Any Name . . .

First, as a practicing broadcast or online journalist, you should consider *anybody* a potential source of information. After you accept that view, you'll start seeing your world differently. A conversation overheard on the subway may give you the idea for a story to investigate; an acquaintance discussing concerns in his neighborhood may reflect emerging issues in the community; a county road project that clogs up rush hour traffic for months may prompt you to call and find out what's going on. Your life observations and experiences will begin to pass through your own internal news filter.

When you *do* get an idea for a story, organize your efforts. Ask yourself *whom can I contact to find out more? How can I verify the information?* Much of what you hear may turn out to be unfounded. Rumor and innuendo that doesn't rise to the level of a news story. But if you keep your finger on the pulse of your community, you'll eventually dig up interesting, original stories. Let your natural curiosity about people, situations, and life be your guide.

There are also many more structured sources of information, including beats, news releases, wire services, the futures file, the competition, the networks, newspapers, local experts, police monitors, unsolicited contacts, and former employees.

Working to the Beat

An important element of sourcery is **beats**. A beat is *an area of interest.*

Within news organizations, some reporters are considered "general assignment," which means they cover any type of story as needed; others may be assigned a beat. Examples of beats are education/schools, police/crime, courts, medical, and government. A beat can also be a specific geographical area such as Loudoun County, Virginia (includes any and all happenings in Loudoun County and the cities and towns within the county). How would the term, "beat," be used in a sentence? A television news director might tell a reporter, "I need you to cover the crime beat next week for Rob while he's on vacation, which means keeping up with the investigation into Leesburg's string of bank robberies."

The advantage of working a beat is that it allows you to specialize and learn more about a topic. It's also much easier to develop sources. For example, a police officer who has dealt with the same reporter on a number of stories through the years is much more likely to talk to—and trust—that reporter than one with whom he's never spoken before.

Your best shot at mastering beat sourcery is through familiarity. Get to know and make yourself known to potential sources. Here's an example of a strategy you could use to develop sources on a newly assigned beat:

Strategy for Starting on a New Beat: Indian River County, Florida

Identify the cities, towns and government, and law enforcement agencies within the county.

Find out when any regular government meetings are, how individual groups and agencies release press information, and how to access meeting agendas in advance.

Identify local officials and press contacts. Obtain their phone numbers and email addresses and make sure they have yours.

Introduce yourself in person to everyone you can and explain your beat.

Every step of the way, let it be known that you're always looking for good story ideas and that you'd like to hear from anyone who has any.

Develop a routine in which you regularly contact agencies and officials, stopping in at their offices daily or weekly, depending upon whatever is practical. This is referred to as "making the rounds."

☞ **TIP:**   A television news director once told his reporters that by the time an important local issue was voted on by a city or county board, the story was nearly over. He advised that the goal of journalists should be to identify and bring to the forefront newsworthy items much earlier in the decisionmaking process: before they reach the final stages of a formal vote. Chatting with "sources," that is, lawmakers and community groups is one way to accomplish this. Regular visits and telephone checks with newsmakers and community advocates can also help you get an early start on emerging issues. Also, instead of waiting for a vote at a government meeting, scan the meeting agenda in advance and identify, investigate, and report on interesting topics.

Regardless of which reporter is covering which beat, others within the news organization should be making additional regular contacts with sources called **beat calls,** also referred to as **beat checks**.

Beat calls are a mainstay of most any news operation. The phrase describes the practice of calling a list of area law enforcement and emergency rescue agencies at regular intervals throughout the news day to find out if any "news" is happening. The list of agencies to call may include police departments, sheriff's offices, fire departments, state troopers, and the Coast Guard.

At smaller radio and television stations, there may be only one or two people doing all the work: writing, anchoring, reporting, producing, editing, *and* making beat checks. At larger organizations, assignment desk personnel often make the beat checks before each and every newscast: morning, noon, evening, and night.

Several years ago, one television news assignment desk person in a major city was known to initiate beat check conversations by asking the voice on the other end of the telephone, "Anything bleedin' or burnin'?"

The following is our slightly more tactful suggestion for beat check protocol.

Suggested Beat Check Procedure

Identify yourself. Ask for the shift commander, watch commander, sergeant on duty, or supervisor: whoever has been established to handle media inquiries. ("Hi, it's Randall Geiger from Channel 13. May I speak to a supervisor?")

When connected to this person, reidentify yourself and ask if any noteworthy events are happening. ("Hi, it's Randall Geiger calling from Channel 13. I'm just checking to see if anything is going on.")

More often than not, the response will be "Nothing, it's pretty quiet." Thank them and end the telephone call.

Sometimes, the response will be something of the nature, "Well, we're working a robbery downtown." At this point, ask for any details available. If no formal report or release is yet available, try to at least pin down a location and any other facts. ("Is it still going on? Was anybody hurt? Can you give me the address? Do you know how much was taken? Is the suspect still on the scene or has he/she left?")

If you're lucky, you'll get enough to get information on a breaking story to send a reporter and/or camera to the scene if it warrants possible news coverage.

When the news isn't breaking, but has already happened, you may get a more formal "report" out of a beat check. Here's an example of information as you may get it from a sheriff's office:

Example of Beat Check Information from a Sheriff's Office

Sheriff's Representative: "Had a shooting at 438 Inglenook Road. Deputy Pauleen Chester responded to a call at 9:13 p.m. tonight. Arrested was John J. Lamary, age 37, charged with attempted murder involving both his wife and neighbor. Both persons were transported to the St. Joseph Medical Center. Mr. Lamary is incarcerated at County Jail. Bond is set at $25,000."

You should ask any pertinent follow-up questions. For example, "Do you have the names of the wife and neighbor? What was the nature of their injuries? Can I assume they both were shot? Do you know how many shots were fired? Who made the call for help? Are there any witnesses? Who called 911?"

At the same time, you need to be thinking of possible elements for the story. For example, radio reporters should ask the sheriff's representative at the outset if they can

Sharyl's Story

When making beat checks, be on the alert for *hints* of stories even where none are obvious. All effective sourcerers are part news detective. One of my biggest local news stories was generated from a beat call. During routine beat checks, a police watch commander on the other end of the telephone reported, "Nothing's going on." Then he added, as an afterthought, "We did have a report that someone stole a baby from Tampa General Hospital, but it turns out it was the mother who took her own baby." That account raised more questions than it answered: What was behind the confusion? Why didn't the hospital initially realize it was the mother who had taken the baby? Why were the police called in? There was another source to consult: the hospital. A nursing supervisor confirmed that a woman had, indeed, slipped away with her newborn baby. What's wrong with that? It turns out the state had assumed custody of the child, based on an anonymous complaint made against the mother. As anchor of the six o'clock news that night, I reported the event as a brief copy story. Shortly after the news, the baby's mother telephoned me from a payphone. She'd seen the story on the news. She was on the run, but wanted to tell her side of the events and agreed to meet with me. It turned out that there was much more to the case than first met the eye. The state had *wrongly* taken custody of the child. It took several months for the case to wend its way through the court system so that the infant could be returned to her mother. I managed to stay ahead of the competition every step of the way, with the mother giving me exclusive interviews and access to her story all because of that initial tip from a simple beat call.

record the telephone conversation as he gives details of the crime; bits of that recording could be used for radio actualities. Television and online reporters interested in obtaining video or other visual elements should ask, "Are your people still on the scene? Is a mug shot of the suspect available to us?"

There's already enough information to guide you to the scene of the crime where you can get more facts and videotape of the scene. Be on the lookout for more potential sources. A neighbor may have seen or heard what happened and be willing to describe it on camera. If so, you've quickly parlayed a beat call into a news story complete with videotape and interviews.

Refer back to the information as given by the sheriff's representative in the beat check. It's hardly written in broadcast or Internet style. It's up to *you* to make it clear, conversational, and concise so that it can be accurately conveyed and diffused. Stop reading this chapter for a moment and take a shot at writing the shooting story in radio, television, and Internet styles.

Our own television version follows:

SHOOTING VO-SOT ANCHOR/ON CAM	(ANCHOR) A Patterson County man is charged with shooting his wife and his neighbor tonight...both victims are hospitalized.
(VO) Font: Patterson County/Tonight	(VO) John Lamary is charged with two counts of attempted murder after the shootings on Inglenook Road shortly after nine-p.m. Nelda Miggins, who lives nearby, is the one who called the Sheriff's Department.
(SOT) Font: Nelda Miggins, Neighbor	(SOT) IN: "I HEARD ONE SHOT..." OUT:...QUIET HERE." RUNS: 10
(VO)	(VO) Lamary is in the Patterson County Jail under a 25-thousand dollar bond. (XXX)

In the interest of practicing good sourcery, consider other potential sources for this story. One is the actual 911 audio recording of Nelda Miggins' emergency call to the sheriff's department. Emergency calls are usually recorded on audiotape by law enforcement agencies and are typically considered "public record," meaning you have the right to obtain a copy.

Another source is the hospital where the victims were taken. Check to see if the facility will tell you their medical conditions (such as stable or critical). The hospital should be temporarily added to your news organization's list of beat checks so that you'll know if either of the victims gets better or worse. If one of them dies, the attempted murder case suddenly becomes a murder case and *that* will be worth reporting.

News Releases

Another element of sourcery is **news releases**. They come from everywhere: civic organizations, churches, political groups, think tanks, schools, universities, and businesses—all attempting to convince news organizations that *they* somehow warrant media coverage.

Although news releases can be valuable sources of information, always keep in mind that they are first and foremost self-serving and cannot be taken at face value. After all, they're not written by journalists who are seeking the truth; they're written by public relations experts who are trained to shed the most positive light on their group, organization or issue.

 ETHICS NOTE: Never, ever publish or broadcast information as it's written in a news release. If you determine the information is newsworthy and accurate, write it in your own words in a clear, conversational, and concise style. Always consider the source; be sure to independently verify all claims that you intend to report from a news release. Keep in mind the releases may present only one side of a controversial or disputed issue.

Next, we'll transform a news release into a news story.

News Release
Date of release: Immediately
RED CROSS BLOOD DRIVE
Lake Anna- The local chapter of the Red Cross is kicking off its annual blood drive with an educational Fun Fair. The Fun Fair will be held at the downtown convention center from 9a.m.-4:30p.m. on Saturday, July 14. This year's theme is "Give from the Heart." We are confident this will be our best and most productive blood drive yet! In addition to trailers with stations for collecting blood from suitable donors, there will be many educational booths, as well as a fire engine, a moon bounce for the kids, and other items of community interest. The Red Cross will also be soliciting donations, which will be used for various Red Cross relief efforts around the world. Last year, the Red Cross raised $14,000 in cash for such relief efforts, and we are setting this year's goal at an optimistic $20,000, a goal we believe can be met if Lake Anna residents truly Give from the Heart! There will be no admission fee to the Fun Fair. Anyone with questions can call Cindy Rider, executive director of the Lake Anna Red Cross at 703-111-1111.
XXXXX

It's not a particularly inspiring news release, but it provides plenty of information for you to construct a brief news story, as in the following example:

BLOOD DRIVE
ANCHOR/OC

(ANCHOR)
THE LAKE ANNA RED CROSS KICKS OFF ITS ANNUAL BLOOD DRIVE WITH A FUN FAIR IN TWO WEEKS. THIS YEAR'S THEME IS GIVE FROM THE HEART. BESIDES ACCEPTING BLOOD DONATIONS, THE RED CROSS IS TRYING TO RAISE 20-THOUSAND DOLLARS FOR RELIEF EFFORTS AROUND THE WORLD. THE FUN FAIR WILL BE SATURDAY JULY 14 OUTSIDE THE CONVENTION CENTER.

(XXX)

Whether a news item such as this would ever win a spot on the news depends in part on how big the city (market) is. Radio and television stations and Web sites serving smaller towns are more likely to report items such as a blood drive, which may be of community interest, but has little actual news value.

When reporting such an item for television, always search for visual possibilities. The videotaped pictures that go along with a story are often called **B-roll** or **cover video**. What are the B-roll possibilities for the Red Cross Fun Fair story? You might resurrect and reuse video that your organization shot at last year's Fun Fair, showing people donating blood and enjoying the festivities. Pictures like that that are recorded on an earlier date are called **archive** or **file video** because they come from the news organization's archives, instead of being freshly shot. When using archive or file video in a story, you must identify them as such so that the viewers are clear that they're watching a previous event. Here's an example:

BLOOD DRIVE
ANCHOR/OC

(ANCHOR)
THE LAKE ANNA RED CROSS KICKS OFF ITS ANNUAL BLOOD DRIVE WITH A FUN FAIR IN TWO WEEKS. THIS YEAR'S THEME IS GIVE FROM THE HEART.

(continued)

(VO)

Font: Lake Anna/last year

(VO)

AT ITS EVENT LAST YEAR, THE RED CROSS RAISED 14-THOUSAND DOLLARS IN CASH DONATIONS FOR RELIEF EFFORTS AROUND THE WORLD. THIS YEAR'S GOAL IS 20-THOUSAND DOLLARS. THE FUN FAIR WILL BE SATURDAY JULY 14 OUTSIDE THE CONVENTION CENTER.

(XXX)

Whether you decide to write a story based on the news release from the Red Cross, it serves to inform you of the date of the happening so that you can mark it on your calendar of future events to consider for news coverage.

The Wires

No matter how good broadcast or Internet operations are at covering the news, they can't possibly have reporters everywhere at once. The reporters they *do* have are usually focused on covering local issues. So how do they stay on top of regional, national, and world news? Usually, with the help of various wire services, collectively referred to as **The Wires**. For a fee, wire services send a constant stream of news stories by computer into every subscribing newsroom. This stream goes on moment by moment, twenty-four hours a day, seven days a week. The Wires have reporters and freelancers practically everywhere news breaks out around the world. The Wire reporters, often called stringers, file their stories from the field. "Filing" a story simply means writing it and transmitting it to headquarters by computer. When stringers are in remote parts of the world where a computer linkup isn't possible, they can file by dictating their story over the telephone to someone at their headquarters who types it into the system.

Wire stories can be broadcast or published exactly as they're written—word for word—without giving credit or attribution to the wire service. This is not considered plagiarism because since it's all part of the agreement between the wire services and subscribing radio and television stations and Internet sites. Radio stations in particular are likely to broadcast wire stories exactly as they're written because they're often churning out many newscasts and don't have time to rewrite the wire stories into their own original versions. It's a practice called "rip and read" because, before computers, the wires were transmitted to newsrooms through an old-fashioned teletype machine that printed the stories out on rolls of paper. Hurried reporters would literally rip a section of wire stories off a roll of paper and read them on the air exactly as they were written.

It's still best, though, to rewrite wire stories before broadcasting them or publishing them on a Web site. This is because the wire writing is often rushed and leaves a lot to be desired, plus you may need a much shorter version.

The following is an example of a breaking news story as it's covered by the Associated Press (AP) wire services. The slug appears at the top of the page. The word "Tops" in parentheses alerts subscribers (television and radio stations) that it's a new, breaking story. At the bottom is the date and time the story "crossed" (was transmitted). After you read it, rewrite it into a :15 copy story suitable for radio.

AP-Hotel Fire (Tops)

Baltimore hotel fire brought under control

(Baltimore-AP)—A four-alarm hotel fire in Baltimore has been brought under control.

Firefighters rescued six people from the burning building. Ladders had to be used to get some people out.

A fire official says there were about 20 people inside The Abbey hotel when the fire broke out late this morning.

He says firefighters found a man on the top floor who was in cardiac arrest. Paramedics were able to restore his pulse before he was taken to a hospital.

Baltimore has been beset by emergencies recently.

A chemical fire Tuesday forced the evacuation of a one-block area.

And a train derailment and fire two weeks ago paralyzed the downtown area.

(Copyright 2001 by The Associated Press. All Rights Reserved.)

APTV-08-02-01 1300EDT

Now, take a look at the next AP story updating wildfires in the western United States. Rewrite it into a :20 VO for television.

AP-Western Fires

Firefighters converge on Yellowstone blaze

(Yellowstone National Park, Wyoming-AP)—Mother Nature could make it tougher on firefighters battling a wildfire at Yellowstone National Park.

Dry, windy weather is expected in the area today.

Yesterday, lower temperatures and calmer winds helped firefighters contain about ten percent of the 18-hundred-acre blaze.

The fire has closed an entrance to the Wyoming park. And getting it open again is a priority—since many lodges and resorts in the area rely on Yellowstone traffic for business.

(continued)

Another fire that caused a major problem in the state has now been contained. Firefighters near Jackson yesterday were able to fully surround a blaze that had been threatening dozens of homes.

Meantime, firefighters near Chelan (sheh-LAN'), Washington are also making progress. They expect to have a 46-hundred-acre fire contained by tomorrow night.

%AP Links

GraphicsBank: search for Yellowstone fire

APTV-08-02-01 1306EDT

The following AP sample shows an example of a NewsMinute: very brief updates on selected top stories suitable for use in a radio hourly newscast.

AP-13th NewsMinute

Somber Vikings practice...Vieques exercises...Panel rejects nominee

(Mankato, Minnesota-AP)—It'll be a shortened practice session today for the Minnesota Vikings. They returned to training camp this morning—a day after the heat-stroke death of offensive tackle Korey Stringer. Fans lined up along the field and clapped for the players, who held hands for a prayer.

(Vieques, Puerto Rico-AP)—The dummy bombs are raining down on Vieques (vee-AY'-kes) again. The U-S Navy has begun a fresh round of training on the Puerto Rican island—despite pleas from politicians and residents to stop. The exercises are the biggest since a stray bomb killed a civilian guard in 1999.

(White House-AP)—They're scrambling on Capitol Hill. Backers of a compromise patients' rights bill are pushing to get it approved by the House before lawmakers go on their summer recess tomorrow. President Bush struck a deal with a G-O-P congressman yesterday that provides for a limited right to sue H-M-Os.

(Washington-AP)—A federal appeals court decision that Microsoft illegally mingled its Windows operating system and its Internet browser will stand. The court has denied Microsoft's request to reconsider its ruling. That clears the way for a lower court to decide the company's antitrust penalty.

(White House-AP)—The White House is blasting Democrats in the Senate—over the embattled nomination of the woman President Bush wants to head the Consumer Product Safety Commission. A Senate panel today voted against the nomination of Mary Sheila Gall. Democrats say she's too pro-business.

APTV-08-02-01 1247EDT

Now, check out the following story from another wire service called Reuters. As you read it, think of how you might turn it into an Internet story, including suggested visuals and links. You can practice by doing this on your own.

BC-TECH-CODERED (WRAPUP 3)

WRAPUP 3-Code Red impact minimized-US Internet watchers

(Updates throughout, previous LONDON)

By Deborah Zabarenko

WASHINGTON (Reuters)—The Code Red worm infected thousands of computers each hour Thursday, with about 150,000 scanning the Internet for more victims, even as U.S. Web watchers said the worm's impact had been minimized.

At the height of contagion, the worm may have attached itself to nearly 240,000 machines during this latest siege. The worm reasserted itself Tuesday and by Thursday about 150,000 computers were infected, said Allen Paller of the System Administration Networking and Security Institute (SANS).

Those fighting the worm were keeping pace with its spread, Paller said, by rebooting to kill Code Red on infected computers and by applying a free software patch to prevent future infection.

By Thursday morning on the U.S. East Coast, fewer than 6,000 computers were being infected each hour, SANS reported.

The patch for computers running Microsoft Corp.'s Windows NT and 2000 operating systems as well as its IIS software can be downloaded from various sites, with instructions *at http://www.digitalisland.net/codered.* Computers running Windows 95, 98 and ME are not vulnerable.

But Paller warned against complacency.

"If we stop, the worm wins," Paller said in a telephone interview from Bethesda, Maryland. "Right now, we've got even with it and we've got to get the rest of the machines patched."

"CAUTIOUSLY OPTIMISTIC"

Jeff Reed of the Pittsburgh-based U.S. Computer Emergency Response Team (CERT), said in an e-mail at 9:30 a.m. EDT his team was "cautiously optimistic that the impact of the infection stage of this particular variant of the Code Red worm, which we will call Version 2, has been minimized."

(continued)

An earlier version of the worm, which stealthily multiplies from computer to computer without the user's knowledge, hit some 350,000 machines in July, and targeted the official White House Web site (*http://www.whitehouse.gov*).

White House technicians had to change the IP address—the series of numbers and dots that identifies the physical address of each machine connected to the Internet — to avoid being shut down by the worm. The current version of the worm is also expected to target the White House site when the worm moves from its infectious stage on Aug. 20 into an attack stage.

It is expected to go fully dormant August 27, Paller said.

The current onslaught has disturbed U.S. Defense Department systems, Pentagon officials said. It also knocked out Web servers at companies of various sizes as the worm commandeered them to scan for new victims, Reed said.

U.S. officials have said they are seeking the source of the worm, which Paller said had been traced to three computers in China. But simply knowing the computers does not pinpoint the source, according to Paller: the computers might have been commandeered by computers users anywhere else on earth, unbeknownst to the registered users.

The worm spreads by latching onto computer servers and then randomly sending itself to 100 other IP addresses, which in turn start scanning the Internet for more computers to hit. Since the Internet has no national boundaries, the worm has quite likely spread globally, and hits have been reported in South Korea, France and Britain.

REUTERS

Reut13:06 08-02-01

The Futures File

Most news organizations maintain a comprehensive file or calendar of future events that may warrant news coverage. It's called a **futures file** and is an invaluable source. For example, if you write a story about a dog catcher getting arrested for abusing animals, it's your obligation to find out what is the *next* step in the case. Prosecutors may tell you that the next step is a court appearance in which the suspect will plead guilty or not guilty. Make a note of the date, time, and place of the expected court appearance and enter all of the information into the futures file so that the story can be followed when that day arrives.

TIP: Even if the broadcast or Internet operation where you work maintains a comprehensive futures file, you should always maintain your own calendar of upcoming events related to stories you've covered.

The Competition

Internet and broadcast news organizations vigorously monitor competing Web sites and radio and television stations, comparing coverage of stories and watching to see if they got beaten or "scooped." (You're "scooped" if the competition gets something first that you didn't get, but wish you'd gotten.) Every news department misses a story now and then, so **the competition** can be an important source.

If the competition *does* get the scoop on a breaking news story, such as a fire, it's not impossible to catch up. You can't just copy the information from their story, but you can use it to call the pertinent fire department, confirm the facts, and find out more. You may already know from the competition where the fire is happening, so you can quickly be on your way to the scene.

When following up a story that was first presented by the competition, it's best to **advance** the story. Advancing a story means adding new, unique elements; moving it further along by reporting the next step in the process; providing a more updated version of the story; or focusing on a related angle. It's great to be the first to report a good story, but, when you're *not*, try to do it *better*. The broadcaster or Web site that's first isn't necessarily the one that covers the story best or most accurately.

 TIP: Most television stations, radio stations, and newspapers maintain Web sites. Some of them update their sites aggressively throughout the day. Check your competition's Web sites frequently.

The Networks

Networks are another important source. Most local radio and television stations have agreements with larger national networks, such as American Broadcasting Company (ABC), CBS, National Broadcasting Company (NBC), CNN, and Fox. The local stations are referred to as network **affiliates**. For example, WUSA-TV in Washington D.C. is a CBS network affiliate.

Networks maintain a constant, organized exchange of news information with their affiliates. First, affiliates send the network packages and video (audio, in the case of radio) that may be of interest to fellow affiliates or to the network itself. The network coordinates the material and distributes it by satellite to all of the affiliates. That distribution is called a **news feed**. Affiliates also have access to material collected by the network's own national correspondents and producers.

Here's an example of a local affiliate serving as a resource for the national network. A hurricane hits Florida. The NBC affiliate in Miami feeds dramatic videotape of the storm, by satellite, to the NBC network headquarters in New York. The network then feeds it to all of the other NBC affiliates around the nation, which use it in their local newscasts. In addition, NBC may use the videotape on its own national news.

Now for an example of a national network serving as a resource for its local affiliates. CNN cameras are first to the scene of an accident where a construction crew is left tenuously dangling from a safety rope on the Golden Gate Bridge. Because

FIGURE 6.1   *Network Feed Room Where Video Is Fed and Received*

CNN serves as a live twenty-four-hour-a-day feed to its affiliates, some of the affiliates immediately put the CNN transmission on the air live as it's happening. Other CNN affiliates record the feed on videotape, which they use in a later newscast.

Newspapers

Newspapers, news magazines, and other periodical publications are not usually considered direct competition to their broadcast and Internet counterparts, but they are excellent sources of information. Printed articles can provide helpful background on issues. They may cover a broader range of topics in greater depth than is typically possible in a traditional broadcast news format. Furthermore, newspapers have much more space to fill and often employ a much larger staff of reporters than do the local radio and television stations . . . so tips on interesting stories and ideas for future stories are bound to be found on their pages.

 ETHICS NOTE: Never write a story based only on information directly from a newspaper; always check it out for yourself with the proper sources. One reason why you should do this is because newspaper reporters, like everyone, can make mistakes. You don't want to be responsible for passing them along. Another reason is that it simply isn't ethical to "steal" a story from the newspaper. If you find yourself in the position where you feel you must write a story based only on the newspaper's account and don't have time to, or are unable to, confirm the story with your own sources, *you must credit the newspaper in your report.*

One of the most valuable functions newspapers can serve is as a source for future stories or new follow-ups. For example, a newspaper reports on a woman bank employee who allegedly helped her husband rob the bank. He escaped; she was captured and arrested. Ask yourself *what's the next step in the case?* Call the appropriate court and find out when her first/next court appearance is. Mark it in your own calendar and submit it to the futures file for possible coverage on that day. In addition, you may want to call law enforcement authorities to find out details of the search for the missing husband. For example, is the manhunt focused on a certain geographic area? Could a separate story be done on this angle?

Local Experts

Many stories can be enhanced with advice, opinions, or expertise from **local experts**. When attempting to find an expert to interview on a given subject, you shouldn't just pick a name out of a telephone book. You should compile your own list of reliable, knowledgeable sources on various topics, such as medicine, education, and politics. Local college professors are good potential sources. A political science professor can discuss an upcoming election, a psychology professor may be consulted about a string of crimes, a history professor may offer some interesting facts about the state's bicentennial, and a law professor may give the legal perspective on a local murder trial. Look for reputable organizations to guide you to experts on other matters. For example, if you need an interview with a doctor, the American Medical Association may be able to refer you to a local expert on the medical issue at hand.

 TIP: Remember you're not looking for just *any* local expert to provide comment for a news report; you want a knowledgeable source who's *also* conversational on radio or television. Talk with experts on the telephone before you commit to doing a formal interview. Make sure they're familiar and comfortable with the subject matter. Don't attempt to put words in their mouth. When you find particularly effective local experts, make a note in your permanent records that they might also be good people to use for future stories. See if they'll give you their home and wireless contact numbers. If you need them on a moment's notice on a future story and it's after hours or on weekends, you can reach them.

Police Monitors

At first, it's annoying and distracting, but eventually, it blends into the newsroom atmosphere. It's the constant sound of an active **police monitor,** scanning and eavesdropping on frequencies used by area law enforcement agencies. Police monitors, also called scanners, are shortwave radio receivers. They allow you to pick up transmissions from within police and fire departments and other emergency rescue agencies as they communicate within their own agencies using their radios. Listening in on these communications reveals what the agencies are working on, what calls they've gotten from people in the community, and what emergencies may be in progress.

Although a valuable source, police monitors won't give you all the information you need to write a story, just enough to pursue one. Police may begin a conversation on one frequency and then switch to another you may not hear. Furthermore, a lot of the initial information conveyed in police calls turns out to be wrong or mistaken. Often, an event that sounds like it could be a big news story turns out to be a false alarm. Never, never air or publish information you get from a scanner without confirming it by calling the law enforcement or rescue agency or verifying it through another source.

Don's Story

In one of my first weeks involved in local television news, there was less than an hour before the ten o'clock Saturday night news. I was helping the anchor, Amy Sutton, write and produce the newscast. It was a small station, so I was also called upon to act as cameraman and videotape editor. It had been a slow day. All of that changed suddenly when Amy and I heard the excited voice of a police officer reporting a fire at a local furniture store. Amy said, "Don, grab the video camera, let's go!"

There was no marked news car available to us, so we jumped in Amy's jeep. She accelerated out of the news parking lot before I even got the door closed and buckled in. We reached some police barricades near the scene of the fire and were blocked by a police officer who obviously didn't know there was a news crew inside the jeep. As he peered inside, prepared to make us turn around and leave, he saw Amy, who was well-known in the local market. "Oh, you're Amy Sutton! Y'all go ahead on through!"

We had, literally, just a few precious minutes to record videotape of the fire and get as much information as we could before we had to get back to the newsroom where we edited the video and wrote the story—just in the nick of time to use it on the ten o'clock news.

Sharyl's Story

When I worked at WTVX-TV in Vero Beach, Florida, in the early 1980s, my photographer and I once used a mobile police scanner in our news car to track the moment-by-moment happenings in a kidnapping case. The young son of a prominent local doctor had been kidnapped; the crook demanded that ransom be delivered to him at a remote site among orange groves in Indian River County. We didn't broadcast the information from the scanner, and we didn't use it to interfere with the investigation (that is, we didn't run up to the site where police believed the boy was being held). However, we *did* use it to track what was happening and to drive to the vicinity. When police found the kidnapper and gunshots were exchanged, we heard about it on the scanner and moved in with our camera. The kidnapper was killed. The boy was rescued, and we were way ahead of the competition because we had heard the events unfold on the scanner.

Unsolicited Contacts

All news organizations are inevitably inundated with letters, emails, and telephone calls from people who believe they have news, or at least a story to tell. Oftentimes, reporters reject such solicitations with the attitude, "if it were news, we'd already know about it!" Yet these **unsolicited contacts** can be valuable sources. To be sure, many tips are from cranks, pranksters, or even well-meaning citizens who don't understand that their noisy neighbor isn't necessarily newsworthy. Hidden among these, through, are nuggets of legitimate stories. There are countless examples within the annals of journalism in which sources were dismissed as "nuts" or "kooks," but ended up having a truly blockbuster story and told it to the one reporter who was willing to listen and investigate it.

When you think you have a hot tip on a good story, you must act like a detective searching for clues, but your mission is to investigate, document, and confirm the truth of the story. Some of the best stories originate with people who may not present it in the most credible or professional fashion at the outset. Maybe they're not well educated, well dressed, or well spoken, but the odds are that *some* of them will have fascinating, legitimate stories.

Disgruntled Employees

When rooting out crime, corruption, and misdeeds within the government or corporate America, ideal sources are people working inside those organizations or agencies who are willing to step forward publicly and expose the wrongdoing. However, because those people usually want to keep their jobs, it can be difficult to convince them to tell all, especially on camera. In such cases, retired and former employees can be excellent sources. Often dismissed as disgruntled by their former bosses, they may nonetheless hold the key to crucial information, documents, or other proof involving important stories. Just because people were fired from a job doesn't mean they're not telling the truth. In fact, who better to drop the dime on their former employer's misdeeds but those who feel as though that employer wronged them.

That having been said, information from these types of sources must obviously be checked and double-checked to ensure that it's honest and accurate. Beware of exaggerations, unfounded claims, and innuendo.

When using a former employee as a source, it's also important to find out the details surrounding his termination from the job by asking both him and the former employer. A brief explanation should be written into the story so that the audience can decide on its own whether it believes the person is telling the truth and what that person's motivations may be. For example, if the story is about a former insurance industry vice-president—Reed Buckland—who's admitting that his company cheated people on their medical claims, you could include a line such as the following: "Buckland says he was fired from his job two years ago because he was blowing the whistle on his company's unscrupulous policies. His company says he was fired simply because he was doing a poor job and is now making false claims because he's disgruntled."

Sharyl's Story

So-called disgruntled former employees have proven to be some of the best sources in some of my biggest stories. It often took a great deal of time and effort to substantiate the information they provided, but it paid off. Examples of such stories include former Firestone tire workers talking about dangerous practices at their plants, a former insurance industry vice president admitting that his company cheated customers out of medical claims, and a former pharmaceutical researcher who was bullied by a drug company into changing the results of her clinical study so that the drug appeared safer than it actually was.

Miscellaneous

There are many other potential sources:

- **Lawsuits:** Lawsuits can be good sources because the legal system essentially has done much of the legwork in researching the conflict at issue. For example, if you're investigating a story on whether wireless phones cause brain cancer, it would be helpful to find a lawsuit alleging that it does. The resulting legal documents may provide background, research, and names of experts. The alleged victim and the accused party may even agree to interviews. If not, attorneys representing each side are often willing to provide information and context.
- **News conferences:** These are basically news releases issued not on paper, but in person by advocates of a certain position or issue. The same caveats that apply to news releases also apply to news conferences; they typically present only one side of an issue and are orchestrated by people trying to advance a position or a cause.
- **Public records:** Public records can provide a gold mine of information if you know where to look and how to obtain them. Members of the public and the press often have a legal right to many documents and information maintained by governmental agencies including police reports, mug shots, official photos of employees, 911 recordings, court documents, internal email, and memos.
- **Depositions:** Depositions are interviews conducted by attorneys for lawsuits. The people interviewed are believed to have information relevant to the lawsuit. You have the right to be present at most depositions. However, attorneys for either side in a case can make a motion to have the deposition closed and have you removed. Even if the deposition is closed, you have the right to obtain the written transcript of the deposition after it's over, unless a judge seals it. Furthermore, many depositions are now videotaped, and you may be able to purchase a copy from the court videotaping service involved.

Be Skeptical

Now that we've instructed you to be open minded to all potential sources, we're going to throw you a bit of a curve: Always **be skeptical**. At first it may seem that the two approaches are at odds, but they're not. Expert sourcerers listen to everyone, believe anything is possible, yet accept nothing as the truth until they can independently substantiate it. Every person with whom you speak has different motivations for talking, some of them ulterior. Consider that when weighing a source's credibility.

Web sites

For more information, check out the following Web sites.

www.newswriting.com/r_holdthewire.htm
Advice on the right and wrong ways to use wire copy

www.poynter.org/dj/060900.htm
Tips on finding experts, from the Poynter Institute

www.poynter.org/dj/tips/broadcast/enterprise.htm
Tips on "enterprising" a story, for the Poynter Institute

crayon.net/using/feedback.html
CRAYON, a tool for managing news sources on the Internet through a free, customized news page you can create

www.cyberjournalist.net/slipups.htm
Center for Media and Public Affairs, tracks network news trends in demographics and topics

Quick Review of Terms

- **Advancing the story:** Adding new, unique elements, moving it further along by reporting the next step in the process, providing a more updated version of the story, or focusing on a related angle
- **Archive or file video:** Videotape shot for a past story, but kept on file for possible use in other stories
- **Beat:** An area of interest
- **Beat calls or beat checks:** Regular contacts with area law enforcement and rescue agencies to find out if any news is happening
- **B-roll:** Videotaped pictures that go along with a television news story and also called cover video
- **Futures file:** A comprehensive file or calendar of future events that may warrant news coverage
- **News feed:** The distribution of news material by satellite from a network to its affiliate subscribers
- **News releases:** Information provided to reporters by groups or organizations, attempting to shed the most positive light on their group, organization or issue
- **Source:** A provider of information
- **Sourcery:** The practice of obtaining information from various reliable sources
- **Wire services:** Companies that provide a continuous stream of news and information to subscribing newsrooms

Review Questions

1. What are some typical sources for broadcast and Internet news?
2. Why shouldn't information from a news release be published on the Internet or used on the air word for word?
3. What's the value of newspapers as a source?
4. How can information from police scanners be accurately used as a source?
5. What's the relationship between networks and affiliates?
6. What are some effective ways to find reliable local experts on issues?

Summary

This chapter has defined some typical sources of information for broadcast and Internet news and described how to use them effectively. Sourcery—the practice of obtaining information from various reliable sources—can only be mastered by journalists who measure each source's credibility, expertise, and motivations. Everyone should be considered a potential source, yet information from sources should be carefully substantiated and/or confirmed before it's broadcast or published on a Web site.

7

Organizing, Interviews, and Leads

Chapter Objectives _____

- To explore methods of organizing to write a story
- To examine effective interview techniques
- To identify poor interview habits
- To define and demonstrate various types of news leads

A fter you have sources for a news story, it's time to organize your thoughts and material, conduct any necessary interviews, and actually write that beginning—or lead—sentence.

This chapter builds on what you've learned so far to help you take those next steps in writing good stories for the Internet, television, and radio.

Organized . . . or Agonized!

The better your basic organizational skills means the more effective writer you'll become, especially under the pressure of strict deadlines. Organizing means lots of things: determining exactly what you need for a story; staying focused on your deadline; taking good notes; keeping a detailed listing of everyone you speak to; and writing standups, wraps, and live shots in the field. Organized thought is also required to conduct interviews and to sit down and compose your story. In fact, we'd go so far as to say be **organized . . . or agonized.**

TIP: Countless writers have learned the *hard* way how important it is to always get—and save—contact information from sources and interviewees. For example, they write a story only to find, just before deadline, they have additional questions. Only now it's after normal working hours, and they don't have the right phone numbers to reach those with the answers! Or, the story is over, but weeks or months later, they're working on a related story, yet have no information on how to quickly reach the excellent sources they spoke to before.

Write as You Go

Pen and paper are indispensable organizational tools, and you'll quickly learn to use them to **write as you go.** That means making notes every step of the way as you gather the information and elements for a story. As you read research, you may come across an idea for a possible interview: write it down. As you travel to a story, you may think of six other crucial tasks you need to accomplish before you write a script: write them down. While in the field, you may think of a descriptive phrase you want to include in your script: write it down. Whether it's possible questions for an interview, interesting video you want to be sure to use, or an especially good sound bite, write it all down.

A crucial time to write as you go is when you're in the field gathering elements for a story. Here, something we call the **Milieu Factor** comes into play. The word "milieu" means *environment* or *surroundings*. The Milieu Factor describes the way your surroundings can help you capture the essence of whatever you're reporting. This means you should make notes of your observations and impressions while in the field, whether you're struck by the utter despair of the relatives of a murder victim or a fire's choking smoke. Writing it down at the moment will keep the memory fresh for when you sit down to write a meaningful, descriptive script.

What Do I Need?

A key part of organizing is constantly determining exactly what's necessary to make your story complete. This means asking at various stages: *What Do I Need?*

Often, the needs are tempered by reality. You might feel as though you *need* an interview with someone who's not available for a week, but your deadline is in two hours. Here are some basic questions you should ask as you constantly assess your needs and compare them with your realities to accomplish your goals:

- Do I have the interviews that I need?
- Do I have the information I need to represent opposing viewpoints?
- Do I have the background, research, and documents I need?
- Do I have the visuals I need (i.e., videotape, photographs, and so forth)?

Writing TV Standups

Typically, television news reporters gather information and elements for a story in the field and then return to the station to write the script. But *before* they return, they must have written and shot (recorded) a standup for their story. You'll recall a standup is the part of the story in which the reporter is seen on camera at the scene of the story.

The dilemma is how to write a standup that will fit the story when you haven't even written the story yet. **Writing TV standups** is another facet that requires you to draw on organizational skills.

While in the field, sketch out a rough outline of the story. It'll force you to organize your thoughts and may give you a good idea for a standup close (which would be the end of the story). The standup close could draw a *conclusion* to your story. Suppose you're working on a story about problems with a city's mandatory recycling program. While in the field, you may not yet know exactly how you're going to write the beginning of the script, but you might already know enough to write a conclusion. The following example demonstrates how your standup close could read:

STANDUP CLOSE: "BECAUSE OF ALL THE PROBLEMS THE CITY IS HAVING ...THE NEW RECYCLING PLAN HAS BEEN PUT ON HOLD. BUT RESIDENTS ARE ASKED TO CONTINUE *VOLUNTARY* RECYCLING UNTIL A NEW CONTRACTOR IS HIRED. ERIC SHAPIRO, NEWS FOUR, FT. MONROE."

You could also write a standup close that alludes to the next step in the story, as in the following. These types of standups work well when you don't have enough information to form a conclusion, but do know enough to describe what's happening next in the story.

STANDUP CLOSE: "NEXT WEEK, INVESTIGATORS WILL PUBLICLY RELEASE THEIR REPORT...AND GIVE DETAILED RECOMMENDATIONS ON HOW TO PREVENT ANOTHER ACCIDENT FROM HAPPENING. ELIZABETH COYLE, CHANNEL TWO NEWS, AKRON."

You may also opt to record a standup **bridge,** rather than a standup **close.** You'll recall a bridge is a standup that appears somewhere in the body of the story rather than at the very end. Recording a standup bridge instead of a close works well when you have no idea how you might eventually end your story, or when you plan to use videotape instead of standup at the end of your story.

STANDUP BRIDGE: "THIS MUD IS SIX FEET DEEP AND A BIG REASON WHY RESCUERS HAD SO MUCH TROUBLE. IT TOOK THEM MORE THAN AN HOUR TO GET INSIDE THE HOUSE."

You can also tell a part of the story chronologically by using a standup bridge, as in the following example:

STANDUP BRIDGE: "BY EIGHT O-CLOCK AT NIGHT...THE LITTLE BOY HAD WANDERED HERE... TO A REMOTE PART OF THE WOODS...WITH THE TEMERATURE QUICKLY DROPPING."

A bridge can also serve to give facts or figures or other information for which you have no good pictures (videotape) to use, as in the following examples:

STANDUP BRIDGE: "COUNTY OFFICIALS SAY WHEN THE ORDINANCE WAS PASSED MORE THAN 50 YEARS AGO...NO ONE HAD ANY IDEA IT WOULD LATER BE USED TO DISCRIMINATE AGAINST MINORITIES WHO WANT TO WORK IN COUNTY GOVERNMENT."

STANDUP BRIDGE: "THE DOCUMENT REVEALS A TORTURED PAST...13 ARRESTS...INCLUDING ELEVEN FELONIES...BEFORE HE WAS 25 YEARS OLD. THE CRIMES RANGE FROM GRAND THEFT TO AGGRAVATED ASSAULT."

Writing Radio Wraps

The radio equivalent to television news packages, you'll recall, are wraps. Both packages and wraps are self-contained stories from reporters in the field, usually containing pieces of interviews (sound bites in television; actualities in radio).

Radio reporters should organize so that they can write and record their wraps entirely in the field whenever possible instead of returning to the studio to record their voice. Audio recorded in a studio with no background noise sounds more formal and can be jarring to the listener when mixed in with actualities of people recorded in the field. From the listener's perspective, it usually sounds more consistent and better for the reporter's audio to be recorded in the field as well.

Organizing Live Shots

Television and radio reporters are often called upon to do live shots: reports from the field that are not prerecorded. Even when live shots are largely extemporaneous, **ad-lib,** they require a certain element of organizing, or scripting, in advance. You have to know if you'll be talking live and then introducing a sound bite or actuality. Will you be talking live while the television audience sees some sort of B-roll videotape or be talking live with no video or interviews at all? Will you be talking live to briefly introduce a package or wrap you've recorded?

Radio reporters delivering live shots can refer to—even read directly from—a script they're written for the live shot on a notepad or computer. They don't have to look into a camera and are never seen by the audience; they are only heard. But the writing and delivery should be conversational, not stilted and formal.

Because television reporters *are* seen, it's not advisable for them to read directly from their notes during live shots. Viewers won't be impressed by a reporter talking with his head buried in a notepad. By the same token, it's not a good idea to attempt to *memorize* a script word for word for a live shot. A good approach is to jot down a few words or phrases as reminders of what you want to address in the live shot and in what order. Then, just talk about those issues conversationally in the live shot. You can briefly look down and refer to the notes naturally during the live shot.

Here are some facts you should consider including when organizing a live shot:

- What's happening on the scene at the very moment?
- What's the issue, dispute, or controversy?
- What are the relevant facts?
- What are some interesting or unusual observations?
- What's expected to happen next?

Suppose you're at the scene of a highway collapse. Here's an example of how you could organize thoughts for your live shot on paper:

Rescuers now trying to save family in van

Unexplained collapse one hour ago

8 vehicles damaged/7 people hospitalized/4 mo. old baby/no details on injuries

Recently/major construction on highway—unknown if related

Highway closed/investigation underway

Now, organize and sketch out notes suitable for a radio or television live shot based on the following plane crash information:

Plane Crash

Cessna plane crashed into a house about a mile from the city airport a half hour ago. Plane is still on fire. Pilot was able to crawl out then fell unconscious and was taken to the hospital. House was hit in the garage; the rest of the home seems undamaged, but the whole thing could burn. Unknown if anyone was or is in the house when the plane crashed.

Using the live shot notes you've made, talk them through aloud as if you're actually doing a live shot. Do you make sense? Do you sound like you know what you're talking about? Do you think you're giving the audience the information it needs?

Use the same set of facts to write a standup bridge that could be used in a recorded package, rather than a live shot. Our version is provided at the end of the chapter.

Interviews

Next we'll discuss one of the most important skills any broadcast or Internet journalist must develop. Anyone can ask questions, but it takes a true *thinker* to conduct revealing and meaningful **interviews.** Many of us have cringed while listening to an unprepared reporter conduct an awkward interview live on the radio or have become frustrated while watching an anchor fail to ask the most obvious follow-up question in a live interview on television. Conducting an insightful interview is an art form of its own, one mastered through organization and practice. Typically, novices hone their interviewing skills through trial and error, for example, returning from an interview only to find that they left a key question unasked. Or they might sit down to write a script only to find that there just aren't the right sound bites or quotes to tell the story.

Sometimes interviews are conducted in **informal** settings (see Figure 6.1) (both on and off camera) as in the following examples:

- An Internet news reporter asks a government official a few questions as he rushes through the airport to catch a plane.
- A radio news reporter interviews a source on the telephone.
- A television news reporter conducts an on-camera interview with a farmer as he walks through his cornfield.

Other interviews are more **formal** and are commonly referred to as **sit-down interviews,** even though they don't always take place while seated. Sit-downs are arranged, or set up, in advance. They're also considered **one-on-ones.** That means you alone, instead of a group of reporters in a news conference setting, are asking the questions as in these examples:

- A television news reporter has a one-on-one interview with the mayor in his office.

- A radio news reporter goes to the home of a community advocate for an interview about fighting crime in the neighborhood.
- A Web news site reporter interviews a member of Congress in his office.

Interview Content and Wording

Reporters independently determine interview content and formulate their own wording. Suppose you're preparing for a sit-down interview with a mother. She's launching a battle against a school for *not* expelling a child who repeatedly bullied her second-grader.

You need to ask three categories of questions:

1. First, you need **basic facts** and **background.** Often, you can ask many of these questions before the formal interview begins. In our example, you need to know things like the child's name, age, grade, and school. You may also get a few details of the actual bullying, which may help you think of relevant questions.
2. Next, you need **the story.** Think of questions that someone in the audience without an extensive background in the subject would want to ask. When and

FIGURE 6.1 *A reporter in Biloxi, Mississippi, conducts a one-on-one interview with the governor.*

how did the bullying begin? How did you find out about it? What did your son tell you about it? Did his behavior at home indicate something was wrong? What, exactly, was the bully doing? Did it involve any physical acts, like pushing or hitting? Were there threats? What was the emotional effect on your son? Did a teacher or another adult witness it? Who did you complain to? What was the response? Was any of this ever discussed with the parent of the bully? What makes you say the school should have done more? What did you expect the school to do? What steps are you taking now?

3. Last, always play **devil's advocate**; think of what critics of your interview might say and formulate some questions around that. How would you answer people who say you're just too protective of your son? How is his story different than what a lot of kids dealt with as a natural part of growing up? Why not put your child in private school that is more responsive to your concerns?

Much of what you discover in the interview will lead to the other areas you must address and to other sources. You'll need a response from school officials. You should find out the school and county policies on bullying and determine whether they were followed in the case at issue. Try to talk to the parents of the bully. See if the parents of the bully and the parents of the victim will let you talk to the respective children. You may want to interview a child psychologist who defines bullying and its damaging effects.

If you're writing for the Internet or television, don't forget to check for all possible visuals, such as relevant home video, photos, and documents. Will the parents give you photos or home video of the children involved? If not, can you get them from another family who has a school yearbook? If the victim was injured, did his mother photograph

Interview "Do"s and "Don't"s

- **DO** make a list of questions, but **DON'T** refer to it during the interview. It'll only distract you from following a natural train of thought and asking logical follow-ups. Check the list at the end of the interview to make sure you've covered all the areas you intended.
- **DO** record the interview (even if it's for written quotes for the Internet) so you **DON'T** have to take copious notes *during* the interview; it'll only distract you. It's also distracting to the interviewee if you have your face buried in a notepad instead of making normal eye contact as you listen.
- **DO** ask simple, direct questions; **DON'T** make it a challenge for the interviewee to figure out what you're asking.
- **DO** listen to the answers; **DON'T** hesitate to ask for clarification if you don't fully understand an answer.
- **DO** ask the questions that ordinary people in your audience would want to ask; **DON'T** simply try to impress the interviewee with how much you know about the subject.
- **DO** always end every interview by asking two things: Is there anything else you'd like to say that I didn't already ask you about? Is there a telephone number where I can reach you after hours in case I have any last minute questions as I'm writing the script?

or document the injuries? Is there a doctor's report substantiating the claim? Did the mother put her complaints in writing? Was there any written response?

 TIP: The most important thing you can get from an interviewee is what's called "color and comment," not just the straight facts. Instead of having the organizer of a parade tell how many people attended, have him describe how he *felt* when he saw the outpouring of patriotism among attendees.

The "do"s and "don't"s on page 124 are general guidelines for interviewing. There will be exceptions, but they're good rules of thumb.

Avoiding Bad Questions

Good interviewing isn't only asking good questions; it's also avoiding **bad questions.** What constitutes a bad question? It could be a question that wastes time, doesn't get to the truth, or is unnecessarily offensive to the interviewee. There are some exceptions to the rule, but following are four categories of questions which you should generally avoid.

Bad Questions

1. **Leading questions:** These are questions that improperly attempt to elicit a response based on your own preconceived view of the story. Such questions often begin or end with, "don't you?" For example, "You do believe we need to spend more money on space research, *don't you?*" A nonleading way to get the same information would be "Do you believe we need to spend more money on space research?" If the answer is no, you can follow up with "Why not?"
2. **Multipart questions:** These are questions that ask for two or more answers. An example is "Do you believe we need to spend more money on space research, and if not, why? Haven't you seen the polls showing that most Americans support the idea of increasing funding to NASA?" If the interviewee were simply to say no, it's not clear which question he's answering. Did he not see the poll? Does he not believe more money should be spent? Multipart questions are confusing and unfair to the interviewee and are typically asked by reporters who haven't given enough thought to what they're saying.
3. **Opinionated questions:** These are questions that include your own, personal opinion. They may unduly influence the interviewee's answer or unfairly make it so that any answer sounds unreasonable. For example, "Global warming is the most serious problem facing the world today; why isn't your plant, Mr. Johnson, reducing carbon dioxide emissions?"
4. **Offensive questions:** To be sure, nothing is wrong with asking aggressive and pointed questions, but needlessly rude questions are offensive. Insensitive questions are, too. For example, a mother has just lost her son in a farm accident. It's insensitive—and offensive—for a reporter to ask, "So how does it feel to know how your son died?" Or worse, "So how does it feel to know your son died, and you weren't there to help?" Such questions are asked all the time, but shouldn't be. Even the audience is offended by hearing them asked.

P.R.O.B.E.

Five principles can help you conduct effective interviews. They form a fitting acronym, **P.R.O.B.E:**

1. **P:** Prepare. Before an interview, you should already have gathered and read research—background—on the topic and, if possible, the interviewee.
2. **R:** Relax. The best interviews are conducted as if they are conversations. When you're relaxed, your interviewee is more likely to feel relaxed and provide a better interview.
3. **O:** Opportunity. It's fine to keep the interview to the point, but, in doing so, be sure to give the interviewees opportunities to say what they want. Don't brush off such points.
4. **B:** Boldness. Exercising appropriate boldness doesn't mean being rude, but it does mean being assertive, and, at times, even aggressive when interviewing.
5. **E:** Example. Learn by example: study journalists who are experts at interviewing.

Troubleshooting an Interview

What happens when interview subjects clam up, get too nervous to express themselves, aren't being clear, or can't seem to find the words to answer questions? It's up to you to change the interview atmosphere. Consider the following:

- You may be asking **too many "yes or no" questions.** Reask them in such a way that the interviewee has to respond with more than one word. Follow up a yes or no answer by saying things such as: Tell me more about it. Why do you feel that way? Can you elaborate on that? Start from the beginning of the story for people who don't know anything about it.
- Encourage the interviewee to speak in simple terms and to **avoid jargon.** If someone seems to be speaking in technical language or using acronyms your audience wouldn't understand (such as "IOC" instead of "International Olympic Committee), try saying the following: When we talk, it would be helpful if you'd try to use simple language for people who don't know as much about this as YOU do. Instead of saying IOC, say the whole phrase International Olympic Committee so that people will know what you're talking about.
- Make sure you've touched upon the emotion by asking questions that the person feels strongly about so you don't get **dull, technical responses.** Try saying: You've given a great description of the race problem on campus, but how did it make you **feel** to have to confront discrimination when that was supposed to have gone by the wayside decades ago?
- If the person seems extraordinarily **uncomfortable** or **nervous,** consider moving to a less formal location where he's more at home. Take a factory manager out onto the floor (wearing a microphone) and ask him to describe how the operation works. Then start asking relevant questions. He's more likely to be comfortable in these surroundings and less cognizant of the microphone and camera.

- When you can't get an answer during an adversarial interview with a politician or a bureaucrat, don't ignore the **evasiveness.** Politely, but firmly, use phrases such as: You're still not addressing the question. Did you know about the fraud? or That doesn't answer the question. Are you saying you don't know whether he'd been arrested before?
- If interviewees are continually **unclear** or you want to emphasize something important they said, try paraphrasing what *you* think they mean. For example, Are you saying nobody ever told you that the teacher you hired had been fired from three other school systems?
- If interviewees seem **confused** or **off point,** make sure you phrase your questions succinctly and clearly in a way they can easily follow.
- Are you glossing over answers you don't understand? If an interviewee is **talking over your head** or using phrases, terms, and words you don't know, it's your responsibility to clear matters up. You shouldn't be embarrassed or shy about it, but many reporters are because they're afraid they'll appear unintelligent. Try approaches such as, "I don't understand what you mean by that." or "I'm sorry, you lost me. I'm afraid our audience might not know what stock 'put' options are, either, so why don't you start over and explain them in simple terms." or "I'm still unclear on the chronology of events. Did you get sued before or after you left the country?" You'll find most interviewees are more than happy to have guidance on how to make themselves clear.

Sharyl's Story

In general, I've made it a policy not to surprise my interview subjects. My style is openness; it's not my goal or desire to catch an interviewee by surprise and unprepared. When conducting controversial interviews that may tend to be adversarial, I usually have a brief conversation beforehand with the interviewees. I tell them that, "I'll be asking some adversarial questions. As you know, this is a controversial topic, but it will allow you to give your best responses to your critics who are asking the same questions. I'm not just doing this with you, but with everyone I'm interviewing. I'll also give you the chance to make any points you want to make." For me, it's more comfortable to ask the toughest questions when I've had a conversation like that up front. The interviewees not only appreciate it, but, instead of feeling defensive in the interview and clamming up, they seem to be able to make their points better and more strongly.

The Beginning: The Lead

Whether you're a reporter who's gathered all the elements for a story, or a writer sitting down to rewrite wire copy, you have to start at the beginning. "Lead" is a word that's used in several different ways, but always refers to a beginning of sorts.

- The phrase **"lead-in"** (also called "anchor intro," which is short for anchor introduction) refers to an anchor's introduction of a television sound bite or radio actuality. It's also the anchor's introduction to a reporter's taped or live report.
- The **"lead story"** (also called "top story") refers to the first story in a newscast or on a news Web site.
- **"Getting a lead on a story"** means getting initial information to help you find out something more about a story. (For example, "I have a good lead on someone to interview about the child abuse story. I found a great article on the Internet, and the guy who wrote it lives here. I just have to find his phone number and see if he'll talk to us.")
- **"Story lead"** mean the first sentence in any story.

The final type mentioned, the leads of stories, is the type we'll examine more closely in this chapter.

Story Leads

Every story has a lead. It's the first sentence in a Web site article, the first sentence in a television news package, the first sentence in any radio news script, the first sentence in a live shot, or the first sentence in an anchor lead-in. In some ways, the lead can be the most important sentence in the whole story. It gets the story started. Its purpose is to provide information, of course, but to do so in a way that grabs the audience's attention and gives people a reason to keep on listening, watching, or reading. Leads have been aptly described as "the bait to hook the audience." Yet, crafting the lead sentence can be the most challenging part of writing a story.

A broadcast or Internet news lead should *not* be phrased like a newspaper headline. Read a newspaper headline aloud, and it's usually a choppy-sounding sentence fragment, or an abrupt phrase. The lead sentence in broadcasting or Internet writing is a complete sentence with a natural, conversational flow.

Here's a newspaper headline in San Jose, California:

Police Arrest Three Youths for Burglary

Here's a lead sentence suitable for broadcast or Internet news:

Three San Jose teenagers are in jail after police say they broke into homes and cars.

Read the newspaper headline aloud and then the lead. Notice the lead reflects the L2W principle. It's **localized** (San Jose), and it describes **where** (again, San Jose) and **what** (teens in jail for break-ins).

There are four basic types of lead sentences. When and how you use each depends on the kind of story you're writing.

1. Boomerang Lead

A **boomerang lead** is where you *throw* the basic information to the audience, and then, during the body of the story, the information comes back—it's repeated in a way that expands upon the story. Here's an example:

Boomerang lead

Police are searching for the hit-and-run driver who killed a Memphis man. Earlier this evening 62-year-old Randolph Baxter was hit by a Jeep as he crossed the street in front of his home . . . the driver didn't stop. Eyewitnesses weren't able to get a license tag number. Police are looking for a late model Jeep with a broken right headlight. XXXXXX

This boomerang lead satisfies the L2W objectives. And on its own, it tells the basic gist of the story: a hit and run in Memphis. The rest of the story serves to repeat and amplify that information. Yes, there's some repetition, but it serves a purpose. Imagine people hearing radio news while typing on their office computers or preparing dinner in the kitchen with the evening news on television. These audience members are in a relatively passive state, sometimes only half-listening until they hear a reason to sit up and take notice. By the time they hear the lead and are paying attention, they need information that confirms—or corrects—what they *thought* they heard when they weren't carefully listening.

The previous example's second sentence restates what the lead already told: someone was hit by a car . . . but it also tells who and gives the victim's age. It repeats the fact that the driver has run, but adds the type of vehicle involved.

The first news director for CBS Radio, Paul White, had a poetic way of looking at the mission of broadcast news scripts. His formula was this:

- Tell them what you're going to tell them.
- Tell them.
- Tell them what you just told them.

It exaggerates a key point in this section. The broadcasting audience can't listen at its own pace. Viewers and listeners have no way to stop and back up if they miss or misunderstand the facts. So it sometimes makes sense to be creatively repetitive. Boomerang it! Toss some information to the audience in the lead sentence and bring it back with more detail in the body of the story.

Use the following information to craft an Internet news story that makes use of a boomerang lead. Our version is presented later in the chapter.

Beached Whale

500-pound pygmy sperm whale beaches itself on the New Jersey coast. Found Thursday morning in Spring Lake in Monmouth County. Rescuers rushed it to the National Aquarium in Baltimore. No one knows what's wrong with the whale. A whale was last brought to the same Aquarium in 1993 and turned out to have balloons in his stomach, as well as trash bags. He was treated and released back into the ocean.

---

2. Breaking Lead

Breaking leads are used in breaking news situations, which means stories that are still developing even as they're being written. They stress immediacy and can be short on the kind of detail needed for boomerang leads. That's because fast-breaking stories may only have facts that are sketchy and vague. When you hear a lead that seems to be stressing an event that is happening at the moment, it's a breaking lead.

Here's an example:

Breaking lead

A tornado has been sighted near the city limits of the west side of Goxton on Highway 72. Eyewitnesses say it has touched the ground and is blowing down trees and power lines. It's said to be moving eastward. Our own Debra Long is in the lobby of a car dealership on Highway 72 and is watching the funnel cloud . . . Debra?

The previous lead satisfies L2W. But what makes it a breaking lead, is that it also emphasizes that the event is happening at the moment: "A tornado has been sighted." Later in the day, when the story is over, the fact that the tornado was sighted won't be in the lead sentence. Instead, the *results* of the tornado will be, as in the next example:

Non-breaking lead

A rush-hour tornado on the west side of Goxton flipped four cars, killing two people. Police haven't released the identities of the victims. Four other people who were in the cars . . . including a two-year old baby . . . were injured and hospitalized. The funnel cloud also knocked down trees and power lines on Highway 72 around four-30 this afternoon. Authorities are still assessing property damage.

XXX

From the following information, write a breaking news lead suitable for radio or television. Our answer is provided later.

Train Wreck

Police say there are burning tank cars piled on top of each other in a chaotic situation, producing smoke that could be deadly, after a train wreck in Eunice, Louisiana. Rescue workers have been dispatched, but it's unknown if there are any injuries. No other information is known right now.

---

3. Softy Lead

The third type of broadcast news lead is what we call the **softy lead.** This lead is appropriate for feature stories, also referred to as soft news stories. As we discussed in Chapter 1, soft news stories aren't necessarily about currently happening events. A soft feature might profile an interesting or unusual person. A feature could be written about a day in the life of the mayor's wife. Features might expand upon a hard news story to give it added meaning and interpretation. For example, following a hard news story about a child being abducted, there could be a feature story discussing how to keep your child safe. Features can cover cooking, gardening, financial tips, travel, and sports figures. There are features about courageous people, charitable causes, and features simply intended to provide comic relief.

These soft news features can have practically any mood imaginable: poignant, pious, ridiculous, or practical. A lot of the basic rules, including the L2W lead principles, go by the wayside with features. The writing should be conversational and clear, but, beyond that, you're limited only by your own imagination and creativity.

Let's look at some softy leads:

Can you believe it . . . The British government has banned musical chairs because they say the game makes children aggressive.

John and Betty Callahan get up at the crack of dawn to milk their cows. The unusual thing about this Eastern Rhode Island couple is . . . they're in their late nineties!

His dream for 12 years has been to run with the ball on the Moses High School football team . . . and after being on crutches for so long . . . Rick Maynorth is laying the crutches down and picking up the football.

Every afternoon for just about 22 years now Winfred Lister has taken a good long nap after eating lunch with his wife Sally . . . but what's so unusual is WHERE Lister takes his nap.

Note: In hard news, the attribution should be given *before* the quote. But in soft news stories, it may not important for the audience to know immediately who a quote is from. It can be effective to use the quote first; so then identify the source afterwards.

"She gets her good looks from me." That's what the father of the newly crowned Miss Texas from Nacogdoches says.

"I'll never eat oysters again." That's what Florida State sophomore Carl Hodnett said after winning last night's Lambda Chi Alpha's oyster-eating contest.

Write your own softy lead based on the following information. Compare it to our version provided later.

What: Dark Shadows Night: three hours of the "best of" the horror soap opera (which aired on ABC from 1966-1971).
Where: McComas Theatre at Mississippi State
Who: Presented by the Dept. of Communications
When: Thursday night

Linking Lead

The last type of lead is called the **linking lead.** Such leads serve to either connect two stories in a newscast or to provide a transition to make one story flow smoothly and logically to the next.

Suppose a story in the newscast is about the local sheriff attending the funerals of four policemen killed nearby in the line of duty. The next story is about the battle between county commissioners over the upcoming year's budget and how the sheriff's budget is a key point of contention. Here's a possible linking lead that provides a transition between the two stories:

(Remember, the previous story is about the sheriff attending a funeral in another city. Here's how the budget story could begin.)

While the Sheriff is away, county commissioners are busy fighting over his . . . and the rest of the county's budget.

Here's another example. Suppose there's a story about violent computer games, followed by a report on a fun festival for children. In this case, the transition lead for the fun festival doesn't attempt to connect the two stories—there is no connection—but serves to avoid an abrupt change in subject.

(Remember, the previous story is about violent computer games. Here's how the fun festival story could begin.)

None of that seemed to be on the minds of kids attending the local fun festival today . . . there was a capacity crowd and smiles all around.

Sometimes, two or more stories that are somehow related are introduced by using a variation of linking lead: **an umbrella lead.** Instead of linking or making a transition *between* two stories, the umbrella lead introduces the first of the related stories.

Imagine a newscast with two stories in a row about President Bush visiting Russia and ramifications of the meeting. Here's an example of an umbrella lead:

Umbrella (linking) lead

(ANCHOR)
Two Presidents . . . one near the end of his term, the other beginning a new era . . . sized each other up today. President Bush is in Moscow tonight for his first meeting with Russia's President. Over dinner, the two leaders held what are being called serious and focused talks on a number of issues. We have two stories tonight—one on the issues at hand; the other about the Russian reception President Bush received. Our first report is from Bill Plante who's traveling with the President.

That umbrella lead introduces one story; then the lead-in to the next story links the two stories:

Linking lead

(ANCHOR)
With missile defenses and the A-B-M Treaty under discussion at the Moscow summit **[this refers to the previous story which the audience just saw]** . . . the U-S continues to honor a ban on testing nuclear weapons **[this begins to introduce the next, related story].** No longer able to explode weapons in the desert, scientists are forced to rely on the next best thing. Sharyl Attkisson has that report:

Now, it's your turn. Write a *linking* lead that could provide a transition between the two following stories:

1. A story about a rabies outbreak
2. A story about the local dogcatcher having to take special precautions because of the rabies outbreak

When you're done with that, craft an *umbrella* lead that could be used to introduce two reports examining different aspects of a local police crackdown on truancy and underage smoking as part of a wider campaign to combat juvenile crime.

Compare your versions to ours, provided in the next section.

Answers

    1. Plane Crash/Standup Bridge

> STANDUP BRIDGE: "THE PLANE HIT THE HOUSE ON THE SIDE...IN THE GARAGE...AND THEN BURST INTO FLAMES. THE FIRE THREATENED TO SPREAD AND BURN DOWN THE WHOLE HOUSE, SO RESCUERS WORKED QUICKLY TO FIND OUT IF ANYONE WAS INSIDE."

    2. Beached Whale/Boomerang Lead

> Rescuers at the National Aquarium are trying to find out what's wrong with a pygmy sperm whale that beached itself in New Jersey. The 500-pound mammal was discovered Thursday morning after it washed up on a beach in Spring Lake, New Jersey. It was rushed to the Baltimore aquarium, where workers are watching it around the clock. The last time a pygmy sperm whale was brought to the aquarium—back in 1993—it had a stomach full of plastic balloons and trash bags. That whale recovered and was later released back into the ocean.
> (XXXX)

    3. Train Wreck/Breaking News Lead

> Rescue workers are now rushing to the scene of a train wreck in Eunice, Louisiana...where possibly toxic smoke is billowing from burning rail cars.

    4. Dark Shadows/Softy Lead

> Thursday night's going to be pretty scary at McComas Theatre at Mississippi State as the Department of Communication presents Dark Shadows Night...three solid hours of the very best from the horror soap that aired on A-B-C 19-66 through 19-71.

    5. Rabies/Linking Lead

> The rabies outbreak means people who come in contact with wild animals are on special alert...including the local dogcatcher.

6. Juvenile Crime/Umbrella lead

> Police are trying a new approach in their fight to combat the growing juvenile crime in the area. They're trying to get to kids before the problem gets out of hand. That means cracking down on truancy...and underage smoking. We have two reports on the novel approach, and how much it will cost taxpayers...beginning with reporter Tiffany Johnson.

Web Sites

For more information, check out the following Web sites:

www.poynter.org/dj/020900.htm
How to land an interview, from the Poynter Institute

www.aptra.org/News%20Pages/palmdesertho.htm
Associated Press Television and Radio Association, interview tips

Quick Review of Terms

- **Ad-libbing:** The practice of delivering news extemporaneously without reading from a script. Often employed in live situations
- **Boomerang lead:** A lead that throws basic information to the story and then repeats and expands on it in the body of the script
- **Breaking lead:** A lead used in breaking news stories that are still developing, even as they're being written
- **The lead:** The first sentence in a broadcast or Internet news story
- **Linking lead:** A lead that connects two stories in a newscast or provides a transition to make one story flow smoothly and logically to the next
- **The Milieu Factor:** The way in which your environment or surroundings can help you capture the essence of an event you're reporting
- **One-on-ones:** Interviews conducted by you, alone, rather than by a group of reporters in a news conference setting
- **P.R.O.B.E.:** Five principles for conducting effective interviews: Prepare, Relax, Opportunity, Boldness, Example
- **Sit-down interviews:** Formal interviews (even if they're not actually seated) that are arranged, or set up in advance
- **Softy lead:** A lead appropriate for feature (soft news) stories
- **Umbrella lead:** A form of linking lead that introduces the first of several related stories

Review Questions _____

1. What are some ways to organize your material and ideas as you prepare to write a story?

2. What are some ideas for writing television news standups in the field, even before the rest of the story is written?

3. How can you organize your thoughts for a live shot?

4. What are ways you can prepare to conduct an interview?

5. When an interview seems to be going poorly, how can you attempt to troubleshoot the problems?

6. What are some interview mistakes to avoid?

7. What are the types of leads, and when is each appropriate?

Summary _____

This chapter explains the importance of organizational skills every step of the way when writing broadcast and Internet news stories. It's a job that requires so much multitasking—researching, determining who to interview, making contacts, and writing—that it's easy to let important thoughts and ideas slip away. Creating story outlines on paper while working in the field is one of the best ways to get organized, whether it's for a standup, a live shot, or to determine what other elements are needed to make the story complete. Conducting interviews requires organized thought, but the interviews should be natural and conversational. When all of the elements of a story are gathered, it's time to organize material and ideas to determine how the story will begin and what type of lead will be used. Students who practice good organizational habits will be better positioned to meet deadlines and write clear, complete stories.

8

Beyond the Basics

Chapter Objectives

- To explain concepts that can make writing more interesting
- To discuss the importance of writing to videotape and graphics
- To explore the use of natural sound and graphics
- To consider the differences between long-form and short-form news stories

Now that you know some of the basics of broadcast and Internet news writing, it's time to take things a step further. You *don't* want to become a newswriting robot that simply transmits factual information to viewers. You *do* want to write stories that are compelling and to ferret out information the audience most wants to know. You then want to relay it in a way that people will remember and diffuse.

It takes years for broadcast and Internet news writers to develop their own styles and learn the finer points of crafting an excellent story. This is whether it's writing a radio feature story with a sense of humor; building a feeling of suspense in a long-form television news magazine piece; conveying a sense of irony in a story for the television evening news; or writing an Internet story so compelling that the audience is moved to click onto links, check out video, or take part in an online survey.

This chapter is to encourage you to think beyond the basics. We'll introduce some advanced concepts for you to consider as you practice writing. The most important thing is getting it right. Yet, if you do nothing more, who'll listen? Concentrating on the skills introduced in this chapter can separate you from your competition and can help you gain advantage over those who simply recount factual information, oversimply or sensationalize their stories.

The Point

Often, a writer will mistakenly sit down and begin working without having thought out the obvious: *what's the main **point** of the story?* Chances are that if you, as the writer, don't know the answer to that question, you're not likely to convey the point very well in your finished product. It's a good idea to decide **the point** of the story before you start.

Read the following set of facts, which come from a police report in Tampa, Florida.

Dennis Carlton was arrested on manslaughter charges. He was at his Tampa, Florida, home when his friend, Stacy Mandera, came to visit. Mandera was distraught, depressed, and intoxicated when she arrived. Carlton said he had tired of hearing her complaints, so admits to giving Mandera a loaded handgun saying, 'If your life is so bad, end it.' That's when Mandera picked up the gun and shot herself in the head.

The main point of this story is that a man actually provided a depressed friend with a gun and encouraged her to commit suicide. Your story should convey this point and the horror of it. Here's an example of how it could be written for a television news broadcast:

SUICIDE
(ANCHOR)

(ANCHOR)
A TAMPA, FLORIDA, MAN HAS BEEN ARRESTED ON CHARGES HE PROVIDED A DISTRAUGHT FRIEND WITH THE GUN SHE USED TO KILL HERSELF.
POLICE SAY STACY MANDERA WAS DEPRESSED AND INTOXICATED WHEN SHE VISITED THE HOME OF HER FRIEND DENNIS CARLTON.
CARLTON ...TIRED OF HEARING HER COMPLAIN...TOLD POLICE HE HANDED MANDERA A LOADED HANDGUN AND SAID— IF YOUR LIFE IS SO BAD, END IT.
AUTHORITIES SAY MANDERA THEN PICKED UP THE GUN AND SHOT HERSELF IN THE HEAD.
CARLTON IS CHARGED WITH MANSLAUGHTER.
(XXX)

Now, it's your turn. The following facts are taken from a press release about a new study. Determine the main point and then write a brief Internet news story. You can compare it to one we provide in the Answers section slugged "Working Americans."

A study conducted by the United Nations measured the amount of annual hours worked by labor forces in various industrialized and nonindustrialized nations. The results among industrialized nations found the average American put in nineteen-hundred-seventy-eight hours in 2000. That compares with nineteen-hundred-forty-two hours in 1990. The new amount is more hours on the job than any other industrialized nation, including Canada, France, Germany, Japan, and the United Kingdom. Among nonindustrialized nations, only South Korea and the Czech Republic worked more hours than Americans. South Koreans logged almost 500 hours more than U-S workers; Czech Republic laborers clocked in 100 hours more.

 TIP: To make this story more meaningful to the audience, translate the number of hours from an annual figure into a weekly figure. The annual figure is meaningless to most people, but most people know that an average work week is 40 hours.

The Meaning

You might be shocked to know how often news stories are written by people who don't really understand them to begin with. The result is bound to be confusing to the audience as well. If the **meaning** of a story isn't crystal clear to you, there's no way you can communicate it effectively to anyone else. Beginning writers sometimes make the mistake of thinking they ought to immediately understand new or complex ideas, often introduced to them in confusing press releases, poorly written police reports, or jumbled wire copy that was written by a writer who also didn't understand the story. There's no shame in asking a colleague for help deciphering a subject or terminology or in getting assistance from someone who's better versed on the topic. The shame would be in attempting to write a story that you, yourself, don't fully understand.

Take the following Associated Press wire copy, do whatever research you have to do to decipher its point and meaning, and transform it into a brief, clearly written television news script. Our version, slugged "China Sanctions," appears in the Answers section.

WASHINGTON (AP) - The Bush administration imposed sanctions Saturday on a Chinese arms producer for selling missile technology to Pakistan, a State Department official said.

China is not supposed to export missile technology to nations developing nuclear missiles, according to an agreement with the United States. State Department officials long have accused Beijing of ignoring the accord.

The Chinese company is China Metallurgical Equipment Corp., which has worked with the Chinese government, said the official, speaking on condition of anonymity. Also punished was the National Development Complex of Pakistan.

"The sanctions were imposed on these entities for their involvement in the transfer . . . of missile technology that contributed to Pakistan's missile program," the official said.

The penalties will keep U.S. companies from issuing licenses to launch satellites on Chinese rockets and, in most cases, will make it illegal to provide technology to China's satellite industry.

The technology the Chinese arms dealer is accused of exporting is considered category 2 technology, which includes flight-control systems for missiles and rocket components.

The announcement comes in the month before President Bush's planned trip to China. State Department officials are hoping his visit will help ease tensions after the crash of a U.S. spy plane and a Chinese fighter jet in April.

U.S. suspicions of arms deals between China and Pakistan have been building for months.

Talks between U.S. and Chinese weapons experts last week over whether China is helping other countries develop missile technology ended with the American side wanting more answers, U.S. officials said.

The officials said they worried that Chinese firms provided missile technology to Pakistan and helped Iraq rebuild air defenses. Vann Van Diepen, an acting deputy assistant secretary of state who specializes in nonproliferation issues, led the U.S. negotiators.

In July, Secretary of State Colin Powell met with Chinese leaders and said that the U.S. felt China was not following the arms agreement.

A Chinese Foreign Ministry spokesman, Sun Yuxi, responded that China was making an earnest effort to comply with its obligations.

Sun contended that the United States has failed to comply with its commitments - an apparent reference to the absence of cooperation on commercial satellite launches.

The Mood

Every story you write should have its own distinct **mood**, whether serious, humorous, ironic, or tragic. To be an effective writer or storyteller, you must decide the mood of each given story before you write it.

Consider the following script:

> BALLOON BUST
> (ANCHOR/OC)
>
> (ANCHOR)
> Police in New York City have arrested a 46-year-old man and charged him with the attempted robbery of a tourist. Witnesses say suspect Kenneth Reed attacked a 13-year-old girl outside the Grand Hyatt Hotel where she was staying with her parents. Reed supposedly tried to grab the child's balloons, but she fought him off and managed to hang onto her balloons.
>
> (XXX)

What would you say the mood of the story is? It's written in a serious tone, but there are so many more possibilities that would make it much more interesting! First of all, the attempted robbery of a tourist is not a story that would usually make it into a typical newscast. It's just not particularly newsworthy, especially since the robber was unsuccessful and the victim unhurt. What makes it interesting is that it's unusual for a thief to attack a child for her balloons, and, furthermore, that she was able to fight him off. Those are the ideas your story should capitalize on and convey.

If you don't know where to begin, think about how you would tell the story to a friend. You might say, "Did you hear about some loser in New York who tried to steal a kid's balloons and she fought him off?" *That's* the gist of the story. In light of the fact that the child was not hurt, it's not a particularly serious story. A more appropriate mood might be ironic, humorous, or surprising.

Consider the following more lighthearted approach below:

> BALLOON BUST
> (ANCHOR/OC)
>
> (ANCHOR/OC)
> Taking candy from a baby might have been easier for a would-be robber in New York... Police say the 46-year-old man tried to grab balloons from a 13-year-old girl outside the Grand Hyatt Hotel. But the child would have none of it...she successfully fought him off and managed to hang onto her balloons. The suspect was arrested nearby a short time later. Maybe he should have picked on somebody his own size...
>
> (XXX)

The story has now been transformed into a more clever, interesting version that would be perfect for ending a news broadcast on a light note. And it's one the audience will probably remember.

Now it's your turn to practice. Use the following facts in writing a broadcast copy story. Make the mood light. Slug it "Hair Apparent." Our version is in the Answers section.

Pennsylvania's attorney general, 56-year-old Mike Fisher, recently underwent hair implant surgery. The transformation took place in advance of Fisher's planned run for the Republican nomination for governor next year. Before the surgery, he was balding. One of his supporters says the change gives Fisher a younger appearance. Fisher says it will be several months before he knows whether the hair implants will take.

Surprise Endings

Many news stories include who, what, and where in the very first sentence. But not all scripts have to be structured that way. There are times, for instance, when it's very effective to withhold some of the key facts until the end of the story. This technique, which we call **surprise endings,** can be best used in feature or soft news stories. One example follows:

Payback

A man was desperately guilt-ridden after he shoplifted from a five-and-dime store. So guilt-ridden that he recently mailed the store—a Woolworth's in Shanton—a letter of apology. In it, he admitted stealing a two-dollar toy and enclosed a money order paying the money back plus interest. But what makes this story even more remarkable is that the illegal deed happened fifty years ago! The anonymous author of the letter confessed his transgression occurred way back in 1952 when he was five years old. Now, at last, his conscience may be clear.

See how effective the story is by not revealing immediately that the shoplifting happened decades ago? The following is an example of the same story written in a style that fails to take advantage of a surprise ending.

Payback

A man who shoplifted from the Woolworth's store in Shanton back in 1952 recently sent the shop an anonymous letter of apology. In it, he said he's been guilt-ridden all these years. The item he stole was a two-dollar toy. He enclosed a money order paying back the two dollars with interest.

Use the following facts to construct a brief radio news story with a surprise ending:

Ronald, a five-year-old beagle, managed to save the day when a prowler entered his master's house. The mutt somehow knocked the telephone off the receiver and triggered the speed-dial button programmed to call 9-1-1. When police took the call, they only heard silent panting on the other end and dispatched an officer to the scene. The burglar was caught red-handed and arrested on the spot.

 TIP: When writing your surprise ending, experiment with withholding the fact that Ronald is a dog.

A Sense of Suspense

Another effective technique you can consider using when writing news stories is creating **a sense of suspense.** As in surprise endings, a sense of suspense is best suited for certain feature stories. It's often used in long-form television news magazine programs, such as Dateline NBC and CBS News' 48 Hours. The theory is that a sense of suspense will help create and maintain a level of viewer interest throughout a story or entire program.

The technique can also be used in shorter stories on radio, television, or the Internet. The following is an example of a brief Internet feature story that creates a sense of suspense.

Aussie Lottery Mystery of Unclaimed Jackpot—Is Solved!

Australian lottery officials searched high and low for the lucky winner of the big lottery in Melbourne. The jackpot was a whopping 14-million dollars, and there was only one winning ticket. But months after the drawing, still nobody had stepped forward to claim the prize! So lottery officials launched an all-out search that included newspaper, radio and television ads publicizing the winning numbers—and the fact that the booty had gone unclaimed. Finally, just two days before the jackpot was set to expire and revert back into the lottery fund, a 47-year-old Melbourne man notified officials that he held the winning ticket. The first question on everyone's mind, of course, was what took him to long. He had only one simple answer, telling lottery officials he just "didn't really need the money."

Compare that to a version of the following story, which is written *without* a sense of suspense.

Aussie Lottery Winner Steps Forward at Last!

A 47-year-old man who said he just "didn't need the money" finally stepped forward to claim his 14-million dollar prize almost a year after the drawing. Australian lottery officials had searched high and low for the lucky winner of the big lottery in Melbourne after the winner failed to step forward even months after the lottery. The winner only turned up to collect two days before the jackpot would have expired and reverted back to the lottery fund.

Writing to Video

When writing stories for television news that use videotape, the best writers have a picture—an idea of the video that can be used—to go along with every sentence they write.

People who aren't used to **writing to video** mistakenly write their stories in a vacuum. They construct a script with no specific images in mind, as if they were writing a newspaper article. They then leave it up to a videotape editor or producer to figure out how to cover all of the words with pictures (videotape). The result is often a confusing or uninteresting story with videotape that doesn't support or match the words.

Catherine Harwood, a former local television news director, and a one-time reporter in Orlando, Florida, and Houston, Texas, tells about words of wisdom she got about matching video and graphics to the copy:

> The most memorable writing advice I ever got came from one of my college professors who taught the concept of cognitive dissonance: the proven theory that people generally can't digest and retain a story if you show pictures of one thing while describing something else. It impairs communication. That simple lesson came back to me so many times when I was sitting at a computer struggling to make sense of a complicated story. The pictures and graphics must reasonably match what you're talking about. It's a simple lesson that seems more appropriate than ever as the television screen is filled up with multiple bits of information competing for attention.

Here are two examples of writing stories in which the copy and the video *don't* match: a combination that's sure to confuse the audience. First, suppose you're reporting a horrifying attack blamed on a terrorist. But instead of showing video of the attack, your story shows video of a terrorist happily shaking hands with some state dignitary. The smiling terrorist *pictures* conflict with the *words* about the vicious attack and impair the message. Another example is you *write* a story about a baby drowning in a flood while showing *video* only of a flooded river nearby. The audience will naturally be looking, in vain, for the baby you're referring to.

In contrast, a story written by someone with a good understanding of what videotape is available, someone who's viewed the videotape before writing will tend to be clearer and more interesting to the audience. *Whenever possible, you should view the applicable videotape before writing every story.* The video will lead you to creative ideas and thoughts and will often help you stay away from descriptions or events or details that have no pictures (video) to support them.

Here's an example of a poorly written package in which no consideration was given to the videotape that was shot for the story. The notes in parentheses indicate the pictures that were used to "cover" the parts of the story in the paragraph that follows the notation.

Poorly Written Package in which Videotape Wasn't Considered

Western Wildfires

(Video: wide shot of wildfire from air/no homes in the picture)

A neighborhood near Montana's Glacier National Park is the latest one being threatened by wildfires that have been raging for more than a week.

(Video: another wide shot of the same wildfire)

Residents are frantically spraying water on their roofs and taking other steps to try to protect their homes. One fire official predicts it's going to get even worse.

(SOT-JOHN TRANSOM, FIREFIGHTER)

IT'S BEING DRIVEN BY THE WIND AT THIS POINT AND THERE'S NOT MUCH WE CAN DO. IT'S GOING TO GET EXTREMELY LARGE. (:10)

(Video: tight shot of firefighters on the front lines of the fire)

The fire's leading edge is about ten miles from Lake McDonald. It's grown to more than 40-thousand acres, and is just one of 22 major fires that have now destroyed more than 222-thousand acres in the west.

(REPORTER STANDUP)

OFFICIALS SAY THE ONLY HOPE AT THIS POINT COMES FROM MOTHER NATURE. A LARGE RAINSTORM COULD HELP DOUSE THE FIRES. FORECASTERS SAY IT'LL BE AT LEAST FOUR MORE DAYS BEFORE THE AREA HAS EVEN A CHANCE OF SHOWERS. ANITA REYNOLDS, WRBQ, NEAR GLACIER NATIONAL PARK.

(XXX)

The first mistake the writer in the preceding script made was referring to a very specific neighborhood being threatened by the wildfires even though no videotape was available of the neighborhood. Instead, a generic (nonspecific) wide shot of the fire scene was used to cover the first sentence of the package, leaving a frustrated audience at home watching and waiting for pictures that will never appear.

The writer compounded the mistake by continuing with details of frantic residents trying to protect their homes by spraying the roofs with water. Again, there is no videotape to support this sentence in the story, so the editor used another generic wide shot of the fire.

When videotape is used that doesn't really match what's being said, it's often referred to in the business as wallpaper video, which is a derogatory term.

How could the story have been written better, considering the fact that only limited videotape of the fires is available? If the writer had looked at the available videotape first, he might have noticed that the most compelling shots were the close-ups of tired firefighters working the leading edge of the fire. That would be a better place to begin the story. Here's an example:

Western Wildfires

(Video: tight shot of firefighters on the front lines of the fire)

Firefighters are frantically working near Montana's Glacier National Park to keep the newest, 40-thousand-acre wildfire from spreading to a nearby neighborhood.

(Video: wide shot of wildfire)

The leading edge of the flames is just ten miles away from a cluster of homes at Lake McDonald. Wildfires have been raging out of control for more than a week now, and one fire official predicts things are going to get worse.

(SOT-JOHN TRANSOM, FIREFIGHTER)

IT'S BEING DRIVEN BY THE WIND AT THIS POINT AND THERE'S NOT MUCH WE CAN DO. IT'S GOING TO GET EXTREMELY LARGE. (:10)

(Video: aerial wide shots of fire scene)

The Glacier Park fire is one of just 22 major fires that have now destroyed more than 222-thousand acres in the west. Officials say their only hope lies in a large rainstorm, but fore-casters say the soonest that could happen is four days from now.

(REPORTER STANDUP)

SO RESIDENTS AT LAKE MCDONALD, JUST A FEW MILES FROM HERE, ARE TAKING WHATEVER STEPS THEY CAN TO PROTECT THEIR PROPERTY, THEY KNOW THEY COULD BE FORCED TO EVACUATE WITHIN A MATTER OF HOURS IF THE FIRE CONTINUES ITS DESTRUCTIVE MARCH TOWARD THEM. ANITA REYNOLDS, WRBQ, NEAR GLACIER NATIONAL PARK.

By simply changing the focus of the story a bit, there's not a speck of wallpaper in sight. We've now taken the best pictures available—the videotaped close-ups of the firefighters in action—and made it the focus of the beginning sentence. The video-tape now supports the words and vice versa!

The first version included details about nearby homes being in danger, and those are important facts. But without videotape to support them, you risk frustrating the audience, or even losing its interest. So in the second version, the same basic in-formation is conveyed in the reporter standup.

☞ **TIP:**   Standups can be used to tell important or interesting facts for which there is no videotape.

Roxanne Russell, a longtime senior producer for CBS News, is not only an excellent writer herself, but has trained more than her share of producers and correspondents in the finer points of writing to video. Here's some advice she provided exclusively for this book:

> Here's a major challenge for the television writer: letting the pictures speak for themselves, not wasting the viewers' time by describing what the pictures clearly tell. How much more difficult it is to find something *other* to say than "the strong winds blew down three cars on the main street" . . . when the pictures clearly show that happening. The *good* writer looks for something else to report, while the pictures are weaving their own magic.
>
> Many times pictures force the reporter to write stories to best take advantage of them. This can be frustrating to a reporter determined to "get the facts out." I remember a story Pentagon reporter David Martin was doing on the christening of a new Navy destroyer at the shipyard in Bath, Maine. His original script began with the basic facts of the launch but, once we got to see the videotape the photographer shot of the event, showing dense fog and the eerie sound of the hammers as the workers released the ship from its ties, the story needed to be rewritten to reflect the ghostly images. It was a better story because of it.
>
> Former CBS News correspondent Bruce Morton was legendary for his skill in "wrapping" pictures from around the country for a story on a vague, general subject, such as "summer heat" or "America celebrates Independence Day." Bruce would never write a word until he saw the pictures. He patiently sat in the edit room while video feed after video feed came in from around the country, watching the images, absorbing the reactions of others in the room to what the images showed. And only after the feeds were complete, would he work his magic with words. The pictures would be woven in a way that let THEM tell the story . . . not as wallpaper to words of the "he came, he saw, he said" variety. Bruce was and is a master of his craft.

Writing to Graphics

Another tool that television and Internet writers have at their disposal is something referred to as **graphics.** Graphics refer to a wide range of visual images other than videotape. You, the writer, create the concept of what will be in the graphic and how it will be used. Typically, a graphic artist will actually create the image that will be used in your story.

A graphic can be a graph, chart, list, still photograph, or other visual image other than videotape. It can reflect facts, figures, poll results, or numbers. A graphic can also be a page of a document with certain words or material highlighted. It can be a written quote from someone who refused to do an on-camera interview. In television news, graphics are especially useful to impart information for which there is no good supporting videotape. In any case, **writing to graphics** is very important.

In the following television news story on page 148, the notation on the left-hand side of the page describes a graphic that the audience will see filling the entire television screen.

POLL
(ANCHOR)

(ANCHOR)
AMERICANS DON'T SUPPORT THE
IDEA OF A TAX INCREASE, EVEN IF
IT HELPS KEEP NATIONAL PARKS
CLEAN AND GREEN.

(VO)
Font: Yosemite National Park File Tape

(VO)
THAT'S ACCORDING TO A NEW
POLL CONDUCTED AT YOSEMITE
NATIONAL PARK LAST WEEK.

(FULL SCREEN GRAPHIC)
National Park Tax Hike?
67% NO
20% YES

(GRAPHIC)
TWO-THIRDS OF THOSE ASKED SAID
THAT THEY WOULD NOT BE
WILLING TO PAY ANY ADDITIONAL
TAXES FOR PARK CLEANUP.

(FULL SCREEN GRAPHIC)
National Park Fees?
63% TOO HIGH
10% TOO LOW
20% JUST RIGHT

(GRAPHIC)
ABOUT THE SAME NUMBER ALSO
THOUGHT THAT THE FEES TO
ENTER NATIONAL PARKS ARE
ALREADY TOO HIGH.

(ANCHOR/ON CAMERA)

(ANCHOR/ON CAMERA)
SOME IN CONGRESS ARE
PROPOSING A 50-CENT PER PERSON
TAX INCREASE THAT WOULD
SPECIFICALLY BE EARMARKED FOR
PARK IMPROVEMENTS.
(XXX)

Refer back to the preceding example. The story begins as most do, with the anchor reading on camera. Then, after the first sentence, the viewers at home would see file videotape of Yosemite National Park. Next, instead of videotape, there would be a full screen graphic showing the results of the poll that's referred to in the copy. The title of the graphic that will appear at the top of the screen or "page" that the audience will see is "National Park Tax Hike?" Underneath will be the actual percentages. Then, a second full-screen graphic titled "National Park Fees?" is used. The anchor comes back on camera for the final sentence.

When using graphics in television news stories, two important principles should always be followed:

1. *Keep it simple:* The information should be brief and basic. Remember, the audience will be trying to read it as it flashes only briefly on the screen. If there's too much material included in a graphic, the audience won't have enough time to read it.

2. *Match the graphic to the copy:* When the wording in a graphic deviates too much from the wording in the script, it confuses the audience. Reading along with a graphic should be relatively effortless to the audience. Remember people have just one chance to understand the story. The words in the script should match the graphic as closely as possible.

The following are several examples of poorly written graphics that contain too much information or do not match the copy. Each is followed by a corrected version.

POOR

(FULL SCREEN GRAPHIC)	(GRAPHIC)
Gallup Poll Regarding President's Position on School and Educational Reform:	43-PERCENT OF THOSE SURVEYED AGREE WITH THE PRESIDENT'S
40% of people do not support the plan	POSITION ON EDUCATION REFORM.
43% of people support the plan	BUT ALMOST AS MANY DISAGREE,
11% of people aren't sure how they feel	SHOWING AMERICANS ALMOST
6% of people refused to answer this question	EVENLY SPLIT.

BETTER

(FULL SCREEN GRAPHIC)	(GRAPHIC)
President's Education Reform	43-PERCENT OF THOSE SURVEYED
43% agree	AGREE WITH THE PRESIDENT'S
40% disagree	POSITION ON EDUCATION REFORM,
17% other	BUT ALMOST AS MANY DISAGREE,
	SHOWING AMERICANS ALMOST
	EVENLY SPLIT.

POOR

(FULL SCREEN GRAPHIC)	(GRAPHIC)
Poll Regarding the Number of Middle School Students Taking Ritalin:	FIVE YEARS AGO, ONLY ONE IN 50 OF THE COUNTY'S MIDDLE
One in Fifty Students, in 1998	SCHOOL STUDENTS WAS TAKING
One in Ten Students, last year	THE DRUG RITALIN. BUT LAST
	YEAR, THAT NUMBER JUMPED TO
	AN ASTONISHING ONE IN TEN.

BETTER

(FULL SCREEN GRAPHIC)	(GRAPHIC)
Ritalin in Middle School	FIVE YEARS AGO, ONLY ONE IN
1998: 1 in 50 Students	50 OF THE COUNTY'S MIDDLE
2002: 1 in 10 Students	SCHOOL STUDENTS WAS TAKING
	THE DRUG RITALIN. BUT LAST
	YEAR, THAT NUMBER JUMPED TO
	AN ASTONISHING ONE IN TEN.

       In the example referring to Ritalin use in middle school, an even better idea for a graphic might be a graph or chart with a line tracing a dramatic upswing in Ritalin use across five years.

POOR

(ANCHOR/ON CAMERA)	(ANCHOR)
	Nobody from Jeraned Pharmaceuticals would agree to be interviewed for our report, but issued a statement saying:
(FULL SCREEN GRAPHIC)	(GRAPHIC)
Statement from Jeraned Pharmaceuticals: "Jeraned Pharmaceuticals, based in Tremont Texas, has the following statement for your report regarding our medicine, Revere. We always consider patient safety first and foremost. We could not have foreseen the adverse events associated with Revere, and acted quickly to withdraw the drug from the market as soon as problems surfaced."	"Jeraned Pharmaceuticals...always considers patient safety first and foremost. We could not have foreseen the adverse events associated with Revere, and acted quickly to withdraw the drug from the market as soon as problems surfaced."

BETTER

(ANCHOR/OC)	(ANCHOR)
	Nobody from Jeraned Pharmaceuticals would agree to be interviewed for our report, but issued a statement saying:
(FULL SCREEN GRAPHIC)	(GRAPHIC)
Jeraned Pharmaceuticals: "Jeraned Pharmaceuticals...always consider(s) patient safety first and foremost. We could not have foreseen the adverse events associated with Revere, and acted quickly to withdraw the drug from the market as soon as problems surfaced."	"Jeraned Pharmaceuticals always considers patient safety first and foremost. We could not have foreseen the adverse events associated with Revere, and acted quickly to withdraw the drug from the market as soon as problems surfaced."

In the first version of the preceding example, the audience reading along with the graphic would be confused by extraneous words never referred to in the anchor's copy: "based in Tremont Texas, has the following statement for your report regarding our medicine, Revere." The extraneous words have been removed from the graphic in the second version.

There are fewer constraints for using graphics in online writing because, unlike television, the Internet audience does *not* view graphics simultaneous to reading the related article; instead, the graphics are viewed before or after. Also, unlike television viewers, Internet audience members have the luxury of spending as much time as they want studying a graphic or referring back to it. Still, Internet graphics should closely relate to the story they're associated with. The language used in the graphics should be similar to the language in the story. Short and simple is usually best.

Write two versions of the following lottery story: one for television using at least one full screen graphic and another for a Web site including at least one graphic, at least one set of facts presented as bullets, and at least three suggested links.

(Brick, New Jersey-AP)—Some New Jersey grocery store workers say even their customers are happy for them.

A group of 33 employees at the Pathmark store in Brick Township share one of the two winning tickets in last night's Big Game lottery.

The jackpot is worth 115 (m) million dollars.

The store's manager had a share of the ticket. But she says she had to spend a lot of her morning telling her fellow winners to get back to work.

They each stand to get about one-point-seven (m) million dollars if they take annuity payments spread over 26 years. They would get about half that by choosing the cash up front.

At least a couple of the workers say they'll stay on at their jobs. But one co-winner says they'll have a different relationship with management. He says—quote—"If they give us any nonsense now, we can walk."

Writing to Natural Sound

Some of the best television and radio news writers are especially skilled at **writing to natural sound.** Natural sound is the sound occurring all around when you're out in the field reporting on a story. It can be as soft as the crunch of fall leaves underfoot, or as loud as an explosion. In television, the natural sound is automatically recorded with the corresponding pictures on videotape. In radio, of course, all sound is recorded without pictures.

Natural sound is often abbreviated as "Natsound" or "Nats."

Here are some examples of natural sound:

- When covering a protest, natural sound could be the sound of demonstrators chanting, "Hell, no, we won't go!"

- When covering a controversy over a shopping mall being built in an environmentally sensitive area, natural sound could be the sounds of the cranes and other machinery, as well as the sounds of birds chirping.
- When covering a funeral, natural sound could be the sound of mourners sobbing or just the wind quietly blowing.

Natural sound is always a component of videotape heard quietly underneath the anchor's voice reading copy or heard softly behind the reporter's audio track. Wise writers also learn to use natural sound to its fullest advantage by occasionally letting it play "full." This means the reporter or anchor's voice stops entirely, and, for a moment or two, the audience hears only natural sound: the wind blowing, a baby crying, or children laughing.

In television, natural sound is recorded in the normal course of shooting any story. But if you, as the writer, happen to be present when the story is being shot, you should make sure the photographer records any pictures and sound that you're thinking of using for natural sound. When you get back from the field, view and listen to the videotape to see what natural sound you actually have and how you might be able to use it in your story.

Roxanne Russell, the senior producer for CBS News whom we quoted earlier regarding writing to video, offers these thoughts about natural sound:

> The reporter is challenged by *sound* . . . knowing when to stop his narration and let the natural sound of the event he is covering play by itself. Because by bringing up that sound, the viewer is immediately brought into the picture and into the story. A narration about a fisherman has deeper impact when the reporter's talking pauses for a few seconds at some point and you hear the sound of the sea and the wind, and of the fish as they splash onto the deck. Coverage of a factory is enhanced by the clanks and groans of the machinery. A good television news reporter must learn to value sound as much as picture and use it to the story's advantage. If that means less time for his words, so be it. Less words does not mean the viewer will learn less about the story if sound and pictures are used to their best capability.

Next is an example of a radio news story that makes creative use of natural sound to turn a story into something fun for listeners to hear: natural sound that helps transport the audience to the scene of the action. The script begins with a natural sound actuality of the kickoff for the "Giant Jump": an official's voice giving the countdown . . . "Three, two, one . . . jump!!"

Giant Jump

[TAKE: NATSOT "3,2,1 . . . JUMP"]

It happened this week . . . the biggest science project ever.

At precisely eleven a-m Friday, a million or more British school children all began jumping up and down for one full minute.

The event was called The Giant Jump . . . the kickoff . . . as it were . . . for Science Year in the British schools.

Organizers hoped that all this hopping would create a very small, but nonetheless measurable earthquake.

Children leapt to their task all over the land—even in the halls of the London Science Museum.

Preliminary seismograph readings DID show some impact. Final results will be analyzed over the next two weeks.

Write two versions of the following beach story: one for radio that makes use of two appropriate natural sound actualities (places in the radio script in which the anchor will pause for a few seconds of specified natural sound) and another as a television news package that has a sound bite and at least two natural sound breaks (brief pauses in the script in which the audience sees video and hears natural sound full with no reporter or anchor narration).

Our versions of each are presented in the Answers section.

(Greenwich, Connecticut–AP)–It's too late for summer . . . but beaches in Greenwich, Connecticut, will soon be open to the public. The town's board of selectmen has voted not to appeal a ruling from the state Supreme Court. The court declared Greenwich's residents-only beaches policy unconstitutional. The town's decision now means Greenwich beaches will be open to the public by mid-September. Tens of thousands of people frequent the Greenwich shores every year, enjoying swimming, volleyball, cooking out, and just lounging around. But by law, those frequenters are legal residents of the town. Outsiders are forbidden. Town officials say lawyers told them the U-S Supreme Court would probably not take the case, and if it did—would likely rule against the town. The decision ends a six-year legal battle that began after a Stamford attorney tried to go jogging on a Greenwich beach, but was told he wasn't allowed.

Short-Form versus Long-Form Stories

Much of the news-writing instruction in this text has centered on the most common **short-form** stories.

Television short-form stories include the following:

- Either copy stories, VOs, or VOSOTs, all read by news anchors, typically ranging in length from approximately fifteen seconds (:15) to one minute (1:00) or so
- Reporter packages generally ranging in length from about one minute thirty seconds (1:30) to two minutes (2:00)

Radio short-form stories include the following:

- Either copy stories, or copy stories with actualities, all read by news anchors, typically ranging in length from approximately ten seconds (:10) to forty-five seconds (:45) or so

- Reporter wraps or actualities generally ranging in length from about twenty seconds (:20) to forty-five seconds (:45) or so

Online short-form stores include fairly brief, single-page reports that are translations of broadcast news stories with additional information, links, pictures, bullets, and videotape added.

No doubt you also know there's another universe of news writing entirely: **long-form stories.** These long-form stories can range in length from three- or four-minute (3:00 to 4:00) features to twelve-minute (12:00) reports on television newsmagazine programs, such as ABC News *20/20* and CBS News *60 Minutes*. News documentaries can run even longer: even an entire hour without commercials. In radio, long-form reports are regularly heard on such programs as National Public Radio's (NPR's) *All Things Considered.*

Clarity remains critical in long-form stories, but the obvious additional challenge is capturing and holding the audience's interest for what's considered a long time, in broadcasting terms. Yet the long-form writer has the luxury of using longer sound bites, more detailed descriptions, additional videotape, and more natural sound to create the mood, make the point, and convey the meaning.

One of the true giants in long-form writing is the long-running program on CBS News called *Sunday Morning.* What sets it apart is the comfortably slow pace of the reporter's delivery, the extraordinary photography, and the liberal and creative use of natural sound.

The following CBS *Sunday Morning* scripts range in length from five minutes ten seconds (5:10) to nine minutes ten seconds (9:10). The sound bites (SOTs) within them are often longer than in the typical short-form news story. Many of them include entire exchanges—questions and answers—between the reporter (correspondent) and the interview subject. Also, note the expert use of natural sound and the skillful way in which the reporter writes to video.

CBS SUNDAY MORNING: WHAT'S COOKING?

Correspondent: Martha Teichner

Producer: Judith Hole

Editor: Grayce Arlotta-Berner

Associate Producer: Allison Page

RUNS: 8:35

SOT: so pronounce your name....tim: zagat, like the cat in the hat..and that's that...

(VO)

ZAGAT...THE NAME THAT...BEGAT...A GUIDEBOOK... "THE" GUIDEBOOK TO RESTAURANTS IN NY AND NOW 44 OTHER CITIES.

(continued)

MEET TIM AND NINA ZAGAT...THEIR NAME IS OFTEN MISPRONOUNCED...SELDOM MISCONSTRUED...AS THE POSTER SAYS..."READ IT AND EAT."

SO IF YOU'RE LOOKING FOR THE BEST STEAKHOUSE IN ATLANTA...ACCORDING TO ZAGAT'S, IT'S CHOPS, " DELIVERS GREAT BEEF TO A POWER BUSINESS CROWD..." RATING—27 OUT OF A POSSIBLE 30.

FOR GOURMET DINING IN BERKELEY, CALIFORNIA, IT'S CHEZ PANISSE....RATING 28. IN ZAGAT SPEAK, "BEAT A PATH TO THIS HIGH ALTAR OF FOOD."

FOR THE SLURPIEST NOODLES IN TOKYO...MATSUYA...RATING 22, "THE EPITOME OF DOWNTOWN SOBA SPOTS." YOU'VE GOT CHOICES...FROM A TO ZAGAT...

CUT TO PARIS...IN SIGHT OF THE ARC DE TRIOMPHE...WHAT BETTER PLACE FOR THE ULTIMATE FOODIE STORY TO HAVE BEGUN...TIM AND NINA ZAGAT, TWO FOOD-LOVING YOUNG LAWYERS WORKING THERE IN THE LATE 60'S...TRADED RESTAURANT RECOMMENDATIONS WITH THEIR FRIENDS...PASSED AROUND THE MIMEOGRAPHED LIST OF COMMENTS...

SOT: nina...when we came back we really discovered that there wasn't any way to make a quick decision about where to go out to eat...and we had grown accustomed to having this little crib sheet you might call it...

(VO)
SO THEY STARTED A NEW YORK VERSION AS A HOBBY...WHEN THEY FOUND THEMSELVES HANDING OUT 10,000 COPIES A YEAR...FREE....THEY DECIDED TO SELL THEM.

SOT: tim: we took in half a million dollars in one month, and that was more than either one of us was earning as a lawyer / / / / /

(VO)
THEY BOTH ADMIT THIS IS MUCH MORE FUN THAN BEING A LAWYER.

THE NY RESTAURANT GUIDE ALONE SELLS 650,000 COPIES A YEAR..TIM ZAGAT IS FAMOUS FOR DRAGGING JOURNALISTS AND PALS ALONG ON BARNSTORMING TOURS OF EATERIES IN THE CITY...OFTEN TAKING IN 20 OR 30 A NIGHT.

SOT:..normally when i go around i'm looking to see whether anything major has changed..:48 i'll ask the chef, has he had any new sous chef...or is there something else that we need to know that we'd only know by asking...mat? do you check out the kitchen...tim: oh sure...i check out kitchens all the time.

(VO)
I DON'T...SO AT THE 1ST STOP...JEAN-GEORGES...RATING 28...."A NEARLY FLAWLESS...CLASS ACT..." ACCORDING TO THE 2001 ZAGAT'S, I GET DISTRACTED.

SOT: 15 / 06:05:10...i smell truffles....ETC.

NARR....TIM ZAGAT INSISTS HE DROPS IN ON ALL THESE PLACES STRICTLY FOR PROFESSIONAL REASONS....I HAVE ANOTHER THEORY.

(continued)

SOT: 06:12:10ish...mat: tim, i think the reason you do this dropping in on restaurants is because you like to...tim: i love it...// i love people and my secret thing is i would have like to have been a politician.//

(VO)

THIS CONFESSION AT STOP NUMBER 2....GABRIEL'S...RATING 22..."...WHILE PRICEY...CAN'T BE BEAT FOR PRE-THEATER CONVENIENCE..."

(nat sot in kitchen)

(VO)

WHEN TIM ZAGAT ENTERS A RESTAURANT, NOBODY STOPS HIM FROM WALKING RIGHT ON INTO THE KITCHEN...THE RATINGS AND COMMENTS IN THE GUIDES ARE NOT WHAT TIM AND NINA ZAGAT THINK, THEY'RE WHAT THE CUSTOMERS THINK...150,000 PEOPLE FILL OUT SURVEYS FOR THE BOOKS, ANOTHER 650,000 HAVE VOLUNTEERED TO COMMENT ON-LINE. YOU COULD SAY, IT'S THE LAST WORD IN WORD OF MOUTH...DINING DEMOCRACY.

WALK INTO THE ZAGAT'S NY OFFICE, AND IT'S UNBELIEVABLY QUIET...

SOT: curt gathje...10/01:14:35ish...we're thinking...that's what that is...

(VO)

CURT GATHJE IS QUIETLY EDITING ZAGAT'S INTERNATIONAL TRAVEL SURVEY..

SOT: 10/01:07...mat? what are you doing...curt: i'm in jamaica...yesterday i was in bora bora...

(VO)

TALK ABOUT LIVING VICARIOUSLY....IT'S HIS JOB TO DIG THROUGH TENS OF THOU-SANDS OF SURVEYS LOOKING FOR CLEVER COMMENTS...LIKE THIS ONE THAT MADE IT INTO THE NY NIGHTLIFE GUIDE.

NATSOT: 10/01:12: 50ish...there's a Latin drag bar on 38th street..."gender here is anybody's guess"...)

(VO)

AT THE NEXT DESK, THE TOKYO RESTAURANT GUIDE IS GETTING A GOING-OVER...

AND THERE'S THE ZAGAT'S WEBSITE..

(NATSOT10/01:22:29 750,000 users come to our site in a day)

(VO)

LAST YEAR VENTURE CAPITALISTS HANDED OVER 31 MILLION DOLLARS TO FINANCE THIS LEAP INTO CYBERSPACE...AND BEYOND.

SOT:..nina..we're planning to expand much further into various other kinds of leisure activities ...mat: like? time...skiing...nina...we haven't made...tim: cruising, cruise ships, fashion, anything people do, and are avid about.

(VO/tour of gray's papaya)

(continued)

LET IT NOT BE SAID THAT ZAGATS' GUIDES ONLY INCLUDE WILDLY EXPENSIVE RESTAURANTS FREQUENTED BY THE RICH AND FAMOUS...STOP 3 ON OUR NY RESTAURANT TOUR WITH TIM ZAGAT...GRAY'S PAPAYA...

(15/ 06:20:15 ish...ny times, then zagat sign outside...best deal)

(inside)...scene w. guy from chicago getting hot dogs...15/06:24:50ish...it's got snap...

(VO)

" STICKY AND SCUZZY...BUT COLORFUL...." .IS WHAT THE 2001 ZAGAT'S HAS TO SAY. IT GETS A 19.

TIM ZAGAT GETS A HOT DOG...

THEN IT'S ON TO VINNIE'S PIZZA A BLOCK AWAY..."YOU WANT ATMOSPHERE...FRILLS...GO SOMEWHERE ELSE..."

NATSOT: 08;02:30...tim: i'm getting hungry looking at it...don't tell anybody///...mat: this is not 5 minutes after the hotdog...tim: well, the hotdog was nothing...nothin...08:02:45

(VO)

FROM THE RIDICULOUS TO THE SUBLIME, YOU MIGHT SAY...FROM VINNIE'S WE HEAD FOR ALAIN DU CASSE...

YOU'RE LOOKING AT NY'S MOST EXPENSIVE RESTAURANT. A FIVE HUNDRED DOLLAR DINNER FOR ONE...EASY...THE BOOK SAYS..."SUPERDELUXE DINING AND DECOR, PLUS SILKY SMOOTH SERVICE..."

SOT:...mat? is service the #1 criticism of a restaurant...? tim...absolutely...nina...by far...mat? even more so than food.? absolutely...

(VO)

THEY SHOULD KNOW...THEY EAT OUT AT LEAST 8 TIMES A WEEK...SO WHAT DO THEY DO WHEN THEY'RE NOT EATING OUT?

THEY ESCAPE TO THE COUNTRY...AND EAT IN.

(NATSOT talking about ingredients...what's cooking)

SOT:...there's a joy that people...that restaurateurs and people who love food all share...and i'd say we share with our friends...

(VO)

BUT NINA ZAGAT IS SERIOUS ABOUT ALL THIS...SHE STUDIED AT THE RENOWNED CORDON BLEU COOKING SCHOOL IN PARIS...

NATSOT is this play for you?...yes, it is...it's play...with playmates that all like to eat.

(VO)

SPEAKING OF LIKING TO EAT...WE ALL HAD DINNER AT THE FINAL STOP ON OUR RESTAURANT TOUR....AT SUGIYAMA...A TINY, UNASSUMING JAPANESE RESTAURANT

(continued)

THAT OUT OF NOWHERE....FOUND ITSELF RANKED FOURTH HIGHEST FOR FOOD OUT OF THE 2000 RESTAURANTS LISTED IN THE CURRENT NEW YORK GUIDE...

JUST AS WE TUCK INTO ONE OF THE DISHES THE BOOK CALLS "SHEER JOY ON THE TONGUE," WHO SHOULD APPEAR, BUT A ZAGAT GROUPIE.

SOT: 09:05:30...japanese guy nat sot>>ends with...i don't care about actors, actresses,...i care about you...this is the best...

(XXXX)

Often, fonts are not used in long-form stories. This means every person who's interviewed in the story must be introduced and identified somehow—set up—in the copy. In the next *Sunday Morning* script, the first sound bite is with Reverend Milton Henry. Notice how he's set up in the sentence immediately preceding his bite.

CBS SUNDAY MORNING COVER STORY: A DEBT OWED?
Correspondent: Rita Braver
Producer: Irene Taylor
Editor: Grayce Arlotta-Berner
Associate Producer: Sandra Malyszka LoPiccolo
RUNS: 9:10

(VO HEAR MINISTER'S VOICE)
CHURCH SERVICE...HEAR SINGING AND SEE SIGN ON CHURCH...."Reparations" etc. THIS CHURCH IS GROUND ZERO FOR A LOT OF EVENTS THAT ARE HAPPENING ON A NATIONAL LEVEL...

(VO STUFF IN CHURCH)
Indeed... Detroit's Christ Church is giving voice to an idea that has increasing appeal to many African Americans...the idea that they are owed some form of reparations for slavery and its aftermath: Reverend Milton Henry:

(SOT REVEREND MILTON HENRY)
WHEN YOU HAVE STOLEN A PEOPLE, YOU HAVE THAT PEOPLE IN YOUR CARE UNDER YOUR COMPLETE DOMINATION, YOU...YOU TAKE THEIR LABOR FOR YOUR OWN BENEFIT...YOU'RE OBLIGATED TO MAKE RESTITUTION IN FULL.

(N'COBRA MEETING)
MAN IN CAP: WHITE PEOPLE OWE US AND THEY KNOW THEY OWE US

(VO)
And a few miles away...the sentiment is the same....at the monthly meeting of the Detroit chapter of N'COBRA...the National Coalition of Blacks for Reparations in America...

(continued)

(SOT)

I HAD DECIDED LAST...WHEN N'COBRA STARTED...

WOMAN: YES SIR...

MAN: TO JOIN THE MOVEMENT!

WOMAN: AMEN...

MAN: BECAUSE I CAN FEEL THE PAIN THE MY FOREBEARS WENT THROUGH DURING THAT TIME...

(VO)

They meet here to make sure that the suffering of those who came before them is not forgotten.....

(SOT)

CUT TO RAY P.22 : MY GRANDFATHER...WAS BORN IN 1855 IN MISSISSIPPI.....WHEN THEY FREED HIM...THEY MADE A SHARE CROPPER OUT OF HIM//AND WHEN HE DIED HE LEFT NO WEALTH TO HIS CHILDREN. IT ALL WENT TO THE PLANTATION OWNERS.

VO RAY IN MEETING...THEN CUT TO HIM AT OFFICE...

This is Ray Jenkins...and for him...this gathering...has a special meaning....

(CUT TO HIM IN HIS OFFICE: SOT)

RAY IN OFFICE, 5:20:25 HOW LONG HAVE YOU BEEN INVOLVED IN THIS REPARATIONS ISSUE....

RAY: I WOULD SAY ABOUT 38 YEARS....

(VO)

Jenkins is proudly known as "Reparations Ray..."

(VO/CUT TO ARTICLES IN PAPER...AND THEN TO STUFF IN HOUSE)

For years he has been writing letters to politicians...and magazines and anyone else he could think of

(SOT RAY)

AND HERE'S A LETTER TO MICHAEL JACKSON ON THE ISSUE OF REPARATIONS.

(VO)

His crusade has drawn a lot of flack....:

(SOT RAY)

WE GOT SOME LETTERS THAT PEOPLE WROTE...SAYS...GO BACK TO AFRICA...YOU DON'T NEED NO REPARATION...AND MY PEOPLE FROM IRELAND...WE COME OVER HERE...AND WE PULL OURSELF UP BY OUR BOOTSTRAPS, SO WHY DON'T YOU PEOPLE DO THE SAME THING?

RITA: WELL, WHAT'S YOUR RESPONSE TO THAT, WHEN SOMEBODY SAYS SOMETHING LIKE THAT?

RAY: MY RESPONSE IS THIS...THAT THEY ARE...THEY CAME OVER HERE...THEY CAME OVER HERE...BUT THEY DIDN'T COME OVER AS SLAVES//THOSE PEOPLE THAT JUST

(continued)

SAID, WELL, WE SUFFER TOO...BUT THEY DIDN'T SUFFER NOTHIN' LIKE THE BLACK PEOPLE SUFFERED..

(VO RAY, THEN CUT TO MONTAGE OF HEADLINES)

For years Reparations Ray and a small band of other advocates around the country have largely been ignored. But suddenly, things are changing. Stories about reparations are everywhere... High powered lawyers are talking about how to formulate new law suits to recover damages for slavery...and influential African Americans like activist Randall Robinson....are taking up the cause

(CUT TO BRAVER AND ROBINSON WALKING AT U.S. CAPITOL)

RITA: IS IT TRUE THAT SLAVES EVEN BUILT THE U.S. CAPITOL?

RAY: THESE SANDSTONES BLOCKS WERE MINED IN STAFFORD VIRGINIA BY SLAVES

(VO BOOK AND OLDER ROBINSON PHOTOS)

Robinson recently wrote "The Debt, What America Owes to Blacks"...arguing the case for reparations. His interest in the cause is significant...because he was a leader in the movements that forced change in U.S. policy towards Apartheid in South Africa...and toward the military dictatorship in Haiti.

(VO SLAVE AND JIM CROW)

Now he says it's time for the United States to formally acknowledge that this country was built on the backs of human beings torn from their culture and their families...time to atone not only for slavery...but also for the years of legalized discrimination...

(SOT-ROBINSON)

AMERICANS DON'T WANT TO FACE UP TO THE SINS OF OUR NATION'S PAST...WE DON'T WANT...THOMAS JEFFERSON TAINTED, WE DON'T WANT TO TALK ABOUT WHAT KIND OF MAN GEORGE WASHINGTON MAY HAVE BEEN...

RITA: SLAVE OWNERS BOTH

ROBINSON: BOTH. WE DON'T WANT TO REVISIT THAT PAST...

ROBINSON: THAT WE DID THIS AWFUL THING TO A PEOPLE...

(VO SLAVERY AND JAPANESE INTERNMENT PICTURES)

The new impetus for the reparations movement has come from the fact that the United States Government...has paid now reparations to Japanese-Americans interned during World War II...and their direct descendants...

And African-Americans are also pointing to reparations paid by Germany and Switzerland to victims of the Holocaust and their families.

(RITA STANDUP AT BALTIMORE MUSEUM)

Exhibits like these in Baltimore bring attention to American Slavery. But so far, the U.S. government has been completely indifferent to the issue of reparations for Blacks...or even the idea of some type of national apology for slavery. Polls show that while most African-Americans favor some form of reparations for slavery...most other Americans DO NOT. And even within the African American community...there are skeptics...

WALK AND TALK WITH LOURY.

(continued)

(10:10 SOT)

RITA: WHAT DO YOU THINK IS THE STRONGEST CASE AGAINST REPARATIONS?...

GLEN LOURY: THAT IT WAS A LONG TIME AGO...AND THAT YOU CAN'T REALLY IDENTIFY WHO IS HARMED BY HOW MUCH. AND YOU CAN'T REALLY IDENTIFY WHO DID THE HARM AND YOU MAKE THEM PAY. IT'S TOO ABSTRACT.

(VO)

Glen Loury is the head of the Institute on Race and Social Division at Boston University. He believes reparations could backfire:

(SOT LOURY)

SUPPOSE WE SUCCEED...SUPPOSE THE CONGRESS OF THE UNITED STATES ENACTS AND THE PRESIDENT SIGNS A STATUE THAT PAYS $20,000 PER FAMILY TO AFRICAN AMERICANS ACROSS THE BOARD. NOW WHAT? .YOU'VE BEEN BEEN PAID, OKAY. WE GAVE YOU WHAT YOU WANTED...NOW YOU'VE GOT IT...SO PLEASE, DON'T BOTHER US, WITH ANY MORE OF THIS TALK ABOUT RACIAL INEQUALITY...ABOUT FAILING SCHOOLS, ABOUT SEGREGATION, ABOUT WHATEVER...YOU'VE BEEN PAID.

(SOT)

RITA TO ROBINSON:

CAN YOU PUT A DOLLAR AMOUNT ON HOW MUCH RESTITUTION NEEDS TO BE MADE...

ROBINSON: I THINK IT'D BE PREMATURE TO DO THAT. I THINK THAT WILL COME OUT IN THE MONTHS AHEAD IN THE DISCUSSION// THE ANSWER I'M SURE WILL RUN INTO THE TRILLIONS OF DOLLARS, DEPENDING ON WHAT ONE DECIDES TO COMPENSATE.

(VO)

But Robinson says money should NOT go to individuals:

(SOT-ROBINSON) CHECKS SHOULD NOT BE GIVEN TO PEOPLE. I'M NOT ADVOCATING CASH PAYMENTS...THOUGH SOME ARE.

(VO MEETING)

Instead, he suggests the federal government should fund education and economic development programs for blacks. And though some in the movement are asking for money...or land...

(SOT WOMAN AT MEETING)

AND I THINK THERE SHOULD BE SOME LAND...WE WORKED THE LAND FOR FREE....(FADE UNDER...)

Reparations Ray Jenkins has changed his mind about that:

(SOT RITA, IN RAY'S HOUSE...STAND UP CHAT)

NOW AT ONE POINT, I READ THAT YOU WERE ASKING FOR A MILLION DOLLARS...

RAY: A MILLION

RITA: FOR EVERY AFRICAN AMERICAN...

(continued)

RAY: OKAY...

RITA: WERE YOU...SERIOUS ABOUT THAT?

RAY: NO, NO...I PUT THE MILLION DOLLARS SO IT JUST KINDA CATCH ON...AND CATCH PEOLE...CATCH PEOPLE'S ATTENTION...

(VO)

Jenkins says he too now favors some sort of education program for African Americans... But Glen Loury asks...who will administer these funds?

(SOT LOURY)

WHAT ARE THESE INSTITUTIONS? ARE THEY HISTORICALLY BLACK COLLEGES...ARE THEY PEOPLE WHO ARE WORKING IN THE INNER CITY TO WORK WITH YOUTH? HOW CAN THEIR BENEFITS BE RESTRICTED TO AFRICAN AMERICANS?

RITA TO ROBINSON:

HOW ARE YOU GONNA DO THIS? HOW ARE YOU GONNA DETERMINE WHO IS ELIGIBLE, WHO NEEDS TO BE MADE WHOLE?

ROBINSON: //NO ONE HAD ANY HAD ANY TROUBLE DETERMINING WHO WAS ELIGIBLE WHEN WE WERE ENSLAVED, WHEN WE WERE DISCRIMINATED AGAINST, WHEN WE COULDN'T GO TO CERTAIN SCHOOLS...AND

RITA: SKIN COLOR...

ROBINSON: EAT IN CERTAIN PLACES...I MEAN THAT'S A VERY EASY SELECTION PROCESS. AND SO IF WE WERE ABLE TO DO IT THEN...THEN WE CAN DO IT NOW...WITH...WITH THE RIGHT INTENT...

NATSOUND CHOIR MUSIC UP FULL
And so it's believed at Christ Church in Detroit....but now the champions of this cause must convince the rest of the nation that only reparations will make the scars of slavery fade away....

NATSOUND CHOIR MUSIC UP FULL WITH PHOTOS
(XXXXXX)

CBS SUNDAY MORINING: DRIVE-IN MOVIES
Correspondent: Charles Osgood
Producers: Peter Goodman/ Ramon Parkins
Editor: Maria Nicoletti
RUNS: 5:10

NAT SOT:("Summer Nights" from Grease; pix of people piling into drive-in; sounds of people buying tickets)

(VO)

A summer night at the Vineland Drive In, one of the last outdoor movie theaters in the movie capital...Los Angeles.

NAT SOT: "We come here a lot, we always bring our family"

(continued)

NAT SOT: music

NAT SOT: "My parents always took me to drive ins, so It's nostalgic..."

NAT SOT: music

NAT SOT: "This is actually our first time..."

(VO)

The drive in is a relic from a different time...a bit of Americana you may have thought ran out of gas years ago.

NAT SOT: "The drive in movie takes care of everything, courtship, babysitting, shelter, food and drink... "

(VO)

Drive ins were the brainchild of Richard Hollingshead, who built the first one in Camden, New Jersey, in 1933, as a way to attract customers to his gas station.

(DON SANDERS SOT)

The first night that Hollingshead did this, it was completely sold out. And, uh, people really enjoyed seeing movies in their car.

(VO)

Don and Susan Sanders chronicled the history of drive ins in two books and a new documentary.

(SUSAN SANDERS SOT)

Americans love the movies and we love our cars. It was the perfect marriage.

(VO)

Slowly, word got out about this new entertainment.

(REDSTONE SOT)

My father built what was the third drive in theater in the United States, which was the Sunrise Auto Theatre.

(VO)

Sumner Redstone remembers selling sodas and popcorn at his father's drive in on Long Island.

(REDSTONE AND OSGOOD SOT)

Q: So you really got in on the ground floor?

A: I was in on the very ground floor, yes.

(VO)

Redstone isn't on the ground floor anymore. That drive-in movie company grew into the media giant Viacom, parent of a stellar cast of corporate characters...including CBS.

(REDSTONE SOT)

It started out with a handful of drive ins which as you know represented really an important nostalgic era in the motion picture business.

(VO)

By World War II, there were about one hundred drive ins in the country. After the war, they sprang up everywhere. Families flocked to them.

(continued)

(SUSAN SANDERS SOT)

The decade of the 50s was the explosive decade for drive in growth.

(VO)

Before long, there were five thousand drive ins in the United States. And it hardly mattered what was showing.

(DON SANDERS SOT)

Drive ins never did get first run product. Drive ins played movies that had been out for two to three months. That's the phenomenon of the drive in. The drive in owner could almost play anything and get a crowd.

NAT SOT: Beach Blanket Bingo

(VO)

And the crowds were getting younger...watching teenage fare like Beach Blanket Bingo.

(SUSAN SANDERS SOT)

Certainly by the early 60s, the drive in was the hangout for teenagers. The movie was always secondary really to why you went to the drive in. If you missed ten minutes because you were making out in the back seat, it didn't really matter because the plot wasn't very complicated.

(VO)

Sam Sherman's Independent International Pictures made movies specifically for drive ins.

(OSGOOD AND SHERMAN SOTS)

Q: What are some of the movies that you did, what are the titles?

A: Dracula versus Frankenstein. Blazing Stewardesses. The Dynamite Brothers. Nurse Sherry. And on and on. I tried to employ some taste, you know. I can't say always the best, but some taste.

(OSGOOD AND SHERMAN SOTS)

Q: I heard the expression of three Bs in connection with some of these movies, is that what these were?

A: Breasts, beasts and blood. We had them. If you had Bs, we had them.

NAT SOT: (Angel's Wild Women) "Angel's Wild Women."

(DON SANDERS SOT)

It just got a little more racy. And eventually the movies just got to where they were just flat out X rated movies.

(VO)

But by then, the drive-in's clock had run out. Daylight Savings Time was one reason, forcing movies to start later on summer evenings. Urban sprawl was a second, as the land became more valuable for malls and housing developments. Air conditioned multiplexes and television also helped drive out the drive ins.

(continued)

(OSGOOD AND REDSTONE SOTS)

Q: Is there any way for this to come back?

A: Not a chance, not a chance. It's part of history, it was an interesting, as I say, looking back nostalgic part of the motion picture industry, but it's gone, it's gone forever, like the buggy whip.

(VO)

Others are more hopeful.

(DON SANDERS SOT)

I think that the drive ins low ebb has passed. And I think a whole generation of people that had missed drive ins back in the 80s or the late 70s are now being re-introduced to them, and kids are going back to the drive ins.

(VO)

Today...there are web sites promoting drive ins. And fan clubs. 500 theaters dot the country. A few are being torn down. But about forty others...either new or restored...have opened in the past four years.

NAT SOT: I haven't done this in ages. And it's really nice.

(VO)

It's not quite a revival...but there's renewed interest in drive ins...triggered by memories...of summer nights.

NAT SOT: music (Summer Nights)

(XXXXXXX)

Eric's Principles of Good Broadcast Writing

We conclude this chapter with some valuable pearls of writing wisdom from someone who distinguished himself as one of the most effective writers in network news: former CBS News Correspondent Eric Engberg:

Talk to the computer: As you write, mouth the words to test how they flow. Remember you or whoever else reads them on the air is going to have to speak the sentences out loud.

Use the medium: In radio, you often have audiotape quotations—called actualities—to incorporate into the story. In television, you'll have the interview on camera. Watch (screen) and listen to the sound bites before you even begin to write. Think of ways, while screening the videotape, to tell the story more effectively by making intelligent use of the pictures. Make notes to yourself while screening so you won't forget about a picture you want to write to. Listen to the advice of your videotape editors on what constitutes a good picture.

Not all parts of speech are equal: In shaping each sentence, put most of your effort into finding the right nouns and verbs to describe the action. Adjectives and adverbs should be used sparely and without hype. Automatically ban the word very and nearly all other superlatives. If an explosion is very damaging, you don't need to say it.

Don't caption: The video should augment the copy. The copy should not be a repetitive explanation of what the video shows. The viewer knows what the video shows; he is seeing it.

In radio, it is a waste of words to set up an actuality by stating what it says. Example:

'The mayor says he opposes the traffic plan.

(SOT-MAYOR) 'I OPPOSE THE TRAFFIC PLAN.'

Sounds stupid, stupid.

Put the best pictures at the top: Unless there is some unusual, overriding reason to save outstanding visual images until later, write the story so that the best stuff can be shown right away. Wasn't it showman P.T. Barnum who said, "Get them into the tent?"

Save a good fact till last: Newspaper and magazine stories empty out onto the page like a spilled bottle of ketchup, ending in a dribble of the least significant information. Television and radio stories, because there's a sonnet-like quality to any audio presentation, have to have a closing line that sounds like a curtain. Try to save one trenchant, interesting fact, or quote to use in that last line of copy to make the close rumble.

Steal from your own interviews: Often the best summation or button for this closing line is something someone said to you in your sit-down interviews. Resist the temptation to use that sound bite in the middle of the story. Quoted or paraphrased by you in the copy, it may be the perfect closing line for the story. Warning: it is considered bad form to steal this line without some form of attribution, but your attribution does not have to be by name. It is just fine to write a close that says, *As one participant in the dispute put it, "the Pelopponesian War took less time than this did." Max Smith, College Park, Maryland.*

Answers

1. Working Americans

> Americans work hard for the money, putting in more time on the job than any other industrialized nation. A new study by the U-N shows the average American labored 38 hours a week in the year 2000, up an hour from the decade before. And that's more than any other industrialized nation, including Canada, France, Germany, Japan, and the United Kingdom. Only two nonindustrialized nations, South Korea and the Czech Republic, worked more than Americans...South Korea topped them all, clocking in 50 hours a week!

2. China Sanctions

> The Bush Administration is getting tough on China, imposing sanctions against an arms producer connected to the Chinese government. U-S officials say the Chinese company violated an agreement with the U-S by selling missile technology to Pakistan. The new sanctions forbid U-S companies from going to China to launch their satellites...something that's been become big business in China. U-S officials say China is helping advance the world's arms race by providing other countries help to develop missile technology.

3. Hair Apparent

They say Image is everything. Just ask Pennsylvania's attorney general Mike Fisher. He's seeking the Republican nomination for governor next year. He's seeking supporters. He's seeking funding. And he's seeking...hair. Yes, the 56-year old recently had hair transplant surgery and is now sporting a new, fuller look. One supporter says it gives Fisher a younger appearance. Fisher says he won't know for several months whether the implants will stick. He won't know until next year whether it helps win him the governor's seat!

4. Public Beaches (Radio Version)

Just in time for fall, Greenwich Connecticut beaches will be open to the public...
(NATSOUND/SEAGULLS)
RUNS: 02
The town's board of selectmen has voted not to appeal a state Supreme Court ruling that declared its residents-only beaches policy unconstitutional. The vote means Greenwich beaches will be open to the public by mid-September. Tens of thousands of people frequent the Greenwich shores every year, enjoying swimming, volleyball, cooking out, and just lounging around.
(NATSOUND/PEOPLE SWIMMING)
RUNS: 03
But by law, those frequenters are legal residents of the town. Outsiders are forbidden. Town officials say lawyers told them the U-S Supreme Court would probably not take the case, and if it did—would likely rule against the town. The decision ends a six-year legal battle that began after a Stamford attorney tried to go jogging on a Greenwich beach, but was told he wasn't allowed.
(XXX)

5. Public Beaches (Television Version)

(VO/beaches)
Greenwich Connecticut beaches are beautiful...
NATSOUND seagulls :02
...they're popular...

(continued)

NATSOUND crowds :02

...and they're for residents only! But that will soon change.

(SOT-HARRY WALKER, TOWN SELECTMAN)

STARTING THIS FALL, OUTSIDERS WILL BE WELCOME ON GREENWICH BEACHES FOR THE FIRST TIME.

(VO/town board meeting)

The town's board of selectmen has voted not to appeal a state Supreme Court ruling that declared its residents-only beaches policy unconstitutional. The vote means Greenwich beaches will be open to the public by mid-September.

NATSOUND swimmers :02

(VO/beaches)

Non-residents have been forbidden from sharing the joys that Greenwich beaches have to offer. But town officials are giving up the fight for that policy after their lawyers told them the Supreme Court probably wouldn't take their appeal and, if it did, would likely rule against them.

(REPORTER STANDUP)

THE DECISION ENDS A SIX-YEAR LONG LEGAL BATTLE THAT BEGAN AFTER A STAMFORD ATTORNEY TRIED TO GO JOGGING ON A GREENWICH BEACH, BUT WAS TOLD HE WASN'T ALLOWED. HEATHER LURAY, CHANNEL 4 NEWS, GREENWICH, CONNECTICUT.

Web sites

For more information, check out the following Web sites:

www.newscript.com/index.html
Writing for radio site, including use of natural sound

www.poynter.org/special/poynterreport/broadcast/broadcast1.htm
Tips on writing for broadcasting, including use of natural sound, from the Poynter Institute

www.poynter.org/dj/052400.htm
Tips on Making great TV graphics from the Poynter Institute

www.straightscoop.org/advice/stu_broadcast.html
Advice on writing for broadcast news from Straight Scoop News Bureau for teens

www.tvrundown.com/cases/cas9821.html
From TV Rundown, case study of long form news story

Quick Review of Terms

- **Long-form stories:** A broad range of news stories and features, such as those lasting more than two minutes on television or radio or investigative and expanded reports on the Internet
- **Natural sound (sometimes abbreviated as "Natsound" or "Nats"):** In radio or television, the naturally occurring sound on a given story that can be heard softly underneath the anchor or reporter's voice *or* can be "brought up full" for several seconds without the anchor or reporter's voice being heard
- **A sense of suspense:** A technique that's best used in features, to create and maintain a level of viewer interest throughout the story.
- **Short-form stories:** A broad range of news stories and features typically found in daily news reports
- **Surprise endings:** A technique best used in feature writing that withholds some key facts until the end of the story
- **Writing to graphics:** In television or Internet writing, effectively using visual images other than videotape, such as charts and graphs, to reflect ideas such as facts and figures
- **Writing to natural sound:** The concept of integrating into a radio or television story various natural sound full "breaks"
- **Writing to video:** The television news concept of having an idea for videotape that can be used to go along with every sentence in a story

Review Questions

1. What are some creative ways to make sure that the stories you write are not ordinary and dull?
2. What are the pitfalls of not writing to videotape and graphics properly?
3. How can natural sound be used to make radio and television stories more compelling?
4. What are some differences in apparent style and feel in the long-form Sunday Morning scripts versus short-form stories?

Summary

In this chapter, we went beyond the basics of good newswriting and explored techniques to make stories *compelling*. It's critical that you consider each individual story's mood, meaning, and point. Doing so will help lead to ideas for structuring the script. News writers must always think of the total picture when putting words on paper: what video, photographs, natural sound, and graphics may be used. Long-form stories are not simply longer versions of short scripts, but have their own qualities that allow for more extended exploration of topics; the challenge is holding the audience's interest.

9

Practical Exercises

_____

- To provide realistic broadcast and Internet news writing scenarios
- To generate opportunities to practice organizing, writing, and interviewing skills

Here's your chance to roll up your sleeves and put to practice all of the concepts you've learned thus far. You may write thousands of stories in your broadcast or Internet writing career. The more you practice now means the quicker you'll become comfortable with the basics, and the sooner you'll be able to devote attention to the finer points of writing effective, compelling stories.

This chapter poses a number of diverse writing challenges. It's designed so that you can do the exercises as a class or own your own. Instructors may choose to assign selected exercises while at the same time exploring the final chapters in the text. Answers are provided at the end of the chapter.

Crime Report

We begin with the following news release issued by the Washington D.C. police department:

Today, from The Washington D.C. Metropolitan Police Department

Double Homicide 300 Block of Seaton Place, NE

At approximately 8:40 am today, Washington D.C. police officers were called to the 300 block of Seaton Place, NE for the sounds of gunshots. Upon arrival they were advised that three people had been shot but left the area. A further investigation revealed that two men went to the Washington Hospital Center's MedStar Unit and a third man to an area hospital.

The two men taken to MedStar died as a result of their injuries. One man is identified as 22-year-old **Marvin Gantt, Jr.,** of the 100 block of T Street, NE. The second man is identified as 18-year-old **Matthew Lindsay** of the 6200 block of 67th Court in Riverdale, MD. The third victim taken to an undisclosed area hospital is a 31-year-old northeast man who was admitted in serious, but stable condition. His name is being withheld because he is considered a witness at this time.

The case is currently under investigation by members of the department's Fifth District.

This is a relatively concise, general description of a double homicide. You should recognize it as a hard news story: not necessarily breaking but a current issue.

When considering how to write the story, obvious police jargon should be converted into language that's more conversational. Look for key words and phrases that would sound awkward or confusing in a broadcast or Internet news story, and come up with alternate wording:

- "Approximately" could be replaced with "about."
- Officers "were advised that three people had been shot" is passive, and "advised" isn't what we'd say in normal conversation. How about "Witnesses told police three people had been shot"?
- "The third victim taken to an undisclosed area hospital. . ." is stilted and so is "The case is currently under investigation. . ."
- After "he is considered a witness," it's not necessary to say "at this time."

Although the press release doesn't contain a lot of detail, some camel squeezing must still be done to turn it into a very brief script. Try to identify details that can safely be omitted:

- The exact time (8:40 a.m.) isn't necessary. You could just say "this morning."
- Depending on your audience, it might not be necessary to state the exact block of town where police responded.
- You can also leave out the fact that the victims were transported by Medstar, that is, unless you're writing a television story and have videotape of a Medstar helicopter making the transport or landing.
- In most cases, you probably wouldn't give the victims' home addresses, but you may want to include age to help differentiate the victims from other men with similar or the same names.
- You may not need to say that police are investigating the crime because it goes without saying. And you don't need to mention the police district involved.

1. Now, using information from the press release, write a brief radio copy story. Assume you now want to take this double homicide a bit further and develop it into something more. You'll need to generate more information, not less:

   - Put your sourcery skills to work. Think of all of the people somehow involved in the story, based on what you've read in the news release. They're all possible sources. Most will not be needed for direct quotes; they're simply providers of information.

- As you collect the facts and talk to sources, be on the lookout for the ones who seem to be the most quotable. Often the best sound bites, actualities, and quotes in a story like this come from people actually affected by or involved in what happened, not the officials investigating the crime.

2. Name some possible sources for more information regarding this story.
3. Describe specifically how you would collect elements to turn this story into a VO-BITE for television news. (Remember, that means you need an on-camera interview.)

When conducting interviews on camera, you're *not* looking for someone to recite the facts stoically from the news release. You want someone to provide context, emotion, flavor, or mood and perhaps a personal insight.

4. List several questions you'd ask the person you chose to interview. For the purposes of this exercise, outline possible answers that person might give.

You now have the elements you need to write a television news VO-BITE, but you must do some serious camel squeezing to come up with a concise script. You'll want to select a sound bite that does more than just give a fact. It should *add* something to the story.

5. Write a VO-BITE that times out to one minute (1:00) or less.

White House News Release

For your next exercise, we'll refer to the hard news story outlined in a press release issued by the White House on page 173:

First, it's important to note that news releases from any source, even the government (some would say *especially* from the government), should be viewed as attempts to perpetuate a specific agenda; they can't necessarily be accepted at face value. In fact, any time that you get information from national, state, and local governments or politicians, someone is trying to push a viewpoint. It doesn't mean that the information can't be believed; it means you'll have to be sure and use your analytical skills to determine what the motivation behind it may actually be. It means the information may be presented as fact when it is a subjective viewpoint. It may only tell *part* of a story, or it may even be an attempt to divert attention from other issues. Throughout the years and various administrations, White House officials have generated positive stories to try to divert attention from their own missteps. Federal safety investigators have been known to insist stubbornly that a safety problem doesn't exist because they're afraid they might be criticized for not acting sooner. Members of Congress defending automakers accused of ignoring safety defects have gotten huge contributions from the same automakers.

White House

Fact Sheet The List of Most Wanted Terrorists

Overview

A new national program has begun to heighten global awareness of America's efforts to locate known terrorists and bring them to justice: the list of "Most Wanted Terrorists."

As part of today's announcement of the new program, the White House Administration identified 22 known terrorists that have been placed on the list of "Most Wanted Terrorists."

The List of "Most Wanted Terrorists"

WORLD TRADE CENTER BOMBING
February 26, 1993
Indicted in the Southern District of New York

On February 26, 1993, a bomb exploded in the underground parking garage of the World Trade Center in New York City, killing six persons and injuring hundreds. The following defendant is included in the Indictment returned in the Southern District of New York:

–Abdul Rahman Yasin

PLOT TO BOMB AIRCRAFT IN THE FAR EAST (MANILA AIR)
January, 1995
Indicted in the Southern District of New York

In January, 1995, the United States learned of a plot based in Manila to bomb 12 commercial jumbo jets of United States carriers flying Asian-Pacific routes. In December, 1994, the conspirators had engaged in a test on a Phillippines airliner using only about 10 percent of the explosives that were to be used in each of the bombs to be planted on United States airliners. The test resulted in the death of a Japanese national on board a flight from the Phillippines to Japan. The following defendant is included in the Indictment returned in the Southern District of New York:

–Khalid Shaikh Mohammed

KHOBAR TOWERS BOMBING
June 25, 1996
Indicted in the Eastern District of Virginia

On June 25, 1996, an explosive device contained within a mid-sized tanker truck detonated outside the perimeter of the Khobar Towers military housing complex in Dhahran, Kingdom of Saudi Arabia. The explosion killed 19 United States Air Force personnel, wounded 280 persons, and severely damaged several military facilities in the complex. The following defendants are included in the Indictment returned in the Eastern District of Virginia:

–Ahmed Ibrahim Al-Mughassil
–Ali Saed Bin Ali El-Houri
–Ibrahim Salih Mohammed Al-Yacoub
–Abdelkarim Hussein Mohamed Al-Nasser

THE BOMBINGS OF UNITED STATES EMBASSIES IN KENYA AND TANZANIA
August 7, 1998

On August 7, 1998, bombs contained with large motor vehicles were detonated outside the United States Embassies in Nairobi, Kenya, and Dar es Salaam, Tanzania. Eleven United States nationals were killed in Nairobi; there were heavy casualties among Kenyan civilians and some foreign service nationals employed by the United States Embassy. In Dar es Salaam, no United States nationals were

(continued)

killed but four were injured; several foreign service nationals who worked at that Embassy were killed. The following defendants are included in the Indictment returned by the Southern District of New York:

–Usama Bin Laden
–Muhammad Atef
–Ayman Al-Zawahiri
–Fazul Abdullah Mohammed
–Mustafa Mohamed Fadhil
–Fahid Mohammed Ally Msalam
–Ahmed Khalfan Ghailani
–Sheikh Ahmed Salim Swedan
–Abdullah Ahmed Abdullah
–Anas Al-Liby
–Saif Al-Adel
–Ahmed Mohammed Hamed Ali
–Mushin Musa Matwalli Atwah

HIJACKING OF TWA 847 June 14, 1985 Indicted in the District of Columbia

On June 14, 1985, TWA 847 was hijacked while enroute from Athens, Greece to Rome, Italy. U.S. Navy Diver Robert Stethem was brutally tortured and murdered during the hijacking, his body dumped on the tarmac of Beirut International Airport. The following defendants are included in the Indictment returned in the District of Columbia.

–Imad Mugniyah
–Hassan Izz-Al-Din
–Ali Atwa

So when exercising your gatekeeping function, consider the source and do the appropriate checking to make sure your stories are thorough and legitimate and are not simply a mouthpiece for someone's agenda.

We've selected the White House press release on Most Wanted Terrorists for this writing exercise because it's fairly factual in nature and doesn't contain a lot of "spin." ("Spin" is an attempt to put forth a certain viewpoint or agenda.) The news release contains a *lot* of information. Camel-squeezing skills are about to be put to good use. When working with an extensive set of facts, no matter what kind of story you plan to write, begin by distilling the most important information. To help, first do the following:

6. Determine the point, the meaning, and the mood. For the *point*, ask yourself what is the basic purpose of the news release? Go a step further in determining the *meaning*. What's the broader context? Why should the information be important or significant to the audience? As far as the *mood*, this is pretty much a no-brainer. It's not going to be a humorous or light story.

Now that you clearly understand what the story is really about, you can begin writing.

7. Using only the information provided in the White House press release on Most Wanted Terrorists, write an Internet news story.

As you've learned, writing for the Internet requires a multimedia mind. Facts that are camel-squeezed out of the story can be used elsewhere in the Internet presentation. In fact, you specifically should *avoid* including all of the available information in the text of the Internet story itself; some of it should be reserved to use in other elements, such as graphics or bullets.

8. Besides the basic copy or text of the Internet "Most Wanted Terrorist" story, suggest possible visuals, graphics, bullets, charts, and links.

Radio news stories, of course, cannot rely on bullets, graphics, and other visuals. Everything must be expressed in words or sound. And the script must be crystal clear without any complexities. An Internet story might name all of the suspected terrorists, but such a lengthy list would never be given in the radio version.

9. Translate the Internet story into a radio news script about thirty seconds (:30) in length.

Corporate News Release

Your next challenge is a hard news-current issue story about online spending that's set forth in a rather complex and dry news release:

Online Spending

Cambridge, Massachusetts - 26 September, 2001 (*PRN*): Forrester Research, Inc. (Nasdaq: FORR), in conjunction with Greenfield Online, today announced the results of the latest Forrester Online Retail Index. According to the 20th survey in this monthly series, total US spending on online sales increased from $3.98 billion in July to slightly over $4 billion in August. The number of households shopping online increased to 14.8 million in August, from 14.7 million in July. Consumers spent an average of $273 per person in August, compared with $270 in July.

"It's impressive that online shopping made such a quick comeback after the big drop in June," said Christopher M. Kelley, analyst at Forrester. "It appears that many consumers may have taken their checks from the unexpected across-the-board tax refunds passed by Congress and the White House to stimulate the economy, and gone online to get ready for school or to buy a hard-earned gift for themselves."

About the Index

Forrester Online Retail Index measures, on a monthly basis, the growth and seasonality of online shopping based on data collected from online shoppers. The Index is based on 5,000 responses during the first nine business days of the month from an online panel developed by Greenfield Online. The survey results for August were fielded from September 4 through September 10, 2001.

The monthly panel is weighted to Forrester Research's Consumer Technographics(r) Benchmark Panel, a survey of 90,000 US members of a consumer mail panel developed by NFO Worldwide, a market research firm. Data was weighted to demographically represent the US population. The Benchmark Panel was fielded from December 2000 to January 2001.

About Forrester Research

Forrester Research is a leading emerging-technology research firm, analyzing technology change and its impact on business, consumers, and society. Forrester's "Whole View" provides clients with a comprehensive set of research that reveals how technology change affects their customers, drives their business strategies, and dictates their investment in technology. Clients receive continuous research and analysis through Forrester eResearch(r) Reports, an array of Advisory Services, Assessment Tools, and topical Events. Established in 1983, Forrester is headquartered in Cambridge, Mass., with North American Research Centers in San Francisco, Calif., and Toronto, Canada. Forrester's European Research Center is located in Amsterdam, Netherlands, its UK Research Centre is located in London, and its Research Center Deutschland is located in Frankfurt, Germany.

With a news release like this, the unimportant information is practically begging to be filtered out right off the bat. Before you try to tell the story in clear, concise, and conversational terms, read the entire news release, step back, and ask: *What's the big picture portrayed by the information? Which parts of it might be most relevant to the audience?*

 TIP: Keep in mind that news releases *always* attempt to promote a person, company, organization, or viewpoint. In the example about online spending, a company called Forrester Research is trying to promote itself. You should attribute the information in your story to the company, but filter out the news release's repeated self-promotional references.

10. Begin by determining the point, the meaning, and the mood in the preceding online spending story.

    • This story deals with an overabundance of precise dates and monetary figures that stand to confuse any listener, viewer or reader. The challenge is to select which dates and figures, if any, are really needed to make the point. Don't forget that numbers can and should be rounded off so they can be more clearly communicated.

    • The audience will tune out this story unless it's written in a way that's relevant to them. Consider capitalizing on something mentioned in the news release that's in common to many people: tax refund checks. An analyst is quoted as saying, ". . . many consumers may have taken their tax refund checks and gone online to get ready for school or to buy a hard-earned gift for themselves." The reference to tax refund checks provides context for the story and gives you a way to begin the script other than writing a sentence as dry as "U.S. on-line spending is up . . ."

11. Use the information from the news release to write a : thirty-second (:30) television news copy story. Include graphics. Hint: camel-squeeze heavily! A *large* portion of the news release is background information you don't need to translate or include in your script in any form.

Advocacy Group News Release

Next is a news release from the public watchdog group, Public Citizen, regarding Unsafe Trucks. Assume for this exercise that Public Citizen is well-established as a credible, reliable source of accurate information. In a moment, you'll use this news release as the basis for a television news package. Carefully read the quotations from sources in the news release. When writing your story, you can use the quotations as if they're sound bites from on-camera interviews.

Today

Nation's Commercial Truck System Dangerously Insecure and Unsafe

Chronic Failures of Federal Government Have Led to Few Key Safety Rules

WASHINGTON, D.C. — Because of chronic failures by the federal government, the country's commercial motor carrier transportation system is so insecure that a large loss of life could occur if Congress doesn't act promptly, Public Citizen President Joan Claybrook told lawmakers today.

Testifying before the Senate Subcommittee on Surface Transportation and Merchant Marine, Claybrook painted a picture of a system in which it is alarmingly easy to get a license to truck hazardous materials, in which truck drivers can mask a criminal record, where they receive little training before they step into a large rig, and where it is far too easy for dangerous cargo to be trucked across U.S. borders.

Many of the shortcomings can be traced to the Federal Motor Carrier Safety Administration and its predecessor in the Federal Highway Administration, which failed year after year to enact dozens of regulations ordered by Congress. This irresponsible lack of oversight and inadequate regulation of the motor carrier industry is particularly ominous in light of the terrorist threat under which Americans now live, said Claybrook, who testified on behalf of Public Citizen and Advocates for Highway and Auto Safety, a coalition of consumer, health, safety, and insurance groups on whose board Claybrook serves.

"The federal agency overseeing trucks has dragged its feet for years on installing the kinds of safety nets needed to help shore up our system," Claybrook said before testifying. "While this has always been unacceptable, the urgency to address this untenable situation is even stronger now. The government's failure to act now can help those intent on mass destruction achieve their goals. We simply can't let this continue."

(continued)

In her testimony, Claybrook said that:

It is far too easy for a person to obtain a commercial driver's license (CDL) to operate a truck or bus in interstate commerce, or to haul hazardous materials. Those applying for CDLs take a perfunctory, written test and a minimum on-road skills test, and many drivers learn how to handle rigs solely through on-the-job training. Applicants in many states who take a test for a commercial driver's license are not required to have any instruction, do not need much driving experience, and can obtain a license that has no restrictions. The FMCSA should institute mandatory driver entry-level training for those seeking to obtain a commercial driver's license.

It is far too easy for a trucking company to obtain operating authority to open shop. The FMSCA awards new operating authority to motor carrier applicants without examining the records of the drivers employed by the company, the operating history of the company, or the quality of its management and equipment.

The U.S. Department of Transportation still has not established basic safety information that new or prospective employers must seek from former employers during the investigation of a driver's employment record. In light of published reports that suspected terrorists have obtained licenses to haul hazardous materials, the FMCSA should issue a rule requiring criminal background checks for applicants for commercial driver's licenses and security investigations for those who seek to transport hazardous materials.

Public Citizen strongly urges Congress to pass new legislation that will require on-site safety evaluations of Mexico-domiciled carriers before granting them operating authority. Further, border inspections of freight and passenger transportation would also be beefed up. Records indicate that an overwhelming majority of Mexico-domiciled trucks don't comply with U.S. rules for transporting hazardous materials.

There is no national database of information about the number of hazardous materials shipments, the quantity of what is transported, its nature, its exact origins, or its destinations. Such a database must be established.

The federal government wants to open a high-level nuclear waste repository in Nevada. This would require huge quantities of radioactive waste to be trucked through neighborhoods and cities in 43 states — greatly increasing the threat of a terrorist attack in an urban setting.

###

 ETHICS NOTE: Remember that even sources that are well-established as credible, accurate, and reliable may be providing subjective information and are usually advocating a position for which there are opposing views. It's not enough to stop with the news release or the information within; you must seek alternate views.

What on earth is the point of this complex story? Let's do some major filtering to see what that first sentence is trying so awkwardly to say! Here's the sentence, interspersed with a common sense translation:

Because of chronic failures by the federal government, the country's commercial motor carrier transportation system **[the trucking system]** is so insecure **[is so dangerous]** that a large loss of life could occur **[many people could die]** if Congress doesn't act promptly **[if things don't change fast]**, Public Citizen President Joan Claybrook told lawmakers today.

That's an example of the mental exercise you should go through when reading the entire news release or any complex information.

Here's the second sentence:

Testifying before the Senate Subcommittee on Surface Transportation and Merchant Marine, Claybrook painted a picture of a system in which it is alarmingly easy **[Claybrook told Congress it's alarmingly easy]** to get a license to truck hazardous materials, in which truck drivers can mask a criminal record **[for people with criminal records to get a license to truck hazardous materials]**, where they receive little training before they step into a large rig **[they're poorly trained]**, and where it is far too easy for dangerous cargo to be trucked across U.S. borders **[dangerous cargo can easily be brought into the U-S]**.

12. Determine the point, the meaning, and the mood of this story. It'll help you decide what you do next to gather elements for a package.

When determining the point, the meaning, and the mood, remember to think about what might make this story most relevant to the audience. Consider the following sentence, from the third paragraph, which provides a great deal of context: "This irresponsible lack of oversight and inadequate regulation of the motor carrier industry is *particularly ominous in light of the terrorist threat* under which Americans now live, said Claybrook."

13. Next, make notes from the news release as you begin camel squeezing. Glean the most important facts and points, synopsizing them as you go. The goal is to narrow down the information so that you can examine the story in a more cohesive light.

   - Don't get bogged down in language such as "the Senate Subcommittee on Surface Transportation and Merchant Marine"; you'd almost never write that lengthy title in a script.
   - Erase any notion of using acronyms such as FMCSA (the Federal Motor Carrier Safety Administration) and CDL (Commercial Drivers License), which would be incomprehensible to the audience *and* would require you to use the entire name in full upon first reference.

Hopefully, with notes in hand, you now have a much clearer picture of the story. The next step is determining specifically what you need to create a television news package.

- When writing a package, it's often helpful to start with a specific example, or a case in point. Doing so helps the audience understand and connect to the issue. It also provides a path for using more interesting specific videotape instead of wallpaper or generic video.
- *Without* a case in point, you might be forced to begin the Dangerous Trucks package with a general sentence such as, "An alarmingly dangerous truck transport system may be putting lives at risk" while showing boring videotape of unidentifiable trucks from a distance driving past on the highway.
- Here are some ideas on how to find a case in point, such as a convict who was mistakenly issued a hazardous material truck driver's license. Conduct an Internet news search using key words such as "truck driver, hazardous materials, license, and convict." Call resources such as Public Citizen—which you know has researched the issue—and ask if they can point you to any specific cases. If they can't, ask them to direct you to other resources that might be able to.

14. Write up a list of things you need to do to turn the Dangerous Trucks information into a television news package.

   - Include specific ideas for videotape you could use, interviews, and a possible standup close.
   - Assume you've found a case in point: truck driver Matthew O'Connor, who was arrested last month transporting hazardous waste in Lansing, Michigan. He had four felony convictions on his record.
   - Also assume that your television station has archive videotape of the arrest.

15. Now, write your television news package for a local audience in Lansing, Michigan.

   - Assume you found an opposing viewpoint from Robert Rowland of the Local Trucker's Society who says that the dangers are exaggerated. In a sound bite, Rowland says, "We're already one of the most regulated industries in America. The truth is there have been very few incidents of renegade drivers transporting hazardous materials. All this is just overblown."
   - Cover other opposing views in your script, if you think it's necessary, but you don't need a sound bite for each one.
   - Use at least one sound bite from Claybrook.
   - With each paragraph in your script, note what VO (videotape) you plan to use to cover that part.
   - Be sure and include a standup. The standup is an opportunity to include an extra fact or to incorporate an interesting point from a sound bite you didn't use.
   - Use at least one natsound (natural sound) break somewhere in the script.

☞ **TIP:** You do not have to cover each and every point in a news release or story; in fact you'll almost never have the time to do so. Covering too much can be confusing to the audience and can become a barrier to clear writing. There's an art to determining what to leave *out* of a story. It's best to select no more than one or two main points.

16. Working from your television news package, translate it into an Internet news story.
17. Translate the Dangerous Trucks story into a brief radio news wrap, with an actuality from Claybrook and one from Rowland.

After you've made sense of the basic story and pared it down, it becomes surprisingly easy to camel squeeze it into shorter and shorter versions.

18. Write the Dangerous Trucks story as a fifteen-second (:15) radio story (with no actualities). It's easiest if you work from the radio news wrap instead of the news release. When you've finished, the facts have been boiled down to their barest essence!

Wire Story

Now we'll move onto a task that might seem relatively easy compared to deciphering the story about Dangerous Trucks. Refer to the following wire story:

Line Standers

Wait no more: Brits will pay good money to get out of line

(London) – There's a company based in London, Great Britain, that offers a unique service: You can hire people to wait in line for you. Of course there's a fee. The "waiters" will que up for anything from concert tickets, to passports, to a line for a driver's license. The company says it has done some research showing that people in Britain spent about a year of their entire lives waiting in lines. Some people just don't want to spend time doing that. How much does the waiting service cost? Twenty-nine-dollars an hour. The company so far has eighty employees, most of them recruited from the long-term unemployed because "It's a job that doesn't require a lot of skill or experience." The one thing it does require is patience.

Obviously, this is a soft news feature story, and the mood is light. After you digest it, think of what you might say if you were telling the story to a friend in a normal conversation beginning with "Did you hear about . . . ?"

19. Write a couple of sentences in the very words you would use to tell the story to a friend. It'll help you develop a conversational, friendly tone that will work well for this type of feature.
20. Working with the sentences you wrote, craft a twenty-second (:20) television news copy story slugged "Waiting in Line."

Now is your chance to see if you have the skills to create something more out of this little wire copy feature. Suppose that you want to develop it into a local television news package. Since the story takes place in London, you have to figure out a way to localize it and make it of interest to your audience.

- Think of sources you could contact to help you make the story local. One idea would be to search specifically for companies in *your* area that offer waiting-in-line services similar to the one mentioned in the wire copy story.
- If you identify such a company, contact the manager or owner and see if you can find a good talker, someone who expresses himself well and appears to be enthusiastic about the job. The most interesting sound bites might actually come from a line-waiting *worker*, as opposed to the manager. Ask the manager to refer you to an enthusiastic employee whom you can actually show on the job (remember, you'll need plenty of videotape to go along with the story).
- You'll need to devise sets of basic questions to ask your sources, both for general information and for potential sound bites. What are the basic facts that need to be told? What are the things *you'd* like to know about the business? What are some questions you could ask the interviewees on camera that would help show their personality?
- Another important piece of telling this story is finding and interviewing an actual customer who hires a linewaiter, preferably the same linewaiter you're interviewing. The company will have to help you make that contact. What are the questions you'd ask the customer?
- What are some possibilities for other interviews and videotape?
- What research can quickly be done to help you give perspective to the story?
- You'll have to identify a good place to videotape a standup.

21. Using the previous tips to help, make a list of things you would need to do to turn the Waiting-in-Line feature into a local television news package. If equipped, you can actually *act* upon your list (refer to our list at the end of the chapter if you need guidance). If you don't have access to a camera, use a tape recorder to record interviews and/or other sound and then write a script for a television package or radio wrap.

   - Before you sit down to write your story, you should **transcribe** any interviews you've done. Transcribing means actually listening to the recording of the interviews and typing up what was said word for word (verbatim). You should note the time code on the recording (a running code displayed on the viewing machine) and the length of potential sound bites. Some people also call this process **logging.** You don't have to log parts of the interview that you know you won't possibly use in your story; you can just take rough notes of information given in those parts if you need it. Be sure to use asterisks or other symbols to mark the sound bites that you think are the best. Later, you'll refer to the log when writing your script. Here's an example of how a brief interview log might look, with the best sound bites marked with asterisks.

JANET CUMBERLAND, "Take the Wait Off" Client

INTERVIEW Jan 13

00:14:00 (She talks about how she heard about Take the Wait Off from a friend and decided to use it the next time she wanted to get tickets for her kids to go to a Muppet Show that always sells out quickly)

00:16:28 WITH TWO KIDS, IT FINALLY OCCURRED TO ME THAT MY TIME IS TOO VALUABLE TO SPEND HALF A DAY OR EVEN AN HOUR JUST STANDING IN LINE (:08)

00:16:42 I WAS FED UP WITH LONG LINES... (:02)

00:16:50 SO FOR, UH, ABOUT 30-DOLLARS, I GOT SOMEONE TO DO THE WAITING FOR ME (:05) (she stumbles a bit when talking—not a great sound bite.)

00:16:57 *****(Question) DID YOU GET THE TICKETS? (Janet) FOUR TICKETS, NO MUSS, NO FUSS...AND BEST OF ALL NO WAIT (she laughs)! (:06)

00:16:57 *****(Question) WAS IT WORTH THE MONEY? (Janet) ABSOLUTELY! I'D DO IT AGAIN IN A HEARTBEAT! (:05) (she's VERY enthusiastic in this sound bite)

00:17:30 (She says she's thinking of hiring the same company to wait in line when she needs to renew her driver's license, which has notoriously long lines...)

00:18:40 B-roll of Janet with her kids, they show their Muppets tickets, etc.

XXXXX

- If you're writing a television script, you should also **screen** your b-roll before you write. B-roll, you'll recall, is the video available to use in your story. Screening it means watching it so that you know exactly what pictures you have to work with. As part of the screening, it's helpful to make a log marking useful natural sound and interesting shots as in the following example:

B-ROLL: "Take the Wait Off" Offices

04:36:27 wide shot exterior of office

04:38:00 wide shot of sign, zooms in to closeup of sign

Chapter 9

04:40:40 inside, secretary answers phone

04:41:15 NATSOUND: "HELLO, 'TAKE THE WAIT OFF' WE DO THE WAITING FOR YOU . . . " (:03)

04:45:07 three employees "waiting" for assignments, wide shots and closeups

04:50:04 manager enters and reads an assignment off the sheet for one of the employees

04:57:30 NATSOUND: "OKAY RANDY, YOU'RE GOIN' DOWN TO THE PROPERTY TAX OFFICE . . . " (:04)

05:00:56 employee Randy Tate walks out of office, camera follows him

05:02:00 Randy gets in his car, ***gives a thumbs up sign, drives off

XXXX

Government Agency News Release

The following news release, "Candy Alert," comes from the government's Food and Drug Administration, the federal agency responsible for issues regarding food and drug safety:

FOR IMMEDIATE RELEASE
CANDY ALERT

FDA ISSUES A SECOND WARNING AND AN IMPORT ALERT ABOUT KONJAC MINI-CUP GEL CANDIES THAT POSE CHOKING RISK

The Food and Drug Administration (FDA) is issuing a second warning and announcing an import alert concerning mini-cup gel candies that contain the ingredient "konjac" (also known as conjac, konnyaku, yam flour, or glucomannan). FDA decided a second warning was warranted (the first was issued several months ago) after consultation with experts on choking from the Consumer Product Safety Commission (CPSC). CPSC confirmed that these candies pose a serious choking risk, particularly to infants, children, and the elderly. In addition, the agency has issued an import alert to address the importation of these candies from other countries.

These multi-fruit-flavored candies are typically packaged as individual, mouth-sized servings, and often feature an embedded piece of preserved fruit. Unlike gelatin products commonly found in the U.S., these candies do not readily dissolve when placed in the mouth.

"The public needs to be aware that these candies pose a choking hazard, said Bernard A. Schwetz, D.V.M., Ph.D, FDA's Acting Principal Deputy Commissioner. "We hope to prevent any more of these products from getting into the country, but in the meantime, people need to beware of konjac mini-cup gel candies that may still be in the marketplace."

The news release is fairly concise. At first glance, the focus may seem to be the fact that a second warning is being issued. But you need to use your news judgment and gatekeeping skills to glean what the *real* news here is. The real importance of this story—from the audience's point of view—is that the tempting candies pose a serious choking risk for children.

In the following example, we've highlighted details that may not be necessary to include—or can be synopsized—in a brief radio or television script.

FOR IMMEDIATE RELEASE
CANDY ALERT

FDA ISSUES A SECOND WARNING AND AN IMPORT ALERT ABOUT KONJAC MINI-CUP GEL CANDIES THAT POSE CHOKING RISK

The Food and Drug Administration (FDA) is issuing a second warning and **announcing an import alert** concerning mini-cup gel candies that contain the ingredient "konjac" **(also known as conjac, konnyaku, yam flour, or glucomannan). [The alternate names for the ingredients could possibly be listed in a graphic.] FDA decided a second warning was warranted (the first was issued several months ago) after consultation with experts on choking from the Consumer Product Safety Commission (CPSC).** CPSC confirmed that these candies pose a serious choking risk, particularly to infants, children, and the elderly. **In addition, the agency has issued an import alert to address the importation of these candies from other countries.**

These multi-fruit-flavored candies are typically packaged as individual, mouth-sized servings, and often feature an embedded piece of preserved fruit. Unlike gelatin products commonly found in the U.S., these candies do not readily dissolve when placed in the mouth.

"The public needs to be aware that these candies pose a choking hazard, said Bernard A. Schwetz, D.V.M., Ph.D, FDA's Acting Principal Deputy Commissioner. "We hope to prevent any more of these products from getting into the country, but in the meantime, people need to beware of konjac mini-cup gel candies that may still be in the marketplace."

---

22. Determine the point, the meaning, and the mood of this Candy Alert story.
23. List some of the unanswered questions you still have after reading the news release. It may be necessary for you to find answers to some of these questions before you are able to write a script. Writing them down can give you ideas as to what sources you can turn to to make the story complete.

Enterprising a Story

Your next assignment requires enterprising a story from start to finish. **Enterprising** means finding on your own something of interest to report . . . something that's not handed to you in a press conference or a news release.

- Begin by visiting the CPSC Web site at www.cpsc.gov. Click on the Press Room (www.cpsc.gov/pr/proom.html), and you'll see a wealth of information.
- Go into About CPSC & General Information to get some background on the agency's role. Then browse through other sections, like Story Suggestions and Press Releases.
- From this material, choose a topic that may be of interest to an audience made up largely of college students.
- Next, you'll use the information on the Web site to enterprise a *local* radio wrap, television package, and Internet news story about that topic. To organize your efforts, do the following:

24. Identify the point, meaning, and mood of your story.
25. Determine what elements you need to make the story complete. You can make use of audio clips, radio sound, and even video offered on the CPSC Web site.

   - You'll have to find a way to include any opposing viewpoints. For example, if the story involves a consumer product that is alleged to be faulty, you should contact the company that makes the product to get its side of the story.

 ETHICS NOTE: Any time you use videotape that's not shot by someone in your own company, you must identify the source for the viewers. This can be done in the script. For example, "As this video provided by the Consumer Product Safety Commission shows, the children's pajamas are extremely flammable." The source of such third-party videotape should also always be identified in fonts on the screen, for example, "video from Consumer Product Safety Commission."

26. Now determine how you will localize the story so that it is of greatest interest to your audience.

   - Try to find out if anyone in your area has been injured by the product in question. Call the CPSC and ask how you would locate such victims. Maybe the agency knows about specific cases in certain geographic areas of the country.
   - If you *can* find that someone in your area was injured or affected by the product, contact them for an interview, that is, *unless* it involves someone seriously injured or killed for whom it would be awkward, insensitive, or inconvenient for them to talk with you since this a class exercise. In that case, for the sake of this exercise only, you can create what you believe their responses to questions would be so that you can have sound bites, quotes, or actualities.
   - Another way to localize is to find a store in your area that sells/sold the product in question. Ask the store managers or owners if they know of any problems or injuries with the product. If they do, ask for an interview.

27. Write out lists of questions for the people you intend to interview. Conduct the interviews, if possible, in person or on the telephone. (If you're writing a television news package and have access to a video camera, work in pairs and videotape the interview. Also write a standup, determine a location for it, and videotape it. Shoot some b-roll as well.)
28. Transcribe the interviews you've conducted and screen any b-roll. You're ready to write. Put together a complete Internet story, a radio wrap, and a television package. (For the Internet, be sure and include elements such as bullets, graphics, and links. For radio, don't forget to include actualities. For the television package, note in each sentence or paragraph of your script the type of b-roll that could be used for each section of copy.)

Answers

1. Double Homicide (radio copy story)

Two men are dead and another injured...after a shooting this morning in north-east Washington D.C. Witnesses reported gunshots in the 300-block of Seaton Place at about eight-40 a-m. When police arrived, they found that three men who'd been shot had already gone to the hospital. Two of them—22-year old Marvin Gantt Junior and 18-year old Matthew Lindsay—died. The third victim is in serious condition...police are withholding his name because he's considered a witness.
XXX

2. Possible sources for more information regarding double homicide story:
Neighbors in the area of the shootings, eyewitnesses, relatives of the men who were shot . . . all of whom could be found by going to the crime scene.
Also, police detectives may provide additional information, and you should periodically call the hospital to check the status of the injured "witness."

3. To turn the double homicide story into a VO-BITE:
Shoot videotape of the scene where it happened. Ask neighbors or relatives of the men involved if they'll share any still photos of the men with you. You could shoot exterior pictures of the hospitals where the men were taken. Check with police to see if any of the three men had a "rap sheet" (a prior record of criminal arrests). If so, you may be entitled to a copy of their mug shots on file. Possible on-camera interviews are a police officer or spokesman, eyewitnesses, neighbors, and friends or relatives of the men who were shot.

4. Questions for interviewees:
For eyewitnesses: "What did you see and hear? Do you have any idea what was happening, or why the shooting happened? Do you know if other people were involved besides the three men? This must have been very frightening for you . . . ?"
For police: "What do you know about why the shooting broke out? Are you looking for other suspects, or do you believe only these three men were involved? Is the victim who survived considered a suspect in the shooting of the other two men?"

5. DOUBLE HOMICIDE VO-BITE

(ANCHOR ON CAM)	(ANCHOR ON CAM) TONIGHT, POLICE ARE INVESTIGATING A DOUBLE HOMICIDE IN NORTH-EAST WASHINGTON D.C.
(VO) font: Washington D.C.	(VO) WITNESSES SAY GUNFIRE BROKE OUT AROUND EIGHT-40 THIS MORNING IN THE 300-BLOCK OF SEATON PLACE.

(continued)

(SOT) HENRY MEYERS EYEWITNESS RUNS: 10 (VO)	(SOT) (IN: I HEARD TEN SHOTS... OUT:...ALL THREE FELL. RUNS: 10 (VO) THREE MEN WERE SHOT—TWO OF THEM—22-YEAR-OLD MARVIN GANTT JUNIOR AND 18-YEAR-OLD MATTHEW LINDSAY—DIED. A THIRD MAN IS IN SERIOUS CONDITION WITH GUNSHOT WOUNDS. POLICE CONSIDER HIM A WITNESS AND AREN'T RELEASING HIS NAME. (XXX)

6. Most Wanted Terrorists
   The point: There's a new Most Wanted list that focuses specifically on terrorists.
   The meaning: The US is putting new focus on terrorist threats after the terrorist attacks on the World Trade Center and the Pentagon.
   The mood: Serious; straight.

7. "Most Wanted Terrorists" Internet story

The White House has announced a new program designed to root out known terrorists around the globe. It's called "The Most Wanted List of Terrorists." Twenty-two men are on the first list issued today, including Usama bin Laden—the man the F.B.I. blames for terrorist acts against Americans worldwide over the past decade.

Also on the list are suspects in the 1993 World Trade Center bombing, 1996 bombing of military housing in Saudi Arabia, and U.S. embassy bombings in 1998.

8. Elements for "Most Wanted Terrorists" Internet story:
   Photograph of Usama bin Laden

   Photograph(s) of 1993 World Trade Center bombing and Khobar Towers bombing

   Bullets: Listing all 22 suspects and events they're associated with or the same information could be presented in chart form

   Links: White House Web site that has entire news release. The story could offer links to former news stories written on the terrorist events, and perhaps a link to the FBI Web site

9. Most Wanted Terrorists/radio copy story

There's a brand new hit-list out today naming the world's top terrorists on the loose. The "Most Wanted List of Terrorists" identifies 22 men suspected of murdering Americans around the globe. Among them...Usama bin Laden...the man the F-B-I. blames for attacking the World Trade Center in New York—twice—in the past decade. The White House started the new "Most Wanted" list to put a spotlight on terrorists around the globe. Also listed are people allegedly connected to the bombing of U-S military housing in Saudi Arabia in 1996...and U-S embassy bombings in 1998. (XXX)

10. Online Spending
The point: Americans are spending more money online.
The meaning: Online shopping seems to be becoming more popular.
The mood: Straight though not overly serious.

11.

ONLINE SPENDING COPY / GRAPHICS	
(ANCHOR ON CAM)	(ANCHOR ON CAM) THOSE MILLIONS OF UNEXPECTED TAX REFUND CHECKS THAT CAME IN THE MAIL LAST MONTH...MAY HAVE HELPED FUEL A GROWING OBSESSION TO BUY ONLINE.
(GRAPHIC) August Online Spending Average: $273 per consumer	(GRAPHIC) A NEW SURVEY BY FORRESTER RESEARCH SHOWS CONSUMERS SPENT AN AVERAGE 273-DOLLARS ONLINE IN AUGUST.
(CHANGE GRAPHIC) August Online Spending Total: $4 billion	(CHANGE GRAPHIC) TOTAL U-S SPENDING ONLINE HIT THE FOUR BILLION DOLLAR MARK...UP SLIGHTLY FROM THE MONTH BEFORE.
(ANCHOR ON CAM)	(ANCHOR ON CAM) ONE ANALYST SAYS ONLINE SHOPPING HAS MADE A QUICK COMEBACK AFTER A DROP OVER THE SUMMER. (XXX)

12. The point of the Dangerous Trucks news release is:

    Federal regulators are asleep at the wheel as the trucking system is alarmingly suscep-
    tible; laws should be strengthened and enforced.

    The meaning: Terrorists could easily use the trucking system to wreak havoc.

    The mood: There's a sense of outrage in this story: how outrageously easy it could be
    for terrorists to kill by exploiting flaws in the trucking system and how outrageously
    ineffective federal regulators have been.

13. Notes from the Dangerous Trucks Public Citizen news release:

    Public Citizen claims that many people could die because the nation's trucking system
    is so unsafe. And that, says the group, is the federal government's fault.

    Public Citizen President Joan Claybrook testified before a Senate committee today,
    saying it's alarmingly easy for even convicts to get a license to truck hazardous materi-
    als, where they get poor training and can truck dangerous cargo across U.S. borders.

    Federal regulators, says Claybrook, have failed to enact regulations ordered by Congress.
    The problem has a new sense of urgency with a growing terrorist threat in America.

    Claybrook: (select possible sound bites in which she is not using technical informa-
    tion and acryonyms such as "FMSCA," which are meaningless to your audience):

    • "Applicants in many states who take a test for a commercial driver's license are
      not required to have any instruction, do not need much driving experience,
      and can obtain a license that has no restrictions."
    • "The U.S. Department of Transportation still has not established basic safety
      information that new or prospective employers must seek from former em-
      ployers during the investigation of a driver's employment record."
    • "There is no national database of information about the number of hazardous
      materials shipments, the quantity of what is transported, its nature, its exact
      origins, or its destinations. Such a database must be established."
    • "The federal government wants to open a high-level nuclear waste repository
      in Nevada. This would require huge quantities of radioactive waste to be
      trucked through neighborhoods and cities in 43 states—greatly increasing the
      threat of a terrorist attack in an urban setting."

14. Things needed for Dangerous Trucks package:

    Conduct an archive search at your own station and an Internet news article search to
    try to find a local example of a convict allowed to drive hazardous waste or some re-
    lated violation. Ask Claybrook if she knows of local examples. (Finding an individual
    case or example is always a great way to make a story interesting and to show how it
    matters in the real world.) Best case: Find an example in which there is existing video-
    tape because your station covered the story previously.

    Get opposing viewpoint(s): Ask Claybrook for names of people who've been major im-
    pediments to getting proper laws passed and enforced. Also contact federal regulators
    to let them answer her criticism. See if a local trucking organization/trucker's union
    will do an interview defending the safety of the trucking system.

    Shoot generic videotape of unidentifiable trucks traveling down the highway. See if the
    station's archives has videotape of hazardous waste that could be used when you refer
    to it.

    A good possible standup might be paraphrasing something Claybrook mentioned in
    her testimony: "The federal government wants to open a high-level nuclear waste

repository in Nevada. This would require huge quantities of radioactive waste to be trucked through neighborhoods and cities in 43 states—greatly increasing the threat of a terrorist attack in an urban setting."

A good location to shoot a standup location is along a highway where lots of trucks drive by.

15. Dangerous Trucks package

(VO/arrest last month)

Matthew O'Connor had four felony convictions...yet he managed to get behind the wheel of what could be considered a lethal weapon...a truck carrying hazardous waste.

(VO/trucks on highways)

It's just one symptom of an alarmingly dangerous truck transport system that's putting many lives at risk...according to citizen activist Joan Claybrook.

(SOT-JOAN CLAYBROOK, PUBLIC CITIZEN ADVOCACY GROUP)

APPLICANTS IN MANY STATES WHO TAKE A TEST FOR A COMMERCIAL DRIVER'S LICENSE ARE NOT REQUIRED TO HAVE ANY INSTRUCTION, DO NOT NEED MUCH DRIVING EXPERIENCE, AND CAN OBTAIN A LICENSE THAT HAS NO RESTRICTIONS.

(VO/trucks on highways, hazardous material)

Claybrook blames federal regulators who are "asleep at the wheel." The result, she told Congress today, is a system where convicts can drive hazardous materials, and it's easy to get dangerous cargo across U-S borders.

(VO/exterior of Dept. of Trans. office)

Regulators we spoke to at the Department of Transportation office in Lansing say they're trying to tighten up the system, but don't have the resources to make changes any faster.

NATSOUND FULL OF ROWLAND STARTING UP HIS BIG RIG TRUCK :02

(VO/Robert Rowland b-roll getting in his truck)

As for the dangers on the highway, Robert Rowland of the Local Trucker's Society says things aren't nearly as bad as they sound.

(SOT-ROBERT ROWLAND, LOCAL TRUCKER'S SOCIETY)

WE'RE ALREADY ONE OF THE MOST REGULATED INDUSTRIES IN AMERICA. THE TRUTH IS THERE HAVE BEEN VERY FEW INCIDENTS OF RENEGADE DRIVERS TRANSPORTING HAZARDOUS MATERIALS. ALL THIS IS JUST OVERBLOWN.

(continued)

(GRAPHIC: bullet list)

Overblown or not, consumer advocates want a national database on hazardous materials shipments that tracks how many, how much, exactly what and where.

(STANDUP CLOSE) AND THERE'S A NEW SENSE OF URGENCY BECAUSE OF PLANS FOR A NUCLEAR WASTE REPOSITORY IN NEVADA. HUGE AMOUNTS OF WASTE COULD BE TRUCKED THROUGH ALMOST EVERY STATE...AND SOME SAY...THAT WOULD GREATLY INCREASE THE RISK TO EVERYONE. MAX REPORTER, CHANNEL NINE EYEWITNESS NEWS, LANSING.

(XXX)

Notes: This story began with a specific example, which helps people relate to the issue. It then briefly described the problem, as told by Claybrook, and named whom she thought was at fault (federal regulators). Then, it presented two alternate viewpoints: Department of Transportation officials who say they don't have the money to work any faster, and a local trucker who said things aren't really that bad. It also Completed the Circle by mentioning a proposed solution, creating a national database on hazardous materials shipments, presented as graphic bullets. Last, the standup borrowed a point from Claybrook's testimony and helped look to the future: a plan to build a nuclear waste repository in Nevada that could increase the risk to everyone.

16. Dangerous Trucks Internet story:

Matthew O'Connor had four felony convictions, yet he managed to get behind the wheel of what could be considered a lethal weapon: a truck carrying hazardous waste. The head of Public Citizen, Joan Claybrook, says it's just one symptom of an alarmingly dangerous truck transport system that's putting many lives at risk.

"Applicants in many states who take a test for a commercial driver's license are not required to have any instruction, do not need much driving experience, and can obtain a license that has no restrictions," Claybrook testified before a Senate subcommittee today.

Claybrook blames federal regulators who are asleep at the wheel. The result, she claims, is a system in which:

- Convicts can get licenses to drive hazardous materials.
- Even legitimate drivers receive poor training.
- It's easy to get dangerous cargo across U.S. borders.

Regulators we spoke to at the Department of Transportation office in Lansing say they're trying to tighten up the system, but don't have the resources to make changes any faster.

"It's easy to blame us," says the head of the local D.O.T. office, "but we've been saying for years that we don't have the manpower or the money to implement changes any faster."

As for the dangers on the highway, Robert Rowland of the Local Trucker's Society says things aren't nearly as bad as they sound.

"We're already one of the most regulated industries in America. The truth is, there have been very few incidents of renegade drivers transporting hazardous materials. All this is just overblown," says Rowland.

Overblown or not, consumer advocates say there's one thing that should be done immediately to make highways safer: establish a national database on hazardous materials shipments telling how many, how much, exactly what and where.

A new sense of urgency is attached to the issue with terrorist threats on U.S. soil becoming more real. In fact, a plan to build a nuclear waste repository in Nevada would require huge amounts of waste to be trucked through forty-three states. Some say *that* would greatly increase the risk to everyone.

OTHER INTERNET STORY ELEMENTS:

Photo of Claybrook testifying, photo of Matthew O'Connor being arrested

Graphic chart:

```
                    Consumer Advocate Proposal
            National Hazardous Materials Database telling:
                    ◄How many shipments
                    ◄How much being shipped
                    ◄Exactly what's shipped
                    ◄Where it's shipped
```

Links:

See Claybrook's entire testimony, plus related testimony, at the Web site for the Senate Subcommittee on Surface Transportation and Merchant Marine.

For more on the view from the Local Trucker's Society, click here.

Visit Public Citizen's Web site.

Notes: This story took the time to elaborate a bit more on the Department of Transportation position, using a direct quote. All sound bites were translated into direct quote format because the audience will read, rather than hear the interviews and story. One list of information (Claybrook's summary of the problem) was presented in bullet form. A separate graphic chart was created to outline the proposed solution (National Hazardous Materials database). Possible links and photos were added.

17. Dangerous Trucks radio wrap:

An alarmingly dangerous truck transport system is putting many lives at risk. That's what the head of Public Citizen watchdog group, Joan Claybrook, told Congress today.

START: CLAYBROOK

OUT CUE: "...NO RESTRICTIONS."

TIME: 10

Claybrook blames federal regulators who—she says—have been asleep at the wheel. Among other changes, she's pushing for a national database to track what type and how much hazardous waste is going where. One local trucker, Robert Rowland, says things aren't as bad as Claybrook makes them out to be.

START: ROWLAND

OUT CUE: "...OVERBLOWN."

TIME: 08

And federal officials say they're working as fast as they can with limited resources to tighten up the nation's trucking system. Max Reporter, WZYX-AM, Lansing.

(XXX)

Notes: At approximately four seconds (:04) per line of copy, and a total of eighteen seconds—ten plus eight (:18) in actualities, this radio wrap times out to fifty-one seconds (:51). We deleted material to make this story brief—a must in news radio. It didn't make sense to start with the individual example about the convict, O'Connor, when trying to write "tight," especially because the radio audience can't see videotape of the arrest. Lists and other information must be pared down to the simplest, most basic form possible since, in radio, they can't be supplemented by graphics or bullets.

18. Dangerous Trucks :15 radio story:

In Congress today, the alarm was sounded over a dangerous truck system where training is poor...it's easy to move hazardous waste across borders into the U-S...and even convicts can get licenses. Consumer advocates blamed federal regulators. But THEY say they're doing the best they can with limited resources.

(XXX)

---

19. Waiting in Line story:

"Did you hear about this company in Britain where you can hire someone to stand in line for you? Costs 29-bucks an hour."

20. WAITING IN LINE/COPY

(ANCHOR/OC)	(ANCHOR/OC)
	WAITING IN LINE IS ONE OF LIFE'S CERTAINTIES— EVERYBODY'S GOTTA DO IT SOMETIME. OR DO THEY? A COMPANY IN LONDON IS OFFERING TO STAND IN LINE FOR YOU...WHETHER IT'S FOR A DRIVER'S LICENSE....CONCERT TICKETS OR A PASSPORT. BUT TIME IS MONEY...29-DOLLARS PER HOUR TO BE EXACT. THAT'S WHAT THE WAITING SERVICE COSTS. THE COMPANY SAYS MOST OF ITS STAND-INS CAME FROM...THE UNEMPLOYMENT LINE. THE ONLY SKILL REQUIRED IS...PATIENCE. (XXX)

21. Things needed for Waiting in Line television news package:

Call local Chamber of Commerce and search the Yellow Pages and Internet for local companies that offer line-waiting services. If there is, find one with an owner who sounds like a good interview, who will let cameras shoot b-roll of the business, AND go on an assignment with a line-waiting worker (a *must*!) Who uses the service? How much does it cost? What's the length of the average assignment? What lines are people trying most to avoid? Are any stories of particularly funny/unusual assignments?

Interview the person who hired the line-waiting worker being profiled. Why did you do it? How much did it cost? Is it worth it? Have you used the service before? What are you doing with the time you saved?

Need lots of b-roll and on camera "man on the street" (MOS) interviews (comments) with people standing in line at various venues: driver's license, concert tickets, etc. Call to get permission first if it requires entering offices. For MOS, ask people whether they hate standing in line, how much they would be willing to pay someone to do it for them, and what's the longest line they ever stood in?

Need standup location—possibly unemployment line if there *is* one or a grocery line might be easy if all else fails.

Search for any official statistics or information on how long people in the United States stand in line, etc. If there is no U.S. info, you can quote the British figure: one year of their lives.

22. Candy Alert
    The point: Innocent-looking gel candies pose a dangerous choking hazard.
    The meaning: The FDA thinks the risk is so great that it's issuing a second warning about the candy.
    The mood: Serious.

23. Candy Alert unanswered questions:

    1. How did the FDA become aware in the first place that the candies posed a choking hazard? How complained? (Whoever first complained might be a good person to interview.)
    2. How many cases have been reported and how much of the candy was sold? (This will help you determine whether the story may affect a large number of your audience members.)
    3. Where was the candy sold, all over the United States or only in certain areas? (This will help you determine whether you can localize the story to your area.)
    4. Who makes the candies? The news release indicates at least some of them are imported. (This will tell you what companies you can contact for a response and their side of the story.)
    5. Why exactly, did the FDA issue the *second* warning? Were there still more choking incidents after the *first* warning?

    To enterprise this information into a news story, you should ask the FDA and/or the Consumer Product Safety Commission (mentioned in the release) for names of people who reported problems or injuries (possible interview subjects). If you have a choice, you should opt for interview subjects in your own local area. You can also conduct your own Web or Nexis search looking for people injured by the candies. Also ask the agencies if they have samples, videotape, or photographs of the candies. It's possible that the CPSC recorded the testing on video and will give you a copy. Or the CPSC might let you videotape them performing a choking test on the candies.

24. **through 28.** Independent work; answers vary.

Web sites

For more information, check out the following Web sites:

www.straightscoop.org/advice/stu_broadcast.html
Advice on writing for broadcast news from Straight Scoop News Bureau for teens

www.poynter.org/dj/tips/broadcast/enterprise.htm
Tips on enterprising a story, from the Poynter Institute

www.poynter.org/special/poynterreport/broadcast/broadcast1.htm
Tips on writing for broadcasting, including use of natural sound, from the Poynter Institute

www.poynter.org/dj/011400.htm
Free story ideas from the Poynter Institute

Quick Review of Terms

- **Enterprising a story:** Refers to finding, on your own, something of interest to report, something that's not handed to you in a press conference or a news release.
- **Screening:** In television, the process of watching available b-roll (cover video) before writing a story to determine exactly what pictures can be used. When screening, it's helpful to make a log marking useful natural sound and interesting shots.
- **Transcribing:** The process of listening to recordings of interviews and typing up what was said word-for-word. The resulting transcriptions or logs should include a time code (a running code displayed on the viewing machine) and the length of potential sound bites. Some people also call this process *logging*.

10

Ethics and the Law

Chapter Objectives

- To explain the importance of ethical practices and morally reasonable decisions
- To discuss the line between private facts and the public's right to know
- To explore legal issues such as defamation and invasion of privacy
- To consider the importance of ethical codes and guidelines

We've peppered this textbook with advice and tips regarding ethical practices. It's critical that you learn to integrate such considerations into your daily decision making. This chapter is devoted entirely to explaining why it's so important for you to become not just a broadcast or Internet journalist, but also an *ethical* journalist.

For the purposes of this text, ethics-related decisions include a broad range of issues. What are the consequences of your writing or of your story? How far would you go to get it? Whom might it exploit or victimize? When should you *not* do as you are directed by your superiors or outside authorities? Is your reporting of the facts fair? Is your representation of various viewpoints accurate? Is it ever okay to stretch the truth or even lie for the "greater good"?

It would be impossible address even a fraction of the real-world ethical dilemmas you'll encounter. However, you *can* become accustomed to the exercise of consulting your own "moral compass" and using it to consider the consequences and impact of your decisions.

There are few, if any, one-size-fits-all answers.

Why Be Good?

Moral choices are a very important part of our profession, and the consequences of those choices can cause either happiness or harm. What exactly does it mean to be *ethical*, and why is it so important?

The word *ethics* comes from an ancient Greek word *ethika*, which means matters having to do with character and involving the virtues of goodness and excellence. Today, ethics is the study of moral behavior and of making moral choices even in the most difficult and perplexing circumstances. Simply put, behaving ethically is *the right thing* to do.[1] Further in this chapter, we'll examine the consequences of both ethical and unethical behavior in broadcast and Internet news.

Whose Ethics, Anyway?

The task of teaching journalistic ethics begs one obvious question: *whose* ethics? After all, moral behavior is very subjective. In some cases, ethical behavior is clear cut, even governed by law. However, you'll often be faced with blurred lines: conflicts between what would make a good story and what is actually the right thing to do.

In the new millennium, there appears to be a positive trend in which more and more mass communication, broadcasting, and journalism departments are requiring ethics courses. Part of the reason for the new recognition of the importance of ethics training in journalism stems from the explosion of media outlets in the 1990s. From cable and satellite television, television news magazines, and the Internet to the proliferation of "infotainmet" (the sometimes awkward blend of news and entertainment), competition for viewers reached a peak. Established media companies found themselves up against organizations governed by different ethical guidelines or, in some cases, governed by no apparent guidelines at all. The traditional media began to bend their own rules, giving rise to more and more questionable tactics:

- NBC's *Dateline* television news magazine fired a producer and demoted a reporter after it was revealed that they had been involved in rigging a pickup truck crash test to create a dramatic explosion.
- An ABC News Washington correspondent was chastised for faking a standup in front of the Capitol in Washington D.C.; she was actually wearing a coat inside a studio with the Capitol generated electronically behind her.
- CNN was forced to apologize to viewers for an incendiary investigative report alleging the United States had used poison gas against its own troops in the Vietnam War. The network admitted the story was poorly sourced, and the correspondent defended himself by claiming he really *had very little to do with the script.*
- *The Washington Post* returned a Pulitzer Prize after it was revealed that the reporter had manufactured facts in her award-winning story (details of this case are discussed further in this chapter).
- A *Boston Globe* columnist was fired after allegedly manufacturing sources and information for some of his columns.
- An ABC News *20/20* correspondent was forced to apologize to viewers after a report criticizing organic food, he had cited "tests" that, it turns out, were never conducted.

If such shocking ethical breaches are happening within such respected news organizations, you can only imagine the challenges that may face you.

Sneaking Suspicions

The truth is, many ethical dilemmas come in less obvious forms than those just mentioned. They have a nasty habit of sneaking up unexpectedly in the ordinary course of business.

Sharyl's Story

One of the earliest dilemmas I recall being faced with was at my first job as a reporter at WTVX-TV, the former CBS affiliate in Ft. Pierce, Florida. At small stations like WTVX, the sales department (which generates the all-important revenue for the station) sometimes attempts to influence or control news coverage.

One weekend, I was given the puzzling assignment of covering the opening of a new bank. Even as a fledgling reporter, I recognized that an ordinary bank opening wasn't worthy of a news story. When I questioned the assignment, asking why we'd devote resources and time in the newscast to covering such a "non-news" event, my superior explained that station management hoped that showing the bank opening on our newscast might convince the bank to buy advertising on WTVX. Nobody in college had ever prepared me for this. I knotted my fingers and fretted about how foolish it would be from a journalistic perspective if I actually did a story on the bank opening! My supervisor made it clear that the only way I could get out of the bank story was if "real" news broke out. If that happened, I would be diverted to the legitimate story. Fate intervened in the form of a killer. I was diverted to the scene of a double murder, and the bank opening went thankfully unreported. Since that time, I've often considered what might have happened if I'd been forced to do a story that I knew was bogus. What would I have done? What decision would I have made? As odd as it may sound, I never saw this at the time to be the clear ethical dilemma that it was. I simply knew I didn't want to report a story that wasn't really a story. I'm glad the whole issue never came to a true showdown. I had no experience or training in dealing with such ethical questions at work. I wouldn't have known where to turn for guidance or support. If I'd outright refused to cover the bank opening—as a 21-year old kid just out of college and hundreds of people standing in line for my $12,000 a year job—I'd have surely been fired without a second thought. That was only the beginning of what quickly grew to be a diverse and complicated laundry list of on-the-job moral and ethical dilemmas.

How far should a reporter go in trying to get the interview with the proverbial grieving widow? What should a writer do when asked to let an advertiser review a script before it appears on the air or online? Is the compelling, exclusive videotape of parents being told that their child has been killed too invasive and exploitative to be aired? Should a broadcast journalist accept or decline the assignment to demonstrate on the air how kids can make crack cocaine? A bomb?

After reading this text, you'll be armed to address such touchy issues, and will be able to point to accepted industry standards in defending the stances you take and the decisions you make.

The Moral of a Story

Moral reasoning is a systematic approach to making ethical decisions, which you can use when faced with difficult choices as a broadcast or online journalist. In a general sense, moral reasoning is nothing more than the thought process of addressing ethical concerns before making decisions and taking action. Effective moral reasoning can be used to defend your ethical judgments against the criticism of others.

Certainly, reasonable people may disagree about the correct solution to an ethical dilemma. Two different people may, through proper reasoning, arrive at opposing, but equally compelling, conclusions about the most ethical decision. The important point here is to learn the exercise of moral reasoning. That skill will come in handy when you're required to defend your decisions to supervisors, colleagues, and the public even in a court of law. True moral reasoning is somewhat like a chess game, requiring very deliberate and methodical moves. So how can it be practical to those of us in a fast-paced profession under constant deadline pressure?

You may never actually sit down and diagram moral reasoning dilemmas on paper. But we're including this background because understanding the principles behind moral reasoning will help you to develop your own system of assessing ethical situations quickly and making appropriate judgments.

The Day Rule

We'll begin by describing a theory that we call **The Day Rule,** named for Louis A. Day, professor of Media Ethics at Louisiana State University. Day believes that knowledge in three basic areas, **context, philosophical foundations,** and **critical thinking,** can equip people to carry out effective moral reasoning.

The **context of moral reasoning** is the environment, or the setting in which something exists. Ethical decisions don't take place in a vacuum. From a cultural and social standpoint, moral decisions that are acceptable in New York City might be totally unacceptable in the suburbs of the Midwest, so those differences should be taken into account. Then, there's your professional context. You must consider the policies of the radio, television, or online company where you work. For example, a television news department might have a policy that prohibits reporters from promising confidentiality to a news source. It's difficult ethically to justify going against an employer's policy. Second, the Day Rule contends that you should know the **philosophical foundations of moral theory.** The following briefly outline some key philosophies:

- The Greek philosopher Plato believed that *good* was a value independent of the standards of behavior prevalent at any moment in society. In his view, a person would be justified in defying conventional wisdom in the name of some higher moral good.
- Another Greek philosopher, Aristotle, gave us the idea of *virtue ethics*. Aristotle believed that virtue lay between the extremes of excess and deficiency, or over-doing and underdoing. His aim was the development of a virtuous person, and he believed that virtue was achieved through practice. The idea was that, through repetitive moral behavior, the notion of *good* will eventually become part of the person's value. This is a major component of moral reasoning; that if it becomes a habit, it can realign your way of thinking about ethics. [2]
- *Duty-based* moral philosophy dictates that a person has the moral duty always to engage in truth telling, even if it might result in harm to others; that moral standards exist independently of utilitarian ends. This philosophy rejects the notion that "the ends justify the means." Duty-based philosophers do not approve of using deceptive practices to achieve beneficial ends.
- *Consequentialists* believe in minimization of harm. They recognize that difficult moral choices sometimes cause injury to others and say that people should weigh the impact of their behavior on others.[3]

The third area of knowledge that can equip people to carry out moral reasoning, according to the Day Rule, is **critical thinking:** analyzing and questioning why something is true. Critical thinking involves evaluating alternatives. It keeps us from settling for knee-jerk reactions and encourages more rational approaches to decision making.[4] Much of the rest of this chapter is devoted to putting into practice that crucial process of critical thinking in evaluating moral decisions.

The Fake Hit of Mr. Black

Now we turn to a compelling real world example of a difficult situation that presented many ethical challenges. We call it "The Fake Hit of Mr. Black."

One reason that this case is so interesting is because it involves media organizations knowingly broadcasting deceptive information—something that seems inherently wrong—but doing so to bring about a positive consequence. Some of the ethical questions raised are these: Do the ends justify the means? Is it ever ethical to report incorrect information knowingly? Is deception of the audience ever defensible?

"The Fake Hit of Mr. Black" began in Hattiesburg, Mississippi, in December 1984 when an unnamed person telephoned *The Hattiesburg American* newspaper with disturbing information. Someone in the town was trying to hire a hit man to murder cattle farmer Oscar Black III, a prominent local citizen. The newspaper referred the informant to police.

Police devised an elaborate hoax to catch the would-be murderer. Mr. Black agreed to the plan, as did city and county law enforcement and the district attorney. Using information from the informant, an undercover policeman pretending to be a hit man telephoned the person who wanted Mr. Black killed and agreed to do the dirty job for a fee of $35,000.

Next, police staged a scene using Black's truck that made it look as though he had, indeed, been murdered. Black was actually safe in police custody. To make the deed appear convincing, investigators decided the "crime" should be reported on the news. They hoped that would convince the hirer of the "hit man" to pay up so that he could be identified and arrested.

The sticky part came when investigators tried to convince the local media to go along with the deception. They told executives from *The Hattiesburg American* and local television station WDAM-TV of the whole plan and asked them to report that a hit man had carried out Black's murder, something that clearly was not true.

Simply put, this is the ethical dilemma the media faced: *Do we violate basic ethics by knowingly reporting a false story, or deviate from our own ethical guidelines to possibly save a man's life?* The newspaper and the television station chose different paths, and both decisions stirred up a hornet's nest of controversy.

Clear versus Limited Cooperation

WDAM-TV cooperated fully with the authorities' request, airing video of the faux murder scene, reporting that Black's truck was found abandoned with a pistol on the floorboard, and that Oscar Black was missing. In doing so, the station put its credibility on the line. But WDAM general manager Cliff Brown said he felt it was worth the risk to try to catch a potential murderer. Brown claims he did not tell his news department that the story was untrue until after it had aired.[5]

In contrast, *The Hattiesburg American's* publisher and its managing editor decided they could not publish a falsehood, no matter what the justification. But they didn't exactly report the whole truth, either. Instead, the newspaper ran a statement, which had been approved by law enforcement authorities, in its police report section. It simply read: "Police are seeking information concerning suspected foul play directed toward Oscar Black III."

Here are some of the ethical issues:

- Although the newspaper did not report false information, it—like the television station—*withheld the truth from the audience:* namely, that police staged a faux murder scene to try to capture a criminal. That withholding of information could be considered deceptive in itself.
- Second, the fact that the newspaper gave law enforcement authorities the chance to preapprove a statement it planned to publish raises its own ethical questions. As a general rule, reporters, writers, publishers, and broadcasters should *not* show their work to outside parties for viewing, reading, or approval before the story appears in print, on television, or online.
- Last, both companies claimed to have considered the good that could be accomplished by reporting this false story, but they also had a duty to consider the possible harm. For example, not even Black's own family knew for a time that his murder was a hoax. Reporting the murder potentially put his family and

friends in serious emotional distress. Black later recalled, "I felt like I was wronging my family by putting them through this."

The Fallout

The fallout of the whole scheme resulted in verbal hand grenades being tossed back and forth among the newspaper, the television station, law enforcement authorities, and even the would-be victim, Black.

Black criticized the newspaper's decision not to fully participate in the hoax to help flush out his would-be killer. *The Hattiesburg American's* managing editor, Frank Sutherland, defended his newspaper's decision and its published statement:

> That statement was accurate, but we still had some reservations about the whole story. We were concerned about our credibility with our readers and the journalistic ethics involved. Despite those reservations, we did decide to cooperate with the police . . . persuading our caller to talk to police directly. We turned all information we had on the story over to police. We also withheld publication of what we knew until police decided to make it public. But we decided that the bond of trust we have with our readers would not permit us to lie to them.[6]

However, U.S. Attorney, George Phillips, and Hattiesburg Public Safety Director, Dempsey Lawler, castigated the newspaper's decision not to participate in publishing the false story. In a prepared statement, authorities said the following:

> We have never seen so much self-righteous, self-serving rhetoric as has been written by *The Hattiesburg American* over the Hattiesburg "Hit Man" story. It is inconceivable that, when this once-in-a-lifetime set of circumstances arose last week and we finally came down to the nitty-gritty of deciding to go with the hoax in an effort to save one and perhaps as many as three lives, *The American* chose to bow to saving their own "credibility" with their peers so many would say, 'Oh yes! Their credibility to the public is most important.'[7]

McCallister, the publisher and president of the newspaper responded:

> To insinuate that we don't care about human life is callous and slanderous. The possibility of a threat to human life was discussed at every juncture in our decision-making process. The facts have been and still are unclear. Mr. Phillips [the U.S. Attorney] told us he would "burn us" if we didn't cooperate, and apparently that threat is now coming to pass.[8]

In the meantime, the general manager of WDAM-TV, Cliff Brown, said he felt it was a choice between journalism ethics and saving a human life.

> The ethics question of course was in mind, but I felt I was dealing with credible law enforcement officers. I acted on the basis of my knowledge of who these people were and how credible they were.[9]

The Right Choice?

At this point, you might be hoping for an objective analysis as to what was right and wrong in the media's moral reasoning involving "The Fake Hit of Mr. Black"; that here would be clearly stated what the newspaper and television station *should* have done. But therein lies the dilemma of this field of study. There is no single answer; there are many. You've read some compelling arguments, defenses, and justifications. The most important lessons you should carry away from this analysis is that both the television station and the newspaper were called upon to justify their ethical decisions, and that those decisions were questioned and examined in a very public forum. What decisions would *you* have made? Would you have been able to defend them?

Ironically, after all the conflict and debate, police were never able to make face-to-face contact with the criminal who attempted to hire the hit man; he was never captured or even identified.[10]

Plagiarism: Don't Copy This

Now a few words about an ethical lapse of the utmost concern to everyone from college professors to journalists: **plagiarism.** Plagiarism is copying someone else's writings, either parts of it or all of it, and attempting to pass them off as your own original work. Plagiarism is also co-opting the ideas or language in someone else's writings, but claiming them for your own. The duplication doesn't have to be exact or entire for you to be guilty. Simply paraphrasing the words doesn't exempt you from a plagiarism charge.[11] Obviously, plagiarizing is something you should never, ever do. In the business of broadcast and online writing, it's considered a cardinal sin.

 ETHICS NOTE: Most online and broadcast news operations subscribe to services such as The Associated Press and Reuters in which it's accepted and understood that the writing provided can be used in its given form without credit or attribution. This is *not* plagiarism because the services are being used for their designed and intended use, and broadcast and online subscribers pay for that service.

Equal Time

Years ago, it wasn't unusual to have a community activist or other citizen approach television news cameras and declare, "I demand Equal Time!" These people were under the mistaken impression that they had an automatic right to have their views on a given subject represented in news stories simply by demanding it.

Here's the truth behind the federal Equal Time provision. First, *only political candidates are entitled to equal time*. Second, *newscasts are exempt*.

Under Section 315 of the Communications Act of 1934, if free time is given to a legally qualified candidate for any public office, equal time must be made available,

Sharyl's Story

In 1998, I was covering Senator John Glenn's "Return to Space" for CBS News. As the first U.S. citizen to orbit the earth in 1962, John Glenn was about to make a dramatic return to space at the advanced age of 77. During his astronaut training, it was revealed that he'd been excluded from a particular space experiment for undefined health reasons. I was one of many reporters who spent a lot of time trying to find out what the ailment was. NASA kept a tight clamp on the specifics, saying only that Glenn was in excellent shape and that his ability to travel into space was not impaired in any way by his health. But we reporters wondered, however, whether NASA, in its attempt to get positive publicity with a popular mission, might be making a risky decision by sending Glenn into orbit. Weeks passed with no further insight, and the issue more or less faded into the background.

The day of the actual launch, I was still digging and finally hit pay dirt. I learned that Glenn had earlier been diagnosed with a heart irregularity known as arrhythmia: an irregular heartbeat. I was confident of the accuracy of the information; my source was Glenn's personal physician. I was excited that I had uncovered original information that hadn't yet been reported by anyone else. But before I leapt, I considered the ramifications.

First of all, Glenn's doctor and others whom I consulted all agreed that Glenn's arrhythmia was "benign" or basically harmless and shouldn't have any effect on his ability to serve as an astronaut. If I led the CBS Evening News by reporting Glenn's heart abnormality, would I be putting unjustified fear into the hearts and minds of the nation or the world? I was afraid that viewers would misconstrue the report and mistakenly conclude that Glenn was in danger, or that NASA had made a foolhardy decision in letting him fly. If I reported the heart abnormality at all, I'd have to make it clear that all the experts said there was no cause for concern. If *that* were the case, why was I reporting the fact at all? It would have made sense to do so weeks before when Glenn was excluded from the experiment in question. Now it seemed to me it only stood to muddy the waters on a day in which the launch itself was the real news.

Of course I discussed all of these concerns with my producer and executive producer, and we made a decision not to report the information that night. It's a decision that took great restraint, but was ethically responsible. Naturally, I held my breath during Glenn's entire mission hoping he suffered no problems. And it turned out to be clear sailing for Astronaut Glenn, other than a bad case of nausea upon his return to earth.

upon timely demand, to every legally qualified candidate for the same office. However, there are several important exceptions: *bona fide news broadcasts, bona fide news interviews, or news documentaries* (if the appearance of the candidate is incidental to the subject matter of the documentary). *On-the-spot and/or live coverage of bona fide news events is also excluded, including political conventions.* The bottom line is that, if you're writing or reporting for a newscast, it's likely the Equal Time provision doesn't apply. Even when it does, only political candidates are entitled to equal time; there's no obligation to give equal time to other individuals, organizations, or advocates of particular issues.

In All Fairness

The main thing you need to know about another federal initiative, **the Fairness Doctrine,** is that it's defunct. It *used* to make "fair coverage" in broadcasting subject to government oversight. The genesis of the doctrine was back in 1949, when the Federal Communications Commission determined that broadcasters had a duty to present conflicting views on controversial issues of public importance. Nobody really argued with the premise, but broadcasters *did* take issue with the concept that the federal government had a right to monitor their fairness. Many news organizations fought the Fairness Doctrine and won their battle in 1987. After nearly forty years, *the Fairness Doctrine was eliminated.*

"Quite a few of us are appalled by such a stupid thing," said former FCC Commissioner Abbott Washburn, who supported the Fairness Doctrine, "Striking down the Fairness Doctrine undermines the very foundation of the Communications Act of 1934—the public trusteeship concept."[12]

In any event, the responsibility to be fair now rests solely with broadcast journalists themselves, which gives even more meaning to the topics examined in this chapter.

Payola: A Bribe by Another Name

Payola is the act of taking services, gifts, or anything else of value from people who want to influence what's being reported. The Federal Communications Commission strictly prohibits broadcasters from accepting payola. Further, you must avoid even the appearance that you're taking something in exchange for or in payment for any sort of favor or mention in a story.

That Infamous Media Bias

Now we'll address a concept that many people refer to as **media bias:** the notion that journalists do not approach stories in a fair-minded way and that they unfairly shape the description of issues to influence the audience to feel a certain way or to believe a particular viewpoint.

Few people would argue that media bias does *not* exist, at least in some fashion. As a general philosophy, broadcast and Internet journalists should make every attempt to represent various views fairly, seek out diverse opinions, and give those under attack the chance to defend themselves.

Sometimes media bias is entirely unintentional. We all bring viewpoints to our writing and reporting, and it is difficult to completely shed the essence of who we are. However, if you learn to recognize some common sources of media bias, you may be able to avoid them. Each of the following examples is taken from real-life scenarios.

Don't Get Locked into Preconceived Notions

It's a common problem in newsrooms. Journalists hatch an idea at the beginning of a story as to what exactly it should say, even before the issue has been thoroughly investigated.

The following example shows how preconceived bias can creep into a newsroom.

Example of Preconceived Bias

A group of television news employees brainstorms story ideas. One of them says, "Let's do a story on why the Republican tax cut plan won't work!" This demonstrates an unfortunate preconceived notion among the group that, in fact, the plan *won't* work: something that is nothing more than an opinion or *preconceived bias*.

Broadcast or Internet journalists starting out with such a conclusion means that they'll likely seek out people who agree with their viewpoint rather than try to investigate the issue fairly. They may inadvertently filter out the voices of people who disagree with *their* premise. The genesis of a fairer, unbiased report would be, "Let's find some of the best minds on both sides of this issue to make the case for why the tax cut plan will or won't work."

It's only human to have ideas or opinions about a story before you write it, but you should allow it to take its own shape as you investigate the truth. Be open to ideas that don't fit in with your preconceived notions or personal biases. Be willing to change your mind and your approach midstream if you find that there's more to a story than you previously thought. Don't simply decide your boss's theory or a newspaper article on a particular subject is "the gospel." Investigate it yourself and find your own way of telling the story.

Don't Fall into the "Good vs. Bad" Trap

It's tempting to draw hard lines when writing a story . . . to choose up sides and characterize people or positions as "good" and "bad," if not explicitly through words, then by implication. It's convenient to make one opinion or set of facts "the truth" and all others "lies," especially when you only have precious limited space to explain a debate on the radio, on television, or online. But remember that life is full of shades of gray. If everything were clearly black and white, there would be little argument on such hot-button topics as abortion, taxes, education, religion, gays and lesbians, military spending, and assisted suicide. The following is an example of a journalist failing into the Good vs. Bad trap.

Example of Good vs. Bad Trap

A first-grader is expelled from school for carrying a sharp nail file to class in his backpack. An Internet journalist writing the story for his Web site immediately characterizes the child as an innocent victim of unreasonable punishment; school officials are portrayed as ridiculous bureaucrats who are obviously misapplying a zero-tolerance weapon rule.

Occasionally, stories *are* this simple, but most are not. Had the journalist bothered to look a little deeper to understand what he obviously concluded was a ridiculous viewpoint—the school's position—he would have discovered thoughtful and well-meaning educators struggling with growing violence in the school district. He would have found out that the child had been warned several times for bringing weapons onto school grounds, that he had pointed sharp items at other children in a threatening manner, and that a note had even been sent home asking for his parent's special attention to the problem.

You may personally feel there's no debate on certain issues or viewpoints, especially in matters about which you personally feel strongly. It may seem as though people on one side of an issue are nice, helpful, reasonable, and honest and that representatives of the other side aren't. But it's your responsibility to seek out and explain opposing viewpoints, not to villainize those who differ. On virtually any topic, there are reasonable people who disagree. Don't make the mistake of choosing up sides when you shouldn't be taking any.

Don't Lapse into Reasonable vs. Weirdo

Another way in which we can unintentionally slant our stories is by quoting reasonable-sounding people on one side of an issue, but seeking out radical weirdos to represent the other side. The following example show how a story can be slanted by the Reasonable vs. Weirdo trap.

Example: Reasonable vs. Weirdo Trap

A television reporter is assigned a story on gun control. Being pro-gun control himself, he interviews a well-respected and reasoned voice representing the gun control issue. Then, he seeks out a strange-looking, gun-toting radical to represent the opposing view. Almost giddy, he tells his colleagues back in the newsroom, "You should see this guy. He was wearing two machine guns around his neck, and we interviewed him in front of his Vietnam War photographs. He looked like a real nut and could barely put two sentences together!"

The reporter was displaying his bias in the way he selected who he would interview to represent both positions. He *should* have attempted to find an anti-gun control activist who could give measured, reasonable discussion on the issue.

Don't Fall for the Independent Trick

One of the most important points to remember as you write news stories is that there's no such thing as an independent analyst, source, group or individual. Everyone has an interest or motive, if not an axe to grind. Journalists working in Washington D.C. quickly learn that organizations boasting to be nonpartisan, independent, not-for-profit, or unbiased, even academic-based research groups, require special scrutiny to discover their true biases or slants. The following example demonstrates how a journalist can fail for the Independent Trick.

Example of the Independent Trick

A radio writer is assigned a story on the potential dangers of a prescription drug. He consults an organization that he's long believed to be unbiased; after all, it's an academic research group in a university setting. In an interview, the head of the group assures the radio reporter that the drug is safe, that the pharmaceutical research on it is sound, and that the talk of danger is overblown.

Had the reporter bothered to scrutinize this so-called independent source more closely, he would have discovered that the group's entire funding is provided *by the pharmaceutical industry*. When questioned about this after the fact, the research group insisted its funding source didn't influence its research or opinions. That may be. However, the reporter certainly would have questioned the group's viewpoints more strongly and would have been tougher in requiring the head of the group to justify his positions, if the funding facts had been known. Further, the source of funding should have been mentioned in the story when introducing the sound bite with the head of the organization so that audience had the chance to form its own conclusions about the credibility that should be given to his viewpoints.

Even neutral-sounding organizations such as the American Enterprise Institute, The Council on Competitiveness, The U.S. Business and International Council, The Center for Constitutional Studies, The National Women's Law Center, The Young America's Foundation, and The Chamber of Commerce have specific political leanings and viewpoints that they may attempt to peddle as unbiased opinion. Most groups, when asked, are more than willing to disclose the source of their funding or support. Ask if they do any legislative lobbying. Find out what other issues they're involved in. Their answers will provide context to their comments and give you clues to help determine "where they're coming from."

Don't Write the Sound Bite

One of the most troubling bias problems in the industry is broadcast or Internet journalists who literally put words in the mouth of an interview subject and, in effect, create or write the sound bite. Nothing is wrong with keeping an interview focused and on track. However, you cross the bias line when you guide the interview in such a way that shapes what the interview subject says. The following is an example of a reporter Writing the Sound Bite.

Example: *Writing the Sound Bite*

An online writer decides to write a story on the ethical implications of human cloning. He interviews a noted researcher.

"The ethical ramifications of cloning are exaggerated," the researcher tells the writer.

"Exact human copies will likely never be achieved, and similar genetic copies would still differ tremendously, even if raised by the same parents in the same environment at the same time. In fact, human clones would be no more alike than identical twins, which occur randomly in nature."

The online writer is disappointed with the answer, and prompts, "But can't you conceive of *some* sort of nightmare scenario?"

"No, not a realistic one," answers the researchers.

"There must be *something* negative about cloning," whines the online journalist, practically begging the researcher to oblige by modifying his answer, "Aren't you very concerned about abuses by unethical Frankenstein-type doctors?"

Finally, the researcher gives in. "Well, I suppose there could be abuses of the technology by Frankenstein-type doctors..."

Obviously, this is not an ethical way to go about conducting an interview. Often, the act of writing the sound bite is much more subtle. Some people so desperately want to appear on television or to be quoted online, they'll give you whatever slant they think you're after in an interview. Others simply want to please or don't want to look silly and so, after repeated prompting, will say what they think you want them to say. You should not exploit this tendency. Interview people to hear what they have to say, not to make them say what *you* want.

Don't Lean on the No Comment Crutch

It happens to all journalists. You call somebody for an interview or information, and the person won't talk: "no comment." This should *not* become a crutch you lean on to get out of telling that side of a story. It's important for ethical journalists to realize that "no comment" is *not* a license to neglect that viewpoint or position. The following shows how a reporter can mistakenly lean on the No Comment Crutch.

Example of the No Comment Crutch

A story crosses the wire services about an insurance company that is refusing to cover damages to homes after a devastating tornado. A television news reporter is assigned to investigate the story. He calls the insurance company to get a response, but a spokesman says he hasn't seen the report and can't comment on it until he hears from his headquarters. The reporter then writes a compelling script about homeowners are being wronged, and sums up the insurance company's viewpoint with a single line: "The insurance company had no comment."

Saying "The insurance company had no comment" is accurate, but it's not fair. The reporter had a duty to make a better effort to discover, understand, and represent the insurance company's viewpoint. There are many creative ways to fairly include the position of someone who refuses an interview opportunity. Here are some techniques you can try:

- Ask the person who won't talk to refer you to somebody who can. In the case of the previous example, the television writer could have asked to speak to somebody at the insurance company's headquarters or to a group that represents the insurance industry.
- Tell the person you're anxious to represent his view fairly, but that it's difficult to do that if nobody will explain it. It's surprising how willing people are to help when they become convinced that you're truly interested in hearing what they have to say.
- If you still strike out, you can offer to talk to the person without quoting him by name, just so you can understand his position and try to explain it in your story.
- If all else fails, inform the person that you'll be forced to write in your story that he would not comment. This may drive home how negative his portrayal may appear to viewers if he is unwilling to take the opportunity to make his side of the story known, and he may change his mind about refusing the interview.

Don't Let Their Lie Be Your Lie

When you're writing a story, you should only write what you reasonably believe to be the truth. Repeating something that you know to be false makes *you* legally liable for that person's lie, and it's ethically irresponsible. (We'll have more on the legal ramifications of reporting false information and your responsibility to the truth in the discussion on defamation and privacy.) The following examples demonstrate how you could inadvertently Let Their Lie Become Your Lie.

Letting Their Lie Become Your Lie

1.   A radio reporter conducts an interview with an eyewitness to a murder. The eyewitness says, "I saw a Black man beat the guy to death before my eyes, and then he ran off laugh-

ing." Later, when chatting off camera, the eyewitness reveals to the reporter that he really couldn't see very clearly and couldn't be even be sure about the race of the suspect, but he "figured it was a good guess." The reporter has a responsibility *not* to use the sound bite now that he knows the eyewitness was being untruthful when he gave his account.

2.   A television reporter snags a terrific interview with another man who claims to be an eyewitness to a kidnapping. The interview is dramatic and poignant and makes "great television." After the camera is off, a bystander approaches the reporter and mentions that the person who was just interviewed is a notorious local "nut" who claims to witness to anything and everything, and has been in and out of mental institutions for years. The reporter is disappointed that he may lose the best element of his story: the compelling eyewitness interview. But, of course, he has an obligation to try to discover whether the eyewitness is, indeed, legitimate before he uses his sound bite on television. If the reporter finds the witness is of questionable credibility, the interview cannot ethically be used.

3.   A government Food and Drug Administration scientist makes fantastic claims to a radio reporter about pharmaceutical companies concealing safety information about profitable, but dangerous, drugs. Obviously, the reporter should seek out further sources and confirmation. But on a very basic level, he should ask: *Do I believe what this person is telling me? Do I have any reason not to believe it? What in his background (job history, experience) either adds to or subtracts from his credibility?* Sometimes it's impossible to know the ultimate truth about opposing claims on a given controversy. But you should reasonably believe people are telling you the truth when they is making such claims, or you could have trouble defending yourself ethically and legally for reporting or publishing the claim if its veracity is challenged.

Media Bias: Case in Point

There are many other ways in which news coverage can be improperly slanted. One is through the process of choosing which stories to cover and which to ignore. The best way to demonstrate the volatility of this powder keg is through a compelling example: the very different reporting on two separate murders. One involves and alleged *killer* who is gay; the other involves an alleged *victim* who was gay.

Matthew Shephard was a Wyoming college student who was murdered in 1998. He was gay and his murder drew a flurry of sympathetic national news coverage. Jesse Dirkhising was a 13-year-old Arkansas boy who suffocated to death after he was bound, gagged, and sodomized in 1999. His alleged killer was homosexual. But the trial wasn't covered by ABC, CBS, CNN, *The Washington Post*, or *The New York Times*, and *those companies were called upon to defend that decision.* Why the different treatment of what some saw as similar crimes?

On March 23, 2001, the *Washington Times* newspaper published a scathing critique of the media coverage decisions, arguing that the same networks and newspapers that devoted extensive coverage to the case in which the homosexual was the victim refused to do the same when homosexuals were the attackers, in Dirkhising's case.

> There were no nationally televised candlelight vigils for Jesse Dirkhising. No Hollywood celebrities mourned the passing of the 13-year-old Arkansas boy. *The New York Times* hasn't reported how Jesse died . . . (his) death has not caused powerful Washington activists to lobby for new federal laws to punish such crimes . . . By contrast, the Shepard murder made front-page news—and the cover of Time magazine—in October 1998. Sen. Edward M. Kennedy and Rep. Richard A. Gephardt were among the politicians who appeared with Hollywood stars like [lesbian] Ellen Degeneres at a candlelight vigil on Capitol Hill to mourn Mr. Shepard's death and demand new hate crimes laws to protect homosexuals.
>
> —*The Washington Times*, Robert Stacy McCain, March 23, 2001.

The television networks defended their coverage decisions in a variety of ways. A CBS News spokesman said, ". . .we have twenty-two minutes to fill on the *CBS Evening News*, and every day the producers. . . have to determine what stories make the broadcast and which don't. . . on the days when [the Dirkhising murder] story was unfolding, the overall editorial judgment was that it couldn't fit into the broadcast that day." Indeed, the trial took place during a heavy news period where many important national stories were competing for space: the stock market was falling, the economy threatened to nosedive, there were shootings at schools, and the devastating hoof and mouth disease threatened the U.S. market.

ABC News offered another reason for excluding coverage of the trial: that it didn't rise to the level of national significance. "It appears to be a local crime story that does not raise the kind of issues that would warrant our coverage," said an ABC News spokesman.

But a columnist for the liberal *New Republic* magazine joined in the criticism for the coverage decisions made by major media companies:

> This discrepancy isn't just real. It's staggering . . . The Shepard case was hyped for political reasons: to build support for inclusion of homosexuals in a federal hate-crimes law. The Dirkhising case was ignored for political reasons: squeamishness about reporting a story that could feed anti-gay prejudice, and the lack of any pending interest-group legislation to hang a story on.
>
> —Andrew Sullivan, April 2, 2001, *New Republic* magazine.

The truth is that both Dirkhising and Shepard suffered brutal, unjustifiable deaths. The decision by the national media to cover, or ignore, either story on a given day can be explained many different ways. The point to emphasize, once again, is that they were called upon to *defend* their choices. Any coverage decisions you make should come only after careful consideration of journalistic issues and should not be a result of either a liberal or a conservative or bias.

Nothing But the Truth

Ethical misconduct can cost journalists their careers and reputations. But what exactly is the recourse for someone who has been injured by a report that's been broadcast or published online? It's courts. Specifically, people may sue for **defamation**, which includes **libel** and **slander**, or they may sue for **invasion of privacy**.

The single most important thing you should know about defamation is that *truth is an absolute defense.* In other words, if what you reported can be proven factual, there are no legitimate grounds for a lawsuit. Privacy is a different matter. Even if what you write is absolutely true, you can still be successfully sued if what you reported is deemed to be an unfair invasion of privacy. Whether invasion of privacy or defamation is the charge, public figures have less protection under the law than do ordinary citizens. What constitutes a public figure? How is defamation defined? We'll look at some of the critical terms in this area of law and then explore some true cases in point.

Defamation

You're guilty of **defamation** in your broadcast or online report if you intentionally report something false about an ordinary person, the report is published or spoken, and it harms that person's reputation or good name.[13] **Libel** and **slander** are two forms of defamation, and both can apply to broadcast and online writing. The burden for a public official or public figure to win a defamation lawsuit is greater than that of a nonpublic person. The public figure must prove that the defamatory statement was published or spoken with malice.[14] *Truth is an absolute defense in all defamation cases.*

Malice

You're guilty of **defamation with malice** against a public person if you knew the information was false, or if you didn't make reasonable attempts to find out whether it was true or false.[15] It's why, beyond the obvious ethical reasons, you must always do your best to determine that what you report, and even what interview subjects say in your report about someone else, is true. If you don't, you could be guilty of defamation *for reckless disregard for the truth.* In any case, *truth is an absolute defense.*

Libel

Libel is the form of defamation that traditionally applies to information published in print, such as newspapers, magazines, or online. However, it's also been found to apply to television and radio broadcasts that "publish" in a different sense: over the airwaves. *Truth is an absolute defense.*

Slander

Slander is the form of defamation that traditionally applies to the spoken word, such as in broadcast reports. Often, someone complaining of defamation in a broadcast or online report will sue for both libel and slander. *Truth is an absolute defense.*

Harm or Injury

Generally, people claiming to be defamed must prove they have been **harmed** or **injured.** That can be a very subjective determination. Harm has been described as negatively affecting a person's reputation; tending to hold that person up to ridicule, contempt, shame, or disgrace; degrading a person in the opinion of others; making someone an object of reproach or diminishing respectability; changing someone's position in society for the worse; dishonoring or discrediting a person the eyes of the public or acquaintances; causing someone to be shunned or avoided; or charging that someone has violated their public duty as a public officer.[16]

Public Figure

Exactly who is considered a **public figure** and therefore must meet the higher burden of showing that a false report was malicious when suing for defamation, libel, or slander? It can be anyone who is either famous or infamous: athletes, artists, business people, politicians, community leaders, or others who have assumed roles of special prominence in society because of who they are or what they've done, whether good or bad. Often, public figures have thrust themselves into the spotlight of conflict or controversy to influence the outcome. In some cases, people have become public figures through no choice of their own. It's important to note that even if people are deemed public figures involving one issue or one aspect of their life, *they are not necessarily considered a public figure for all aspects of their life and for all time.* People who are temporarily in the spotlight, such as the victim of an infamous crime, could arguably be considered private persons when the spotlight fades.

The following table compares defamation of public and private figures:

Elements of Defamation (Libel or Slander)

Ordinary, Nonpublic Person Must Prove:	*Public Official/Public Figure Must Prove:*
Report is false.	Same
Report is communicated (published or spoken).	Same
Result is injury to reputation or good name.	Same
(No malice requirement)	Report is made with malice, and reckless disregard for the truth.
Truth is an absolute defense.	Same

The Case of the Forged Documents

In 1997, CBS News' *60 Minutes* aired a report about documents that supposedly described unsavory activities by John F. Kennedy, others in the Kennedy family, and Marilyn Monroe. A man named Lawrence Cusack was circulating the documents as authentic. *60 Minutes* found they were phony and suggested it was Cusack who forged them. After the report, Cusack sued for defamation and so did investors who had purchased the documents claiming that the CBS report hurt their value.

As Cusack's defamation case dragged on, he was at the same time prosecuted in federal court for fraud. In his criminal case, Cusack was convicted of fraud for perpetuating the hoax and circulating the unauthentic documents. His sentence was more than nine years in prison, plus a demand to pay $7 million in restitution to the investors he'd cheated.

The judge hearing Cusack's civil defamation suit then threw out his complaint, saying that the fraud conviction prevented Cusack from arguing that the documents were genuine. The judge also found that *60 Minutes* had *not* been "grossly irresponsible," and that the program discussed valid matters of public concern. It helped that *60 Minutes* had gone to great lengths to determine the truth, even consulting handwriting experts who concluded that the papers were fake.[17]

The Case of the Eye Surgery Fraud

While the CBS *60 Minutes* lawsuit was going on, ABC was defending a defamation suit of its own. In a segment on an eye clinic, *Prime Time Live* correspondent Sam Donaldson reported that clinic employees had "fixed" a diagnostic machine to make it seem as though elderly patients needed surgery when they actually didn't. The clinic, Desnick Eye Services, sued for defamation. Interestingly, Desnick Eye Services was deemed to be a public figure. Therefore, it would have to prove not only that *Prime Time Live*'s report was false, but also that it was made with malice—reckless disregard for the truth.

In the end, a judge dismissed the suit against ABC, finding that the statement about employees tampering with the diagnostic machine couldn't have hurt the clinic's reputation any more than other statements in the segment, to which the clinic did not object. The judge also said there was no "actual malice" on ABC's part, and that Desnick Eye Services offered no proof that the statement in question was false or that ABC had reason to suspect it was false and deliberately closed its eyes to the truth. [18]

The Case of Internet Libel

In 1997, a groundbreaking lawsuit was filed against maverick Internet publisher, Matt Drudge. It was groundbreaking because it raised many legal issues about Internet journalism for the first time.

On August 10, 1997, Drudge published a story on his Web site accusing a former Clinton aide, Sidney Blumenthal, of abusing his wife and covering it up. The story created quite a splash and was repeated (diffused) in political and media circles around the nation. Drudge refused to name his sources and made the mistake of *not* calling Blumenthal for comment. Drudge simply said he didn't know how to reach Blumenthal, which is an excuse that could be seen as "reckless disregard for the truth."

Soon after the publication, Drudge apparently questioned his own information, telling one reporter that he believed someone was "using him" to attack Blumenthal, and he quickly issued a new statement on his Web site: "I am issuing a retraction of my information regarding Sidney Blumenthal that appeared in the DRUDGE REPORT on August 11, 1997."

Sidney Blumenthal was not satisfied with the retraction and sued Drudge for $30 million in federal court. He also sued America Online (AOL), which carried Drudge's column. AOL argued that it was not acting as a publisher in this case because it neither supervised nor edited Drudge's column; it simply reprinted it. The judge agreed and released AOL from liability.

Four years after the case was launched, Blumenthal dropped the suit against Drudge and even agreed to pay some expenses to Drudge's attorney for a cancelled deposition. What are the lessons learned? Blumenthal said that suing was the right thing to do to make it clear that Drudge's story was false and malicious, but it cost him tens of thousands of dollars in legal fees. The accused libelist, Matt Drudge, said simply "the First Amendment protects mistakes. Surely Sidney Blumenthal can understand that. The great thing about this medium I'm working in is that you can fix things fast."

Privacy: Don't Be Cruel

Now onto another touchy legal issue: privacy. In its most elemental form, *privacy* is defined as "an individual's right to be left alone."

Not long before his death on August 16, 1977, the great rock-and-roll star, Elvis Presley, lamented he'd gladly give a million dollars for just a single day of peace and quiet. In his search to be left alone, he was known to arrange middle of the night visits to Liberty Land in Memphis, Tennessee, so he could stroll through the park by himself, eating popcorn and cotton candy, and enjoying the rides without being mobbed by fans. Elvis' desperate search for solitude demonstrates the value of privacy and how elusive it can be once it is lost. He was, of course, the consummate example of what we call a **public figure.** He spent much of his life seeking the limelight and, as such, was not legally entitled to much privacy. His every move was considered fair game to be reported upon, photographed, and scrutinized.

As we've discussed, it's not only singers and movie stars who fall into the category of public figures, but also elected and appointed officials, those who lead and organize movements, and other people who intentionally put themselves front and center on the stage of life. There are varying degrees of what's considered an acceptable invasion of their private affairs, but, in each case, *their* protection is limited by their undeniably public status. The fact that they've chosen life in the limelight suggests that they're willing to suffer the consequences of scrutiny of their personal lives.

In contrast to people who become public figures by choice, some people become **public figures by accident,** or even against their own will. A person who's accused of a crime, victims of crimes, witnesses to crimes, and relatives and associates of public figures all can unwittingly become public figures in the eyes of the law and lose much of their legal expectation of privacy.

Ordinary private citizens, on the other hand, are granted many more privacy protections than are public figures by choice or by accident.

As in defamation cases, it's possible for people to become **temporary public figures,** that is, people who are deemed public figures for one story or for a limited period of time. When the spotlight fades, and they do not seek it, they may again be considered ordinary, private citizens entitled to additional privacy protection.

To summarize, when it comes to decisions about privacy, the following table shows the four basic categories of people.

Privacy Categories

Types of Figures	Description
Voluntary public figures	**People who are voluntarily in the public eye,** such as elected officials, movie stars, and heads of organizations. The legal expectation of privacy is less for this category of people than for ordinary citizens because voluntary public figures have chosen to put themselves in the spotlight.
Involuntary or accidental public figures	**People who are involuntarily in the public eye,** such as victims of crimes or relatives of famous or infamous people. Those who are thrust into the spotlight against their will still have the right to some privacy, yet the law recognizes the possible newsworthiness of their involvement or mention in news stories.
Temporary public figures	**People who are public figures only for one story or purpose, or for a limited time,** then fade back into life as ordinary, private citizens with greater privacy protections.
Ordinary, private citizens	**People who remain private,** including most ordinary citizens. This category has the highest expectation of privacy.

Broadcast and online writers threaten the privacy of people on a daily basis. Some invasions of privacy are necessary and, as we discussed, legally protected in reporting the news. But the question to always consider is *where's the line between a person's privacy and the public's right to know?* What is legal is not necessarily what's ethical. From an ethical perspective, special consideration should be given before reporting private information, even about a public person.

Here are some things to ask yourself when faced with reporting private information about *anyone*, whether private citizen or public figure. There are no "right" or "wrong" answers; the questions should simply be considered to ensure your decisions are ethical and morally defensible.

Privacy Questions

- What category of person am I reporting on (public figure by choice, public figure by accident, or private citizen)?
- What's the purpose for which the information will be used? Is it legitimate and important?
- Does the public *need* to know, or merely *want* to know?
- Is invading an individual's privacy the only—or the least offensive way—to get the information?
- How can I minimize the harm done by my story?
- How would *I* feel if the story were being done about *me*?

You should not invade privacy except in cases of overriding public need (normally, private information about private individuals needs to meet a defined public interest in order to be published) or to meet a vital public interest. Second, private information of a private individual should not be made public unless the need can be met in no other way than through publication of that private matter.

Invasion of Privacy

What constitutes an improper **invasion of privacy?** It can be the unwarranted appropriation or exploitation of one's personality; publicizing a person's private affairs that are of no legitimate public concern; improperly scrutinizing someone's private activities resulting in mental distress, suffering, shame, or humiliation. As in defamation cases, public figures have less protection under the law than do private persons, but there is an important difference. *Truth is not an absolute defense in matters of privacy invasion.*

The Case of the Clinton Conundrum

Never, perhaps, was there more debate and conflict among journalists about the private lives of public people than during the Clinton presidency from 1993 through 2000. Never before were the bounds between good journalism and bad taste so sorely tested.

The President of the United States is considered one of those consummate public officials for which nearly anything goes; very little about his life is considered off-limits to public and media scrutiny. However, when Arkansas Governor Bill Clinton ran for President, the media found itself constantly struggling with issues of privacy and ethics.

From the start, President Clinton invited scrutiny of matters that might otherwise have been left alone by addressing them openly during his first presidential campaign in 1992. With his wife by his side during an interview on CBS News' *60 Minutes*, the couple answered questions about Clinton's past affair with a woman named Gennifer Flowers. The conversation produced Hillary Clinton's now-infamous comment in which she defended her loyalty to her disloyal husband, "I'm not sitting here like some little woman standing by my man like Tammy Wynette." (Wynette was the voice behind a popular rendition of the country-western song, "Stand By Your Man.")

That, of course, was only the beginning of eight years during which the media got uncomfortably up-close and personal to the First Couple's private lives. Congress even impeached President Clinton, in part based on false information he gave under oath involving his private affairs.

Then there was President Clinton's relationship with a White House intern named Monica Lewinsky. There was talk of a semen-stained dress that supposedly provided concrete evidence of her affair with the President, which Mr. Clinton denied at the time. In an interview, editor-in-chief of the *Economist* magazine, Bill Emmott, talks about how he first reacted when one of his writers referenced the stained dress.

Emmott deleted the mention, deciding it was gratuitous and salacious. Later he reconsidered. As it turned out, the dress became a key piece of evidence in an official investigation. Of his original decision to omit mention of the dress, Emmott said, ". . . in hindsight, my decision was wrong, but I think that on the basis of the information at the time, it was correct. People were writing about the case with a sort of salacious delight under the cover of public interest in that it involved a president."[19]

Sharyl's Story

For me, a memorable assignment as a CBS News Washington correspondent was covering independent counsel Kenneth Starr's investigation of President Clinton, which culminated with a 445-page report to Congress in September of 1998. My job was to read pages from the report live in a Special Report with Dan Rather moments after the document was printed and handed to journalists. It was an awkward moment, to say the least.

Without the opportunity to prescreen the pages, I had to simultaneously read, translate and paraphrase, editing out some of the most salacious words and sentences involving intimate details of the President's illicit affair with Monica Lewinsky. My challenge was to report the essence of the investigative findings, without crossing into matters that were more salacious than substantive.

What, exactly, about the President's sexual relations with an intern deserved legitimate media attention? There are many ways journalists justified devoting so much coverage to the Clinton-Lewinsky affair. The President's critics—some of them members of his own party in Congress—asked whether the President was carrying on affairs of the heart while conducting the affairs of State. Did his private secrets influence his public performance? Did he perjure himself under oath when he denied an affair? Did his behavior reflect something about his character that voters had a right to know about? Was it grounds to question the legitimacy of his very presidency?

Yet all of us working on the story knew that there was more than a little prurient interest in the President's life behind closed doors. When polled, Americans reported being disgusted by the pursuit of President Clinton's private matters, yet, at the same time, they couldn't seem to get enough of it. That, alone, is never a legitimate reason for journalists to oblige.

The Case of the Private Attack

As mentioned earlier in this chapter when defining defamation and libel, it's much more difficult to justify invading the private lives of ordinary citizens who are not seeking the limelight. One case of interest involves news accounts of an attack against a female sheriff's deputy by a Human Immunodeficiency Virus (HIV)–positive jail inmate in Monterey, California. The deputy claimed she was ostracized after the media published her name and revealed she had received medical treatment for possible exposure to HIV from the attack. She sued *The Monterey County Herald*.

The Herald argued the case was newsworthy and that its story was based on testimony in open court and public records. The Superior Court Judge who heard the case agreed with the newspaper, dismissing the deputy's suit: "It is clear that the matter reported was of legitimate public concern. It involved a criminal offense on a police officer, the problems of HIV exposure, and issues of punishment," Judge Richard Silver stated in his ruling. He also concluded that state laws barring disclosure of HIV test results do not apply to the news media, "particularly where that information is obtained from public records or in the course of public judicial proceedings."[20] The judge also noted that the U.S. Supreme Court ruled that a Georgia television station could not be penalized for using a rape-murder victim's name, after obtaining it from public records.

However, it's very important to note that these legal rulings don't take into account the question of ethics. As broadcast and online journalists, we are obligated to ask these questions: Even if it was technically legal to invade these individual's privacy, was it ethically justifiable? Who would be harmed by the story? How could that harm be minimized? Wouldn't the story about the attack on the sheriff's deputy have had the same news value and impact if her name hadn't been disclosed? In fact, another newspaper, the *Salinas Californian*, reported the story, but chose *not* to disclose the deputy's name or the nature of her treatment.

The Case of Arthur Ashe: Forced Admission

The last privacy example we'll briefly explore involves a forced admission from former tennis champion Arthur Ashe.

In April 1992, *USA Today* was pursuing rumors that Ashe had Acquired Immune Deficiency Syndrome (AIDS). In response, Ashe hastily called a news conference to acknowledge that he did, indeed, have the deadly disease, and that it was the result of a blood transfusion. But the pursuit of the story, and Ashe's reluctant admission raised serious public debate about whether the public had the right to know such painful private information about this public figure.

The Society of Professional Journalists analyzed the case and found no black or white answers.

> It is not adequate to argue "newsworthiness" about a public figure without some supporting list of social benefits. For example, Ashe's case may confirm to some people for the first time that the disease is not solely a sex-and-drugs product, creating a very different example of a celebrity victim for audiences to observe . . . (Others) would argue that having AIDS is a private matter, and one should retain the choice over when and how it would be revealed . . . Whether the benefits outweigh the anguish is still the decision of the individual reporter or editor . . . (who) should publicly justify their action, explaining how and why they decided as they did.[21]

Once again, journalists were called upon to defend their decisions. At one time or another, you will be, too. Be sure you have thoughtful, legitimate answers ready before you're asked the tough questions.

Let Your Conscience and Code Be Your Guide

With so many ethical challenges facing us as professional broadcasters and online writers and reporters, you might find comfort in knowing that there are some resources we can turn to for guidance. First, there's a code of ethics developed by the Radio-Television News Directors Association (RTNDA). It's not legally binding, but serves an important purpose by setting standards against which conduct can be measured and evaluated.

These codes of ethics have many benefits. They help ensure that standards are set internally, by professionals in our field, rather than having either the courts or the legislatures intrude and assume this responsibility. They provide ideal standards to help us evaluate our own value and performance as an industry and as individual writers and reporters.[22] They offer reasonable standards and guidelines that help the public discuss, debate, and measure the media's performance. They can protect us from unrealistic expectations, demands, and criticisms and can help the public express reasonable demands and criticism of the media when it is warranted.[23] Finally, they provide a reference point that can be used to protect us from internal pressures that might otherwise threaten to force us to violate our own consciences.

The following excerpts are from the code of ethics developed by the RTNDA.

RTNDA Code of Broadcast News Ethics

Strive to present the source of nature of broadcast news material in a way that is balanced, accurate, and fair. Evaluate information solely on its merits as news, rejecting sensationalism or misleading emphasis in any form. Guard against using audio or video material in any way that deceives the audience. Do not mislead the public by presenting as spontaneous news any material that is staged or rehearsed. Identify people by race, creed, nationality, or prior status only when it is relevant. Clearly label opinion and commentary.

Avoid conflicts of interest, real or perceived. Decline gifts or favors that would influence or appear to influence judgment.

Respect the dignity, privacy, and well-being of people.

Recognize the need to protect confidential sources. Promise confidentiality only with the intention of keeping that promise.

Respect everyone's right to a fair trial.

Broadcast the private transmissions of other broadcasters only with permission.

Actively encourage observance of this code by all journalists.

Decoding the Code

Now, onto decoding some of the elements within the RTNDA Code of Ethics.

First is "getting it right." **Accuracy** is always of paramount concern to any journalist. But the RTNDA code gives equal emphasis to the need for **balance, fairness, and impartiality.** It's not enough that reporting be accurate alone. The following are examples of fairness considerations.

Examples of Fairness

1. Naming a rape victim in a public news report certainly is not inaccurate, but neither is it fair to the victim who could be embarrassed or hurt by such a disclosure.

2. You're writing about somebody accused of serious wrongdoing. You place one telephone call, can't reach the person who is accused, and write in your story that he "couldn't be reached for comment." That technically may pass the accuracy test, but it sure doesn't pass the fairness test. You didn't make enough of a legitimate effort to reach the person who is about to be the subject of an unflattering portrayal in a story.

It's also your responsibility to **avoid sensationalism.** Sensationalism in a very basic sense is the appeal to morbid curiosity, ridicule, and/or voyeurism. The following examples demonstrate sensationalism.

Examples of Sensationalism

1. Showing videotape of a gory car accident on the television news not because it's newsworthy, but because a certain segment of viewers may be attracted to the sight of "blood and guts."

2. Showing suggestive videotape of a stripper to tease an upcoming "investigative" report on organized crime.

3. Showing any videotape or telling any story simply for its shock value.

So how do we **evaluate information solely on its merits as news?** The answer is in the eyes of the beholder. What is legitimate "news" differs from person to person and from audience to audience. What may be of high news value to one individual could be low to another. In making this subjective determination, you must be mindful and sensitive to the interests of your specific audience. The following is an example of news value considerations.

Example of News Value

In a news market where the demographic balance of your audience is higher than age 65, you would probably not load up a newscast with high-tech references and stories. You'd be more inclined to pay special attention to stories that have to do with health care and stories that hit viewers in the pocketbook. On the other hand, if you're writing for a Web site, you already know you're dealing with an audience that is probably more technically oriented than average, so there's no need to shy away from stories about computers, software, and technical innovations.

You must always truthfully and accurately reflect what happened at an event. You wouldn't want to cover a mostly peaceful protest by showing only video of a small group of violent demonstrators, as if the entire protest had been violent. Further, you should take great care to ensure that videotape and audiotape of interviews and events is never edited out of context, but instead accurately reflects the nature of the interview or event. It's critical for you to **avoid staging:** the act of actually setting up something that is to be videotaped or recorded in a way that it did not occur naturally. The following are examples of staging.

Examples of Staging

1. An Internet photographer arrives at a protest after it's over and asks the demonstrators to regather and march around so he can get the picture he missed. That is staging, and it should never be done.

2. There's the infamous case of a network television news magazine that was doing a report on allegedly dangerous trucks, but, when the truck tests they recorded didn't turn out the way the reporter and producer wanted, they took part in having an explosive placed on a test vehicle to create a fireball upon impact, which they recorded and reported without making any mention of the explosive device. That, too, is staging in the extreme.

Staging is also more subtle acts of placing people and/or moving objects around so that it suits your picture visually, but doesn't represent what you actually found when you arrived at the scene.

 ETHICS NOTE: It is *not* staging to simply move or to adjust an object that's blocking a camera shot, as long as doing so doesn't affect the substance of the story; it's okay to arrange people for an interview so that they'll fit in the camera's view. Staging refers to substantive changes that force, urge, direct, or even subtly encourage somebody to do something they wouldn't ordinarily do, or would not have done on their own without your suggestion.

Do not identify people's race, creed, nationality or prior status unless it's relevant. One instance in which you'll have to decide whether to make such identifications is in the case of a criminal suspect, as described in the following example.

Example of Identification

The race of a murder suspect, whether Black, Asian, or White, is typically not relevant. Mentioning a specific race only stands to feed into the perception of potential bias. On the other hand, race may be relevant under different circumstances. If police are looking for a murder suspect and putting out a detailed description so that the audience can identify that suspect, race may clearly be a significant factor. Second, if a crime is believed by reputable sources to have been racially motivated, race could legitimately be mentioned. An example would be a case of a group of White "skinheads" who target a Black victim.

As a journalist, you should generally **keep your opinions to yourself.** Likewise, opinions of others should always clearly be stated as such so that they are not confused with absolute, established fact. The following example describes a case in which opinion is considered.

Example of Opinion

If you're writing a story about a protest by environmentalists outside a factory, and you believe, or have been told by the factory owner, that the protesters represent only a small fringe group of extremists, you should *not* report: "Although these protesters claim to represent thousands of Americans, they, in fact, are extremist in nature and have very little support in the general community." However, if you independently substantiate that claim, if it's relevant to your story, and if you've given the protesters the opportunity to defend the claim, you could be justified in this type of statement: "The owners of the factory say that the protesters are merely a fringe group with very little backing in the general community."

The primary goal is avoiding errors in the first place. But when mistakes are made, you should be sure to acknowledge and **correct or "retract" the errors** in a fashion that is as public as the way they were originally reported.

You must **avoid real or perceived conflicts of interest.** A great deal of people are willing to give you gifts, favors, entertainment tickets, or other special offers because of the type of job that you have and your potential to influence public opinion. Accepting such offers or payola could put you in the uncomfortable position of feeling as though you "owe" that person something in return, whether it's a favorable mention in a news story or a positive interpretation of an issue that person is concerned with. Even if you don't feel as though you owe that person something in return, merely taking such gifts can create the appearance that you do and make your future conduct appear suspect when scrutinized by your peers and superiors. It's just as important to avoid the *perception* of conflict as it is to avoid *real* conflict.

Respect everyone's **right to a fair trial.** No matter how guilty a person may appear to be, that person is entitled to a fair trial to determine innocence or guilt. Whether reporting on an arrest or a trial itself, even when the facts seem obvious, many factors could play into a person's ultimate innocence or guilt in the eyes of a judge, jury, and the law. There are endless cases in which a person has been pinpointed as "guilty" by their relatives, police, and prosecutors, but turned out to be entirely innocent. Remember police have been known to manufacture or destroy evidence, witnesses have lied, and conclusions that seem obvious at one point have turned out to be entirely different when more information is revealed. The following example shows how misinformation was reported (and diffused) because of presumed guilt.

Example of Presumed Guilt

In Tampa, Florida, in the 1980s, police rushed to investigate a complaint about a little boy who was allegedly being neglected or even abused. Authorities were horrified by what they'd found: an elementary school aged child who appeared to weigh half what he should and could neither walk or talk! They leaked news of the case to the local media and invited cameras to come and take pictures of the poor child to expose the abuse. Police even spoke on the record about the case saying it was one of the most extreme cases of abuse they'd ever seen. A young child—they concluded—was obviously being starved by his mother and was so neglected that he'd never been taught so much as how to speak or walk. Reporters, equally horrified by the child's plight, reported the news. But within a few hours, the whole story had to be retracted. It turned out upon further investigation that the boy had a muscular disease that accounted for his slight weight and the fact that he could neither walk nor talk. He had been wheelchair bound (but had somehow crawled out of his wheelchair), and his mother, by all reports, was actually very devoted to her handicapped son. What had been reported by police—what seemed so obvious to all of the reporters—turned out to be entirely untrue when the true facts came to light.

CBS News Standards

Many individual news organizations have adopted their own ethics guidelines or standards tailored to the challenges of their organizations. The guidance is often extraordinarily specific and detailed. Before you write your first news story at a radio station, television station, or online, you should have already read a copy of your organization's ethics guidelines, if they exist.

Here's a sampling of highlights from the most recent standards adopted by the CBS News network:

Excerpts from CBS News Standards

CBS News employees should not, even in their personal lives, take any side in a controversial issue and should not actively participate in politics and political campaigns.

Staging is prohibited.

Interviews must be unrehearsed; questions may not be submitted to the interview subject in advance. Words or ideas must not be put in a subject's mouth or mind. Someone who grants an interview may not later prohibit it from being broadcast.

Avoid victim or next-of-kin interviews except when they are essential to shed light on what happened. Exercise restraint and decorum in such interviews. Do not stick a microphone or camera in the face of a victim or next-of-kin if prior permission hasn't been granted and do not interview a person who appears to be in a state of shock.

Rarely, withholding your identity is the only way to adequately report an investigative story. In such cases, it must be approved in advance by senior management after consultation with the CBS law department.

Federal and state laws governing hidden cameras and recordings are varied and complex. Before any secret recordings are made, the CBS Law Department and CBS News management must be consulted and grant approval. Among the legal questions involved are: Is the location public, semi-public or private, or is it not clear? Is there an expectation of privacy? Does the applicable law require consent of all parties to the recording? Is the material for broadcast or for note-taking? (Use of hidden cameras is permissible in public or semi-public places, such as streets, public park and buildings, restaurants and stores but may only record what would reasonably be seen by others in such locations.)

On the Internet, e-mail may be used as evidence in investigative reporting in much the same way that we use written correspondence unless if was intercepted or obtained illegally.

When covering demonstrations or riots, when the presence of our cameras is sustaining the event, we should stop our coverage and withdraw, regardless of what other news organizations do.

When government officials in any nation attempt to restrict our coverage, it is CBS News policy to protest respectfully but firmly to the highest appropriate authority. If unsuccessful, you should follow the instructions of the government officials rather than subject yourself to arrest or worse, then notify the nearest CBS authorities. The restrictions imposed upon us should always be part of our report.

In rare cases, such as troop deployments or law enforcement actions, if we are asked to withhold or delay broadcast of material or information, such request must be referred immediately to the president of CBS News.

Editing should reflect fairly, honestly and without distortion what was seen and heard by our reporters, cameras and microphones. Even a short sound bite should accurately reflect the spirit of the entire interview.

Supers or fonts should identify the interviewee's relevance to the story. For instance, in identifying a political pollster who has long been associated with one political party, the super should not just say "political pollster," but "Democratic pollster." When identifying Jane Doe of Widgets Corp., it might be clearer to identify her as Jane Doe, "chief engineer" or "assembly-line worker," than to name the company.

The use of music in hard news reports can rarely be justified unless the music itself is part of the event, as in parades, ceremonies and reports involving music.

Editorializing (advocating a course of action) is not allowed, but news analysis and commentary are permitted, provided such material is properly identified and not confused with straight news reporting.

To ensure that the audience does not confuse live with taped coverage, we should never give the impression that a news event described on tape is, in fact, taking place at the time of the broadcast. In switching between a live anchor and a recorded report, there should be no impression that it is all "live." For instance, it would be wrong to simulate a live situation by having correspondent John Doe sign off in a recorded story by saying, "Now back to you, Sam,"or to have the live anchor say, "Thanks, John" to a previously recorded report.

In cases of libel, the press can be held liable for reporting allegations made by one person against another, even if the allegations are accurately reported and clearly attributed to the source. Care should be taken to ascertain the reliability of the source and, where possible, to corroborate the charges. Allegations contained in filed legal documents or set out in official documents, proceedings or meetings, may generally be reported without fear of libel action, as long as the report is accurate and fair, and discloses the source and context of the allegations. A journalist is in a vulnerable position when the sources of allegations against a person or company are confidential ones, to whom anonymity has been promised. Such allegations should generally not be broadcast without corroboration by at least one non-confidential source.

It is CBS News policy not to reveal the identity of sources to whom we have pledged confidentiality and to resist in court subpoenas seeking such disclosure. Strict adherence to this policy is essential to maintain the trust of potential news sources. However, if a CBS News employee is threatened with legal action and/or jail for refusal to disclose a source, he has the right to decide to reveal his sources since his personal liberty may be at stake, and CBS cannot order him to risk imprisonment or other punishment. Employees who fight to avoid naming sources will have the full support of CBS News and will be provided counsel from CBS News and the CBS Law Department.

Breaking the Code

Now that you have a good idea of the ethical guidelines by which broadcast and on-line news writers should operate, you might find it interesting to explore the consequences of breaking the code. One of the most infamous cases involves one of the most prestigious newspapers and a Pulitzer Prize winning reporter, who seems to have blatantly disregarded some of the most basic ethical guidelines.

In 1980, a twenty-six-year-old *Washington Post* feature writer authored a compelling, poignant,and tragic series about a little eight-year-old boy she called "Jimmy."

Jimmy, according to Cooke's articles, was a third-generation heroin addict, who lived in a dismal southeast Washington neighborhood with his mother, an ex-prostitute, and her lover. Later Cooke reported that the lover was a dope dealer, responsible for Jimmy's heroin addiction. The stories even described a disturbingly detailed scene of the little boy getting his fix of heroin.

The horror of what was written in the article so disturbed the public and city officials that Washington's police chief demanded to know Jimmy's true identity so that he could be helped. Cooke refused to reveal the name, the police chief threatened to subpoena Cooke to get the information, and the Mayor ordered a search for a child matching Jimmy's description. All the while, Cooke told her editors that Jimmy's mother's lover had threatened to kill her if their identities became known, so she had to keep them secret. Her editors, including the Pulitzer Prize winning Watergate journalist, Bob Woodward, stood by her. Jimmy was never found. Cooke won the Pulitzer prize for the series. That's when her uncanny deception began to surface. Cooke's biographical information was published nationwide, revealing discrepancies in her background. *The Washington Post* investigated and discovered that facts on Cooke's resume didn't check out. What's worse was that Cooke soon confessed that Jimmy didn't exist. She said that she fabricated the character as a composite of young addicts whom she had heard about from social workers. The events her story described had never taken place.

Cooke was forced to resign and *The Washington Post* returned the Pulitzer Prize.[24]

This chapter only scratches the proverbial surface of the infinite ethical and legal issues, situations, and dilemmas you'll face when writing and reporting broadcast and Internet news. The point is to make sure you let your conscience be your guide in this important profession that gives you the ability to improve, change, and destroy lives. Now, your conscience has some valuable food for thought.

Web sites

For more information, check out the following Web sites:

www.ldrc.com/LDRC_Info/libelfaqs.html
Libel Defense Resource Center

www.cyberlibel.com/repman.html
A defamation checklist for politicians

usinfo.state.gov/usa/infousa/media/unfetter/press08.htm
U.S. Information Agency (federal government); libel law in the United States

www.presswise.org.uk/Plagiarism.htm
International policies on plagiarism from Presswise Trust, a UK-based media ethics charity

law.about.com/cs/defamationlaw/
International stories of libel and defamation including Internet cases from the Consumer Project on Technology

www.fair.org/
Fairness and accuracy in reporting discussions from a watchdog group that critiques the media

www.ou.edu/class/standers/3633/ethics.html
Ethics questions to consider from Dr. Steve Anderson at the University of Oklahoma

www.rtnda.org/trades/writing6.shtml
Ethics discussion regarding use of videotape

Quick Review of Terms

- **The Day Rule:** The theory that knowledge in three basic areas—context, philosophical foundation, and critical thinking—can equip people to carry out moral reasoning.
- **Defamation:** Intentionally reporting something false and harmful about an ordinary person. Truth is always an absolute defense in defamation cases.
- **Invasion of privacy:** Publicizing private affairs that are of no legitimate public concern resulting in suffering, shame, or humiliation.
- **Libel:** The form of defamation that traditionally applies to print, but also may apply to broadcast material.
- **Media bias:** The concept that journalists unfairly shape coverage to advance their own particular viewpoints.
- **Payola:** The unethical practice of taking anything of value from people who want to influence what's being reported.
- **Plagiarism:** The unethical act of copying someone else's writings or ideas and passing them off as your own work.
- **Public figure:** Anyone who is famous, infamous, or has assumed roles of special prominence because of who they are or what they've done.
- **Slander:** The form of defamation that traditionally applies to spoken word, including broadcast reports.

Review Questions

1. To what do the three areas of The Day Rule—context, philosophical foundations, and critical thinking—refer?
2. What's the basic lesson behind "The Fake Hit of Mr. Black"?
3. Why are the Fairness Doctrine and the Equal Time Provisions largely not applicable to broadcast news writing?
4. What are some unintentional ways the media can display bias?
5. How does the presence of malice apply to defamation cases?

6. Describe how various types of public and private figures pertain to defamation and privacy law?

7. How is "harm" measured in defamation and privacy cases?

8. What's the point of having a professional codes of ethics or ethical standards?

Summary

This chapter examined the concept of moral and ethical practices and applied them to real-life situations. Some matters of ethical conduct are regulated by the law, specifically by defamation and privacy laws. These laws afford the greatest protection to ordinary private citizens and more limited protection to public officials. On other matters, such as staging and bias, there are standards and codes of ethics to which we can turn. Following their guidelines helps protect journalists, the companies for which they work, and members of the public. However, no hard and fast rules will apply to every situation. It's up to individuals to consider the implications of their writing and reporting. The consequences of failing to do so are potential harm to members of the public, to one's own reputation, and to the company for which an individual works, and could lead to costly and damaging lawsuits.

Notes

1. Wimmer, Roger D. and Joseph R. Dominick. *Mass Media Research, An Introduction*, 6th ed. (Belmont, CA: Wadsworth Publishing, 1999), 66, 67.
2. Day, Louis A. *Ethics in Media Communications: Cases and Controversies.* (Belmont, California: Wadsworth Publishing Company, 1991), 49.
3. Day, 55.
4. Day, 56.
5. Braswell, Janet, "Officials Condemn Paper's Hoax Decision," *The Hattiesburg American*, December 15, 1984, sec. A, p. 12
6. Braswell, Janet, "Hoax to Stop Hit," *The Hattiesburg American*, December 15, 1984, sec. A, p. 1
7. Braswell, Janet, "Hoax to Stop Hit," *The Hattiesburg American*, December 15, 1984, sec. A, p. 1
8. Braswell, "Officials Condemn Paper's Hoax Decision," *The Hattiesburg American*, December 15, 1984, sec. A, p. 1
9. Braswell, Janet, "Authorities Stand by Hoax Decision," *The Hattiesburg American*, December 14, 1984, sec A, p. 12
10. Braswell, Janet "Hoax to Stop Hit," *The Hattiesburg American*, December 15, 1984, sec. A, p. 1
11. *O'Rourke v. RKO Radio Pictures*, D.C.Mass., 44 F.Supp.480, 482, 483.
12. Copyright 1987 Reed Publishing USA, *Broadcasting*, August 10, 1987, Vol. 113; Pg. 59.
13. *Black's Law Dictionary*, 6th ed., s.v. p. 417.
14. *New York Times Co. v. Sullivan*, 376 U.S. 254, 84 S. Ct. 710, 11 L.Ed.2d 686.
15. *Black's Law Dictionary*, 6th ed., s.v. p. 417.
16. *Black's Law Dictionary*, 6th ed., s.v. p. 1388.
17. Judge Kapnick, "Defamation Suit Arising from *60 Minutes* Broadcast Dismissed for Plaintiff's Conviction; Cusack v. *60 Minutes* Division of CBS, Inc." *New York Law Journal*, Monday, July 2, 2001, p. 17

18. *Desnick v. American Broadcasting Companies, Inc.*, 233 F.3d 514, 2000 U.S.App. LEXIS 27038 (7th Cir. 2000).
19. Kramer, G. "All that's Fit to Print—Journalism in a Globalized World." *Harvard International Review* 23, no. 2 (2001): 76–79
20. Superior Court Judge Richard Silver, March 14, 1999, Monterey, California.
21. Black, Jay, Bob Steele, & Ralph Barney. *Doing Ethics in Journalism: A Handbook with Call Studies.* (Boston: Allyn & Bacon, 1993), 171.
22. Gordon, A. D., & Kittross, J. M. *Controversies in media* ethics (2nd ed.). (New York: Longman, 1999), 62
23. Gordon and Kittross, 62
24. Day, 20

11

Careers

When you graduate from college, you may have the education you need to help scratch the insatiable itch to become a broadcast or Internet news journalist. But how do you get your foot in the door? What career options are out there? How do you get started looking for a job? What will it pay? This chapter touches on some of the exciting possibilities.

Getting the Experience

The arena of broadcast and Internet news is so competitive that it's difficult to become gainfully employed without having some measure of experience. That concept leads to a circular question: How do you get experience if no one will hire you unless you have experience? Fortunately, there are some practical answers.

Some of you are lucky enough to be attending a college or university that has experience opportunities **on campus.** Students in the College of Journalism and Communications at the University of Florida, for example, actually run two commercial radio stations and produce daily, competitive television newscasts that are heard and seen beyond campus grounds. At Mississippi State University, students research, write, and deliver live daily newscasts at the campus radio station that reaches three counties. Because working at the stations is often a class requirement at those universities, graduating seniors often leave college with a resume tape in hand, reflecting the kind of experience prospective employers are looking for.

Another obvious way to get experience is through professional **internships.** Most colleges will help you investigate and apply for internships, which are available at many local radio and television stations, national television and radio networks, and Internet outlets across the country. The vast majority of such internships are unpaid because so many people are vying for them. Most students intern during the summer before their junior or senior year of college. A growing number of companies also offer intern opportunities in fall and spring. Such off-peak internships may be somewhat easier to get.

Making the Most of Your Internship

Getting an internship is one challenge; making sure it serves your needs is quite another. How can you cross over from being someone who simply answers telephones or conducts mundane "gofer" tasks to a valued worker who is assigned serious responsibilities and can get hands-on experience?

In most newsrooms, you'll discover that, after you prove you're smart, interested, and willing to work hard, a lot of people will be eager to help you out. Here are a few tips for making the most of your internship.

Define goals: Schedule a meeting with the news director or other person of influence in the newsroom before the internship actually begins so that goals are spelled out: yours *and* theirs. Discuss specific ways to accomplish both. For example, you may decide that two of your goals in an internship at a television station are to learn how to write stories and to actually shadow—follow along with—reporters when they go out on interviews. Ask how and when you may be able to do these things. Convey that you're willing to work extra time beyond your normally scheduled hours to get the opportunities you're asking for; it'll be worth it. Plus, such displays of devotion and eagerness will get noticed by people who may be in a position to provide you with job recommendations or help you find work down the road.

Prove yourself first: The first impressions you make during an internship will be enduring. Approach any task you're given with enthusiasm and dedication, no matter how unexciting it may seem. If you give short shrift to such jobs as answering the telephone efficiently and politely, or if you duck and hide when you think someone is looking for you to fix a paper jam in the copy machine, nobody will be eager to help you take on more responsibility.

Turn mundane tasks into more: Perform even the most mundane tasks with eagerness and efficiency. That way, both you and your employer will get more out of the experience. Prove you're the type of worker who's proactive, has ideas, and follows through. A simple example is if somebody asks you to scan and e-mail documents to a certain location, you should accomplish the task, make sure the original documents are reassembled in the proper order, and return them to the person who asked you to do the job with a notation telling him/her what time the fax went through. Once, an intern really impressed me by telling me that she had, on her own, followed up on my request for her to fax material by calling the recipient to confirm that he actually received the material.

Volunteer for extra tasks and hours: Let your supervisor and coworkers know that you're interested in helping out on your own time, even if it means coming in at night or on weekends. At a television station, you can offer yourself up to go out on shoots with photographers when no reporters are available. At a radio station, you can offer to research stories or help answer the phones on a shift when help is needed. If you're interning for a Web site, offer to monitor what other Web sites are posting to help ensure your company remains competitive.

Be persistent, not pushy: Most newsrooms are constantly bustling with activity. As a result, your requests for help on certain issues, or promises made about what you'll be allowed to do may be overlooked or forgotten. Practice patience and persistence. Approach people with gentle reminders when they seem to be less busy, not during the frenzy right before a newscast.

Don't be negative or critical: You may hear employees make negative or critical remarks about each other, their newscasts, or even the company for which they work, but it's bad form for an intern to join in. Interns who attempt to demonstrate their intelligence and confidence by providing harsh critiques of newscasts, reporters, anchors, and writers risk coming off as brash and uninformed. It's one surefire way to guarantee nobody will want to help you.

Volunteering

Besides getting experience on campus and through internships, you can also seek out opportunities by applying for low-level paid or **volunteer positions** at broadcast and Internet companies. Why should you stoop to mundane work for little or no salary? Because it will allow you a wealth of opportunity, including the chance to meet connected and experienced people, to ask questions, to learn about the profession, and to become familiar with the professional environment.

Beginning the quest for such an opportunity is as simple as identifying companies in the area where you live and contacting the news director or other appropriate manager to volunteer your time and effort, or to ask how to apply for paid entry-level positions. Explain that you're a broadcast or Internet journalism student looking to get some exposure to a real working environment. Offer to do most anything, even if it means cleaning up the newsroom or getting coffee. Ask for the chance to come in on weekends and observe a newscast as it's being is designed and executed.

If you impress the right people, you might eventually position yourself to be able to help write copy and even to practice reading it on the set. You could get the chance to go along as a story is being covered from start to finish and to record and write your own version, which could become part of your resume tape. Granted, the material won't have actually aired—you'd have to make that clear in any job application—but it will give prospective employers a hint of your potential, as well as a glimpse into important characteristics such as how well you convey a story, how you write, how you sound, and, for television, how you present yourself on camera.

Career Choices

The number of possible jobs is infinite, and, with the expansion of the Internet, the range is growing broader by the day. Here are some basic examples of typical job opportunities with brief descriptions of how each position may involve an element of writing.

In radio news, positions can include the following:

★ **Anchor:** Makes beat calls for possible actualities and/or information for stories, researches news topics, write and revises news copy, generates story ideas, and often makes decisions on which stories and actualities will be aired.
★ **Reporter or correspondent:** Gathers, researches and presents the news story on the air; generates story ideas; and often writes in the field where the story is delivered.
★ **News director:** Oversees news operation, may also generate story ideas, research news topics, revise and write stories, anchor newscasts, and direct which stories will air on a newscast.

In television news, positions can include the following:

★ **Anchor:** Makes changes to final scripts before reading them on air. Generates story ideas. Often writes some original scripts and is involved in newsgathering, reporting, and producing.
★ **Reporter or correspondent:** Generates story ideas, gathers and researches a topic from start to finish, and then writes the script for that story and delivers it on air. Also delivers spontaneous "live" reports in the field, often with little or no preparation or formal writing.
★ **Executive producer (EP):** Oversees an entire newscast or group of newscasts. Has editorial control of content. May edit scripts and generate story ideas. Often includes writing responsibilities.
★ **Senior producer:** One step under the EP. Mostly found at networks and some large local markets. Controls a particular newscast or group of newscasts. May edit scripts and generate story ideas. Often includes some original writing and newsgathering responsibilities.
★ **Line producer:** Usually reports to a senior producer or EP. Responsible for organizing one specific newscast. Puts various stories into order on a rundown. Times newscast down to the second. Assigns who writes which stories in the lineup. Decides how long each story or script should be. May include writing, newsgathering, and generating story ideas.
★ **Field producer:** Performs various tasks that can include organizing a shoot for a reporter or anchor. May conduct research, generate story ideas, assist reporter

or anchor with writing responsibilities, and have possible newsgathering duties. This position exists mostly at networks and some large markets.

★ **Associate producer or assistant producer (AP):** Performs various tasks designed usually to help the line producer or EP. Can include writing, researching, newsgathering, and booking (finding and arranging) interviews or guests for a live broadcast. May generate story ideas.

★ **Broadcast associate (BA):** Performs various tasks that can include writing, researching, newsgathering, and booking guests. Another position mostly found at networks. Is entry level.

★ **Production assistant (PA):** Performs various tasks that can include writing, researching, newsgathering, and booking responsibilities. Mostly found at networks. Is entry level.

Internet news positions may include the following:

★ **Assistant or associate producer:** Mainly deals with technical issues, such as live Webcasts and the recording and streaming of audio and video clips. With experience, may do some writing. Is entry level.

★ **Producer:** First acts as reporter, gathering the facts from all sources. Then writes the piece. Next, searches, chooses, and processes any still photos for the story. Also works with the assistant and associate producers to add appropriate audio and video clips. Searches the site and the Internet for related stories. Writes a headline and bullet points.

Television producers oversee a live newscast in the control room

★ **Assignment editor:** Decides what stories are covered, who covers them, and how they're ranked in order of importance on the site.

The Job Hunt

The job hunt may be the single most intimidating task college students will face. Graduating seniors preparing to enter the work force often feel overwhelmed and simply want to know *where do I begin?* Contemplating the mere question has been known to throw some of the most promising jobseekers into stifling paralysis.

If you try, you can probably invent a number of creative methods and systems for searching out jobs. The most important step is taking some sort of action. It makes sense for college students to begin looking for work about three months before they graduate. You can do research and begin general inquiries long before that, but remember a news director is unlikely to agree to keep a competitive position open for months and months, awaiting your graduation.

Many industrious students are fortunate enough to have jobs waiting for them as soon as they walk off campus the last time. However, it's not unusual for graduates to be out of school for months before receiving a viable offer.

One good way to get started is by examining comprehensive lists of broadcast and Internet companies so you can get a look at all of the places you could apply to for a job. There are many excellent references that you can turn to. In the field of broadcasting, radio and television stations are typically listed in these references according to their **market size.**

What's market size? It's a ranking assigned to a geographical area on the basis of population. For example, the city of New York and its surrounding areas make up the nation's most populated and, therefore, largest market. It's assigned the market size number one. The Los Angeles area ranks second in population and has a market size of number two (second largest in the nation). Chicago is number three. The list goes all the way down to number 225 (the smallest market in the nation). Every single place in the United States is grouped into one of these 225 markets. Because population growth shifts over time, a given market size may grow or shrink from year to year. For example, the Tampa, Florida, area grew in market size from number seventeen (seventeenth largest in the nation) to number thirteen (thirteenth largest in the nation) in the mid-to-late 1980s. As a general rule, the larger the market means the more sophisticated the news operation, the more skill and experience that is required to work there, and the higher the salaries. Therefore, beginners usually apply for jobs in smaller markets and work their way up over time.

A couple of terms you may run across in reference books that list radio and television stations are **Areas of Dominant Influence** (ADIs) and **Demographic Marketing Areas** (DMAs). Think of them as just two more phrases that basically mean market size, but as determined by two different companies who may use slightly different population estimates and/or use different geographic groupings.

A systematic and effective way to begin a job hunt is by identifying markets where you'd like to work and then applying to the radio or television stations within those particular markets. Whether you manage to send out only two written resumes a week or ten resume tapes a week, *beginning the search is the most important step.* Create a file on computer or in a notebook that keeps track of the places where you've applied, the responses received, and any comments or follow-up necessary.

There's nothing wrong with applying for a job after you hear of an opening, but it's probably even better to go ahead and apply to places even when no job openings are posted. That way you'll have the chance to catch the eye of news directors before they've even announced a position is available. By the time jobs are actually posted, news directors have often already made up their minds as to who will fill them. Even if they haven't, they get flooded by so many tapes that it may be hard to get noticed among the clutter. So it's better to apply to places when they're not actively soliciting.

Later in this chapter, we recommend some specific resources for finding listings of radio stations, television stations, and Web sites.

Do I Need an Agent?

Students often want to know if they need an agent to help them look for a job and represent them in contract negotiations. The reality is, when you start out, you don't need an agent, and a good one probably won't consider taking you at this stage, anyway. Be wary of someone who solicits you straight out of college or early in your career. Industrious beginning journalists should be able to come up with jobs without an agent's help by sending tapes and resumes to targeted areas. You also don't need an agent just to make sure your employment contract or salary is reasonable.

For many, the best course of action is to hire a lawyer who charges an hourly fee to review your employment contract when you're offered a job. An attorney who has experience in media-related contracts or litigation is the best choice. The worst choice is some relative who happens to be an attorney and works cheap, but has never practiced media or contract law.

In a starting job of $30,000 a year for three years, you could pay an agent a ten percent fee totaling $9,000. In the process, you may have also bought yourself an ongoing obligation to the agent whether you're happy with that agent or whether you even need or use those services down the road. In contrast, an hourly rate attorney should only cost you a few hundred dollars up front. It may be difficult to make that kind of investment when you have so little money to begin with, but do the math yourself. Which is the wiser business decision: a $6,000 bill and lengthy commitment to an agent, or a few hundred dollars up front with the freedom to choose any agent down the road if you want to?

Typically, you shouldn't need an agent to ensure your resumes and tapes are getting read, seen, and heard by prospective employers. In fact, hiring an agent can exclude you from many potential jobs and here's why. When there's a job opening, no agent submits tapes of *all* of his clients for that opening. After all, what kind of credibility would an agent have with a news director if he submitted a hundred tapes for each opening? Instead, the agent sends only a few, and the odds are, for any given job, your tape won't be among them. At least if you send tapes to prospective employers on your own, you increase the chances they will be viewed.

The Climate

The profession you're considering has been described in many ways, including viper's pit, cutthroat, and lion's den. It can be all of those things. For any single job opening, there are dozens—even hundreds—perhaps thousands of candidates. That type of competitiveness tends to breed extraordinary aggressiveness.

This is a good point to mention two often-evoked sayings in the business. The first is "What goes around comes around." It means that any evil things you do unto others will surely come back to haunt you at some point. Broadcast or Internet journalists who stab others in the back to get ahead inevitably find themselves victim to the same type of viciousness later in their careers. What goes around comes around. The other saying along the same lines is "You meet the same people on the way down as you met on the way up." It's another truism that means people you step on during your climb to the top will have the chance to stomp on you on your way down.

Those sayings should be constant reminders as you attempt to ascend. There's nothing wrong with being aggressive, but you can be aggressive by working hard and being creative rather than stealing opportunities from others behind their backs or taking credit where it isn't due.

In the end, you may want to know what separates the wheat from the chaff. What guarantees you'll get ahead in your career and not become stuck in a job you don't like with the inability to move ahead? Here are some key points.

Hunting for Jobs Aggressively

One of the single-most important factors is obvious, but often overlooked: aggressive job hunting. Countless talented broadcast and Internet journalists wither on the vine at jobs they don't like because—though they spend a lot of time complaining—they can't seem to buckle down and get their resume together. It takes a kind of organization and discipline that many people lack. If you conduct aggressive job hunts that begin several months in advance, you'll automatically separate yourself from a host of candidates who just don't have the motivation.

The easiest way to be prepared for your *next* job hunt is to keep a current cache of your work on hand at all times. For television reporters and anchors, this means making sure you retain copies of your best stories and broadcasts *as you go*, even if it's a year before you'll actually be looking for a new job. If you don't do this, you'll be faced with the job hunt and will find you can't remember when your best stories were, or won't be able to locate the video recordings of them. Not to mention that it becomes embarrassingly obvious if you run around the newsroom right before your employment contract expires desperately looking for copies of your best work. Even worse, if you find yourself unexpectedly fired and escorted from the building (it *does* happen, even to the best!), you'll be out of luck if you haven't been keeping your own copies of your work.

For radio reporters and anchors, save recordings of your best material as you go. For Internet writers, keep records of your work by printing out screens and articles *and* retaining them in a personal computer file that's not controlled by your company.

Overcoming Discouragement

Another quality that will help you get ahead is the ability to overcome discouragement. Lots of discouraging things can happen during your career. It's often said, "You're only as good as your last story." It means you can create a dozen wonderful stories that your supervisors rave about, but make one mistake and you find you're in the doghouse. You may have prospective employers say you're not cut out for the business or worse. The easily discouraged should not pursue a career in broadcast or Internet journalism. The ones who stand the best chance of getting ahead are those who can displace feelings of discouragement with determination, not an angry or bitter determination, but a resolute one. Be determined to succeed. Be determined to become better at your job. Be determined to make each story its best.

Accepting Constructive Criticism

Another factor that's extremely important in succeeding is the ability to accept constructive criticism. You'll get plenty of it. You should welcome it. Consider it a chance to improve or free advice on how to become better at what you do. Not everyone who weighs in with an opinion on how you write, look, or sound will be correct, but they're worth listening to. When you notice a consistent theme, it's time to take a good hard look at making the recommended change. Remember that superiors who are launching criticism your way don't just want to hear you defensively explain why they're wrong; be grateful that they're actually giving you the chance to correct the problem before it keeps you from getting promoted, or maybe even gets you fired.

Soliciting Feedback

Last, you should solicit feedback at regular intervals. The industry isn't known as one where bosses provide good feedback to employees. In fact, the last saying we'll pass along is "You're great, you're great, you're great . . . you're fired!" It means that some employers will tell you you're terrific until the day they fire you. The best way to avoid such nasty surprises is to ask how you're doing along the way. Find out what you can do to improve and really *listen to the answers.*

Getting to the Nets

"The networks" are national radio, television, and Internet news networks such as ABC, CBS, NBC, CNN, and FOX. As competitive as the world of local news is, multiply that a hundred fold when it comes to the networks. Many set out aspiring to become part of network news. Few will get there.

The same qualities that will help you get ahead in local news increase your chances of making it to a network. However, you'll typically also need a generous dose of serious experience, plus a certain flair—whether it's writing style or on-air presentation—that makes you stand out away from the crowd. It's often subjective and indefinable or what the French call *je ne sais quoi*. If you don't have it from day one, it doesn't mean you can't develop it as you gain experience and confidence.

What's It Worth?

Typically, when it comes to radio and television, salaries in the larger markets are higher, but there are many exceptions. Because jobs in larger markets are so desirable, companies can sometimes get away with paying their employees less than some smaller markets. And stations located in places that are sunny and warm year round often pay less because, they "pay in sunshine." This means your salary isn't too great, but there's a nonmonetary benefit to living in that wonderful weather.

Newcomers to broadcast and Internet journalism constantly worry that they're somehow getting the shaft on their salaries, that other people working around them are making twice as much, or that they should have negotiated harder when they signed their first contract. However, an informal survey among news directors finds salaries don't vary as much within a company as you might suspect. Reporters who don't use agents *aren't* making thousands less than reporters who do. Predetermined budgets often dictate what salaries are offered for certain positions within a company. For example, suppose a weekend reporting job at a particular television station pays anywhere from $35,000 to $45,000. What determines whether you'll be able to get the low end or the high end of the range? It's factors such as previous experience and whether you have competitive offers from other television stations.

Sharyl's Story

Most employers will make a salary offer and do expect you to negotiate for a bit more. I've never accepted terms of a first offer, no matter how meager my quest for an upgrade. For example, in 1982, I was offered $11,500 to begin reporting, producing, and anchoring at a local television station in Ft. Pierce/West Palm Beach, Florida. Okay, it was an infinitesimal salary, but I was starting from a zero base, so I was thrilled. Still, I figured I should propose a counteroffer. I held out for—and received—a whopping $12,000.

Though salaries vary tremendously, there are some concrete examples of what people have earned in recent years in different broadcasting positions. The information comes from a landmark survey conducted by The American Federation of Television and Radio Artists (AFTRA) in 1999 and released in 2000. It's not a scientific study, and only had a 31 percent response rate among those asked for the information. However, it's one of the best pictures available of salary data, which is *very* difficult to obtain. The data provide a decent barometer by which to measure offers in similar-sized markets and cities. Remember, this doesn't mean you should march into a station and demand the given salaries. Your experience, and whether you have competing offers weigh in heavily on the salary you can command.

Results of the survey are shown in Table 11.1. We begin with a sampling of smaller markets (the 76th largest in the nation through the 225th largest in the nation) and work up to the biggest markets in the country (New York and Los Angeles). Each category lists television anchor and reporter salaries followed by radio anchor and reporter salaries.

Unions

Most television and radio stations and news Web sites in America are not unionized. However, a number of local markets and many of the national networks are. If you're hired at one of them, you'll be required to join a union and pay annual dues determined by the city in which you live and your individual salary.

The union that represents on-air television and radio broadcasters is AFTRA. Here's a description of AFTRA and its services, as provided by AFTRA specifically for this textbook:

> The American Federation of Television and Radio Artists ("AFTRA") is a national labor organization representing approximately 85,000 members, including anchors and reporters at radio and television stations and networks across the country. At stations where employees have chosen AFTRA as their collective bargaining representative, AFTRA negotiates contracts establishing minimum terms and conditions of employment for bargaining unit employees. AFTRA contracts guarantee minimum pay scales, severance pay upon termination of employment, and impartial and binding arbitration for the resolution of disputes related to employment issues. AFTRA agreements allow members to negotiate their own personal services contracts to provide for wages and other terms over and above the floor of the AFTRA agreement. The minimum terms contained in the AFTRA contract provide union members with additional negotiating strength when they negotiate their own agreements.
>
> AFTRA contracts may also provide for participation in the AFTRA Health and Retirement Funds, an employer-paid, comprehensive plan with fully-paid medical, hospital, vision and dental coverage. The AFTRA Funds also provide one of the most generous pension plans in the industry; participation in the pension plan can be maintained by a member through employment at many different AFTRA employers over the course of his or her career.
>
> In addition to negotiating collective bargaining agreements, AFTRA lobbies state legislatures to pass laws banning so-called "non-compete" provisions from the personal services contracts of broadcast employees. AFTRA's legal and other professional staff advise and assist members in negotiating personal services agreements and mediating or arbitrating contract disputes. AFTRA also testifies before Congress and has met with and submitted position statements to the FCC on legal and regulatory issues of interest to broadcasters, including the effects of corporate mergers, broadcast ownership limits and equal employment opportunity guidelines.
>
> Although AFTRA membership is open to any one who wishes to join, most broadcasters do not join AFTRA until they become employed at a station where an

TABLE 11.1 *AFTRA Salary Survey, March 24, 2000*

	Television Salaries		Radio Salaries	
	Anchor	*Reporter*	*Anchor*	*Reporter*
Small Markets 76–225	15.4% < $20,000 38.5% = $20–34,999 23.1% = $35–49,000 7.7% = $50–74,999 15.4% = $75–99,999	71.4% = $20–34,999 28.6% = $35–49,000	No meaningful data available	
Medium Markets 31–75	12.5% = $35–49,999 12.5% = $50–74,999 12.5% = $75–99,999 18.8% = $100–124,999 12.5% = $125–149,999 18.8% = $200–249,999 6.3% = $250–299,999 6.3% = $300–399,999	34.2% = $20–34,999 28.9% = $35–49,999 28.9% = $50–74,999 5.3% = $75–99,999 2.6% = $100–124,999	100% = $20-34,999	100% = $20–49,000
Markets 21–30	10.5% = $50–74,999 36.8% = $75–99,999 10.5% = $100–124,999 5.3% = $125–149,999 5.3% = $150–174,999 15.8% = $175–199,999 10.5% = $200–299,999 5.3% = $300–399,999	4.9% = $20–34,999 17.1% = $35–49,999 63.4% = $50–74,999 7.3% = $75–99,999 7.3% = $100–124,999	40% < $20,000 20% = $20–34,999 20% = $50–74,999 20% = $75–99,999	33.3% < $20,000 33.3% = $35-49,999 33.3% = $50-74,999
Markets 6–20	50% = $100–124,999 50% = $300–399,999	15.8% = $35–49,000 42.1% = $50–74,999 36.8% = $75–99,999 5.3% = $100–124,999	14.3% < $20,000 57.1% = $20–34,999 14.3% = $35–49,999 14.3% = $75–99,999	20% < $20,000 40% = $35–49,999 20% = $50-74,999
Baltimore	25% = $200–249,999 25% = $250–299,999 50% = $300–399,999	23.6% < $34,999 17.6% = $35–49,999 17.6% = $50–74,999 17.6% = $75–99,999 18% = $100–124,999 5.9% = $150–174,999 5.9% = $250–299,999	50% = $35–49,999 50% = $100–124,999	No respondents
Pittsburgh	33.3% < $20,000 33.3% = $200–249,999 33.3% = $250–299,999	18.2% = $35–49,999 45.5% = $50–74,999 27.3% = $75–99,999 9.1% = $125–149,999	50% = $35–49,999 25% = $50–74,000 25% = $75–99,999	50% < $20,000 50% = $50-74,999
St. Louis	16.7% < $20,000 16.7% = $50–74,999 16.7% = $75–99,999 16.7% = $175–199,99 16.7% = $250–299,999 16.7% = $300– 399,999	25% = $20–49,000 62.5% = $50–74,999 12.5% = $75–99,999	25% = $35–49,999 25% = $50–74,999 25% = $100–124,999 25% = $125–149,999	33.3% = $20-34,999 33.3% = $35-49,999 33.3% = $50-74,999

AFTRA Salary Survey, March 24, 2000 (continued)

| | Television Salaries | | Radio Salaries | |
	Anchor	*Reporter*	*Anchor*	*Reporter*
Seattle	66.7% = $75–99,999 33.3% = $250–299,999	3.3% = $35–49,000 56.7% = $50–74,999 36.7% = $75–99,999 3.3% = $100–124,999	25% = $35–49,000 25% = $50–74,999 50% = $75–99,999	14.3% < $20,000 42.9% < $20–34,999 28.6% = $35–49,000 14.3% = $50–74,999
Washington DC	16.7% = $20–34,999 33% = $100–124,999 16.7% = $125–149,999 16.7% = $150–174,999 16.7% = $500–999,999	14.6% = $74,999 26.5% = $75,000–99,000 17.6% = $100–124,999 11.8% = $125–174,999 17.6% = $200–299,999 8.9% = $300–499,999	10% < $34,999 35% = $35–49,000 25% = $50–74,999 15% = $75–99,999 10% = $100–149,999 5% = $150–174,999	10.5% < $20,000 21.1% = $35–49,000 26.3% = $50–74,999 21.1% = $75–99,999 15.8% = $100–124,999 5.3% = $150–174,999
Boston	9.1% < $20,000 18.2% = $150–174,999 27.3% = $175–249,999 36.4% = $250–399,999 9.1% = $400–499,999	10.7% = $20–49,000 28.6% = $50–99,999 25% = $100–124,999 17.9% = $125–174,999 17.8% = $175–249,999	25% = $35–49,000 25% = $50–74,999 25% = $75–99,999 25% = $100–124,999	50% = $35–49,000 50% = $50–74,999
San Francisco	28.6% = $20–49,000 28.6% = $75–99,999 28.6% = $125–174,999 14.3% = $300–399,999	13.5% = $35–74,999 29.7% = $75–99,000 24.3% = $100–149,999 24.3% = $150–174,999 8.1% = $175–249,999	18.2% = $35–49,000 27.3% = $75–99,999 27.3% = $100–149,999 18.2% = $150–199,999 9.1% = $400–499,999	20% = $35–49,000 20% = $50–74,999 60% = $75–99,999
Philadelphia	25% = $100–124,999 25% = $175–199,999 50% = $500–999,99	13.3% = $50–74,999 20% = $75–99,999 20% = $100–124,999 13.3% = $125–149,999 20% = $150–174,999 13.3% = $175–199,999	88.9% = $50–74,999 11.1% = $75–99,999	25% = $35–49,000 75% = $50–74,999
Chicago	12.5% = $100–124,999 12.5% = $300–399,999 75% = $500–999,999	29.6% = $50–99,999 37% = $100–149,999 14.8% = $150–174,999 11.1% = $200–299,999 7.4% = $400–999,999	33.3% = $35–49,000 33.3% = $50–74,999 22.2% = $75–99,999 11.1% = $100–124,999	16.7% = $35–49,000 66.7% = $50–74,999 16.7% = $75–99,999
Los Angeles	6.7% < $20,000 6.7% = $50–74,99 6.7% = $150–174,999 13.3% = $200–249,999 13.3% = $250–399,999 26.7% = $400–499,999 6.7% = $500–999,999 20% = $1 million	8.9% < $34,999 10.7% = $35–74,999 32.2% = $75–124,999 33.9% = $125–174,999 10.7% = $175–249,999 3.6% = $250–399,999	13.4% < $34,999 26.7% = $35–74,999 40% = $75–99,999 20% = $100–124,999	21.4% < $34,999 14.3% = $35–49,000 28.6% = $50–74,999 35.7% = $75–99,999

AFTRA Salary Survey, March 24, 2000 (Continued)

	Television Salaries		Radio Salaries	
	Anchor	*Reporter*	*Anchor*	*Reporter*
New York City	17.7% = $50–99,000 23.5% = $200–249,999 29.4% = $300–399,999 17.6% = $500–999,999 11.8% = $1 million	7.9% < $49,000 24.3% = $50,000–99,999 20% = $100–149,999 21.4% = $150–199,999 18.6% = $200–299,000 2.9% = $300–399,000 4.3% = $500–999,999 1.4% = $1 million	12.2% < $34,999 17.2% = $35–74,999 29.3% = $75–99,999 31.7% = $100–149,999 9.7% = $150–199,999	22.3% < $34,999 33.3% = $35–74,999 33.3% = $75–99,999 11.4% = $100–149,999

AFTRA agreement is in place. More information about AFTRA is available at its Web site, located at www.aftra.com.

Advice from Professionals in the Field

We asked some successful notables in the field what they'd like to tell prospective newcomers about writing or about a career in broadcast Internet journalism. Most of the people we've quoted have backgrounds in local television and radio news, as well as at various networks. Here's their advice, provided exclusively for you, the readers of this textbook!

Lou Waters, former CNN news anchor and correspondent:

What always surprised me most of all [about broadcast writing] was how stiff and stale news stories could be. Most news writers stick to facts and figures without regard for a well-told, interesting story. I've always felt it's ALL about story telling, and that should be the joy of writing: telling a darn good yarn. That most often entails a narrative complete with conflict, drama, mystery, controversy, or debate—articles of intense interest assembled in a conversational, easy-to-follow series of thoughts. Broadcast writing, after all, is for the ear, not the eye.

Lou Waters

News writers often fall into the trap of rewriting newswire copy almost verbatim, with print words such as "slain," "the former," "the latter," and references digested only after rereading the piece. That can't be done in broadcast; you only get one chance. Writing today becomes even more important as more broadcasters, print media, and Internet entities fight for the attention of an ever-shrinking audience. My feeling is attention spans are short. The hook needs to be sunk early. And only the strong will survive.

Arlene Dillon, CBS News "The Early Show" senior producer

Arlene Dillon

Every morning when you wake up, look into the mirror and say to yourself "That was a great eight hours worth of restful sleep." (Do this no matter what time you are getting up and no matter how much sleep you actually did get. Hopefully, your subconscious will believe you are well-rested and ready to face another day.)

Never believe that you are the only person who can do your job (everyone is expendable).

Teach someone else how to do your job so you can either get promoted or go on a very restful vacation when necessary.

NEVER EVER betray a source because what comes around really does go around.

When interacting with your coworkers, use the terms "WE" and "US" as opposed to "I" and "ME."

John Hartge, CBS News Radio reporter

In radio, there are no pictures to show, so you have to help listeners visualize the story. Paint radio pictures with your words, the natural sounds from the scene of the story, and the words of newsmakers and eyewitnesses.

When you're reporting from the scene, describe what you see, what's going on at the moment. If there are sounds in the background, make sure the listener can hear them. Put the listener at the scene with your description and the sounds around you.

Use newsmaker or eyewitness sound bites to tell part of the story. These sound bites are quotes for radio.

Keep your writing simple and direct. Your listeners don't have a chance to rewind our story or ask you questions if they don't understand you the first time. They will only hear you once. Make sure they get it.

Mary Helen Bernknopf, former CNN producer

In broadcast writing, you should always keep it simple and clear. In TV, the best-written stories are written to the pictures. It doesn't matter how great a story if it doesn't go with what the viewer is seeing. It causes confusion, and then the viewer is lost. Obviously, some stories lend themselves to video better than others.

Let the pictures tell the story when possible. Always use natural sound where possible. It enhances a story and breaks up the monotony of audio track.

When writing feature stories or kicker stories, don't give away the story until the end. You want to draw in the viewer or listener first. One of the best at this: radio's Paul Harvey.

Teases do just that: tease. Don't tell the whole story in the tease, only give a hint.

If you are writing for someone else, make sure you know *their* style. Nothing is harder for an anchor or reporter than to read material that is awkward for them.

Know your story. This sounds obvious, but I knew many writers who just wrote from wire copy and never studied the story further. Their writing showed that lack of understanding.

Dick Meyer, CBSNews.com senior producer

If you would like to have your cake and eat it, head for the Web. Producing news on the Internet truly combines the skills—and pleasures—of print and broadcast journalism.

The most valuable skill in an online newsroom is the ability to write clean, clear, and accurate copy under deadline. The words will be read, not heard. Good writing on the Internet is much like good writing in a newspaper or magazine. Since Web sites can publish instantly, the deadline pressure is intense. But the words stay on the screen; they do not disappear into the airwaves. So there is no room for sloppy writing and dirty copy. And unlike television, pictures may accompany a story, but they are separate and they cannot tell the story by themselves. The sentences matter most.

But the Internet is not print. A good online journalist should have a sense of visual elegance like a television producer. A good online story is one that is enhanced by material form other media sources—video, still pictures, documents, interactive productions, and other Web sites. A good on-line piece doesn't just tell a story, it gives the user more tools to explore a story.

For a creative journalist, writing news on the Web gives you the space to tell the full story in writing and to explain the story further with your own mix of video, graphics, documents, and sound. It's a treat.

Kerry Sanders, NBC News correspondent

How did I get my first job? My mother spoke to my uncle in Lima, Peru, and told him I wanted a job in TV news. My mother explained to him that it's difficult to get a job in this business without contacts. He was politically connected, so he, of course, could make things happen. I flew to Peru (where I had lived and attended some of my high school studies). It was 1981. I was impatient, excited, and thrilled that I would soon be working in the TV news business.

A week passed, and I didn't see my uncle or hear from him. Another week passed and not a peep from him. I called my mom, who tracked him down on the family farm in the north. He finally called me and said: "I haven't been down to Lima to help you because the maid tells me your tools have not yet arrived."

"Tools? What tools?" I asked.

He said: "Your tools to repair TVs."

"Repair TVs? What do you mean?"

Kerry Sanders

He told me: "Your mother said it's hard to get a job learning to repair TVs in the U.S., but here I can help you. So when your tools arrive, I'll get you a job."

YIKES! I had traveled this far for nothing.

After finding out this devastating news, I coped with a few Pisco Sours (local powerful drink) and headed down to the U.S. Embassy and explained my problem. Here to work, and no job. As luck would have it, there was a radio station that needed someone to prepare a newscast in English for the local British and U.S. audience. I took the job and began my first professional gig in the news business.

Peter Maer, CBS News Radio correspondent

Radio writers and reporters must know how to write and broadcast accurately, concisely, quickly and at times, under extreme deadline pressure. Deadlines are constant in local and network radio. There is very little margin for error and often no luxury of time. It is important to know how to write in the *active* present tense while not overusing it. The style lends immediacy to radio news.

Good radio news people know how to weave in the element of sound, just as television news people write to the picture. A former boss once told me, "turn your microphone into a camera." Of course that means turning your eyes and voice into a camera. Radio reports with the sound of a storm, a cheering crowd, music, etc. are so much better than a staid report inside a studio. The goal is to make the audience visualize the scene.

On the job front: Unfortunately, deregulation has led many smaller stations to abolish local radio news departments. There are fewer places for aspiring radio reporters to *learn on the job* in small and medium market settings. I advise young journalists interested in radio to do what we have always done. Knock on doors. Be willing to sweep the floor, answer phones, print copy, and other menial chores. That's how I won my first radio job while in high school. Practice writing and recording. Try to find a mentor to critique your work.

Catherine Harwood, former reporter at KHOU-TV, local news director

As for getting a job, your cover letter is the first sample of your writing that a manager sees, so never start it with the boilerplate line: "I'm writing to apply for the reporter's job advertised in blah, blah magazine." That tells me as a news director that you can't think of a creative way to grab your audience's attention. Also, make sure this short, concise letter tells what you will do for the station. You wouldn't believe how many letters are all about what the applicant wants from the station, not what he can do for the station, and, of course, include your phone number and email on every piece of correspondence and your tape. It's surprising how often applicants fail to include contact information.

When I hired reporters, I wanted great writers. Good reporting starts with good writing. If you can organize your thoughts into clear sentences, paragraphs, and ultimately stories, then you know how to ask the questions and track down the interviews you need to write a memorable, easy-to-follow story. I remember I once was very close to hiring a seasoned producer from one of the large cable news organizations for a position as a local news producer. She seemed overly concerned about the amount of writing involved, so I suggested a writing test. She failed the test and failed to get the job.

When writing, factor in the best video you have, and your story can almost write itself. For example, crime stories are often written with a reverse chronology because you have video showing the crime scene—the end of the crime spree. You start with that and work back from there to tell the story. A boring county commission meeting can come to life if you show video of the problem, then write toward the proposed solution, downplaying the less-than-exciting videotape of the commission meeting.

Troy Roberts, 48 Hours correspondent

Troy Roberts

When writing for a network news magazine show think about the structure and pacing of feature magazine articles or a good short film. Our stories are largely character driven and our job is to make the viewer want to invest time in getting to know them and their stories. A great character can practically write the story for you. We're not too concerned about presenting all the facts of the story in a cluster high up in the piece. Rather we want to reveal the facts naturally. Let the story evolve. Because of the length of our pieces we have the luxury of being more descriptive in our writing, adding texture and nuance to the pieces than a one-and-a-half minute long evening news story. And because our stories can sometimes run eight minutes or sixteen minutes in length (for two-parts), pacing and rhythm are even more critical. Finally, don't be boring and don't lose sight of the central theme to the piece.

Eric Engberg, former CBS News correspondent

The ear is a decidedly second-rate instrument for word processing. When it comes to communicating information to the brain in a meaningful way, the eye has the brain beat in every respect. A person reading a news story on paper chooses his own pace of digesting the material and has the option of pausing to RE-READ a phrase repeatedly until it makes sense to him. Visual cues like paragraph indentions, commas, and periods help move the reader along.

When you write for broadcast, you don't have those tools. If you put the classic Who-What-Where-When-Why-How of newspaper style into the lead, you will drown your listener. Dole it out in digestible portions.

So the first rule of writing for broadcast is short, simple sentences. I had an excellent writing teacher many years ago who used to repeatedly intone, "One idea to a sentence." Anytime I'm in a writing jam now, I mentally revisit that advice. It almost always helps get me through the maze. "One idea to a sentence."

David Bernknopf, former CNN vice president and senior producer

Right now in the world of journalism, it's vital to build up multiple skills. The more any journalist knows about writing (*all* styles: print, wire, and broadcast; video shooting, video editing, and sound teching), the more marketable they are.

This is a new era for journalists. Newspaper and magazine writers routinely appear on television. Broadcast journalists are now often handed small digital cameras and told to shoot their own video. In some cases, they may need to act as a sound technician for their camera person. With editing done on laptops, television reporters and producers ought to become familiar, if not expert, in the use of laptop computer editors.

Never before has it been so important to be multiskilled in a marketplace that demands multitasking.

Roxanne Russell, CBS Evening News senior producer

When I think about broadcast writing, I think about how different are the challenges of writing to pictures, compared to sitting down with pen and paper. No matter how important the information, no matter how scintillating the information, a television reporter has to have images with which to *convey* the information. A television news reporter can't go into huge detail about something that is impossible to visualize—truly a challenge to reporters, and one of the many reasons television is faulted for so-called "superficial" coverage of complex ideas.

Roxanne Russell

What television makes *up* for, of course, is bringing the story directly into the homes of the viewers in a way writing seldom can. Print writers can describe the impact of a hurricane or natural disaster; television lets viewers share what the victims of the disaster are experiencing.

Job Resources

- *Broadcasting and Cable Yearbook* (REF TK 6540 B852): One comprehensive listing of radio and television stations is the *Broadcasting and Cable Yearbook*. It's updated annually, and, although it costs several hundred dollars to buy, you can find it at many libraries. It even lists names of news directors at each station. However, be aware that the position of news director changes frequently. Before addressing a resume to a news director listed in the book, you should confirm the name of the news director by making a telephone call.
- *Television and Cable Factbook* (REF TK 6540 T463): Arranged geographically.
- *TV and Radio Directory* (REF Z6951 W6 v.3): Broken down by DMA.
- *Editor and Publisher Media Links* (REF PN 4700 E42)
- *Gale Database of Publications and Broadcast Media* (REF Z 6951 A97): Three-volume set.
- *Working Press of the Nation:* TV and radio directory, arranged geographically. Lists stations by Arbitron Metro Market and DMA.

Job Resources on the Web

- *ajr.newslink.org/joblink.html*   Job link for journalists
- *www.hooked.net/~cosmo/jjobs.htm*   Insite's journalism jobs pages
- *poynter.org/index.cfm*   The Poynter Institute for Media Studies
- *www.nab.org*   National Association of Broadcasters:
- *www.ithaca.edu/library/bibio/mediasc.html*   Ithica College Library media sources for print, radio, television, and cable markets
- *emedia1.mediainfo.com/emedia/*   Editor and publisher media links: Search for media links around the world
- *www.tvinsite.com/broadcastingcable/index.asp?layout=webzine*   Tv Insite broadcasting and cable
- *tv.zap2it.com/resources/stations/*   Zap2It
- *www.internetnewsbureau.com/journalist/*   InternetNewsBureau
- *writetools.com*   Write Tools, a compilation of Web-based references for professional writers and editors
- *www.writenews.com*   The Write News, resources for media and publishing professionals and also job listings including jobs openings in Internet writing
- *www.Journalismjobs.com*   Journalism Jobs, job board for media professionals

Summary

This chapter has outlined ideas for ways to get experience before obtaining a first paid job in broadcast or Internet journalism. It also provided pointers on how to go about the business of job hunting, listed specific print and Internet resources, and included descriptions and salary-range information for various jobs. Students who use their ingenuity will be able to graduate from college with some experience, and perhaps even a resume tape, that will make their job-hunting prospects brighter. They can use previously mentioned resources to guide them in their job search, and to help them know what salary range they might expect.

Appendix A

Broadcast News Style Guide

Numbers and Money

    a. *Spell out the numbers "one" through "eleven."*

    b. *Translate other numbers and amounts into digits and words.* You would never write "$12,000,000.00" because it would require the anchor to stop, count zeroes, and hunt for the decimal point. Instead, it's "12-million dollars."

    c. *Avoid dollar and cents signs and decimal points.* In the newspaper version of the turtle egg story in Chapter 2, "$1.5 million" was used. But for broadcasting, it's either "one-point-five-million dollars" or, more simply, "one-and-a-half million dollars."

    d. *Round out complex numbers* so that they take less time to say and are easier for the audience to absorb as they go by in a flash. A report on "a $7,998,457.02 budget" would be written as "a seven-point-nine million dollar budget" or "a budget of almost eight million dollars."

    e. *For dates prior to the twenty-first century or far in the future, hyphenate the year.* For example, "1937" would be "19-37." This reduces the risk that 1937 could be read as "one thousand nine hundred and thirty-seven." The year "2027" should be written as "20-27."

    f. *More contemporary year dates are usually understood in their normal form.* For example, the year "2003" need *not* be written as "two thousand three" or "20-oh-three."

Punctuation

    a. *Avoid colons, semicolons, and quotation marks;* they can be difficult for the anchor to read.

b. *Use three dots (...) or a dash (--) to indicate where the anchor should pause.*

c. *Use hyphens to indicate words or letters that are connected* and should be read without pausing.

d. *Use hyphens to separate "non-anti-co-semi" prefixes,* for example, non-factor, anti-war demonstrations, co-worker, semi-conscious. This is the **non-anti-co-semi rule.**

e. *Do not use hyphens to divide a word* at the end of a line and continue it on the next. In broadcasting, words are *never* divided between line-to-line; if there's not enough room for the whole word, move it to the next line.

Abbreviations

a. *Don't abbreviate unless you want the word, phrase, or name read in abbreviated form.* If the anchor is to say "American Telephone and Telegraph," then don't write "A-T-and-T."

b. *Only use abbreviations that are widely known to the audience.* Examples include N-F-L, A-M, P-M, U-S, G-O-P, F-B-I, C-I-A, P-S, F-D-A, and P-O-BOX. Assume most abbreviations are not widely known, such as A-B-A (American Bar Association) and SCOTUS (Supreme Court of the United States).

c. *Abbreviations that are not widely known may be used in second references,* for example, "The treasurer of the Area River Rescue Fund has been charged with embezzling money from the charity . . . the A-R-R-F was founded in 19-84."

Contractions

Use contractions when they would be used in ordinary speech. Your goal is conversational writing, so "The Mayor says *he's* pleased with the clean-up," sounds better than "The Mayor says *he is* pleased with the clean-up."

Direct Quotes

a. *Use actual interviews rather than direct quotes.* Notice that, in the turtle egg example in Chapter 2, the broadcast version did not use a written quote from the Key West worker; instead, it included videotape of an actual interview with the worker. The selected piece of an interview is called a "sound bite" in television and an "actuality" in radio and is preferred over written quotes.

b. *Use direct quotes occasionally for impact.* Direct quotes *can* be used when they're pointed or dramatic and when no better sound bite or actuality is available. An example is "When the jury announced the guilty verdict . . . the suspect shouted—quote—you'll die for this!"

c. *Consider paraphrasing.* Instead of using a direct quote, consider paraphrasing it in concise, clear language. For example, instead of "The mother-to-be said—quote—I will never be able to find a way to possibly tell the police officer how much I truly appreciate the things that he did and thank him for helping me so much," you could write "The mother-to-be said she doesn't know how to thank the police officer who helped her."

Names and Titles

a. *Only use names in the lead sentence of a story when they're widely known* by the audience. Examples of names likely to be widely known are prominent community activists, the mayor, a governor, or a celebrity. Keep in mind that names that are familiar to you may be unfamiliar to your audience. Someone who is very well known in one town may be an unknown in the next.

b. *Always give a title or context when using lesser-known names.*

c. *Use no name at all if it's not important to the story.*

d. *Generally, do not use Mr., Mrs., or Miss* when mentioning names in stories. Leaders of nations are exceptions. They *always* get a "Mr. or Mrs." in front of their last names when their leadership titles aren't used. For example, "President Bush" can be called "Mr. Bush," but is never simply "Bush."

e. *Use the title "doctor" when mentioning someone who has a medical degree.* A person with a doctorate (Ph.D.) is *not* called "doctor," but may be referred to as "professor."

f. *Use appropriate titles for clergy.* Roman Catholic Clergy should be referred to as "The Reverend" and in each subsequent reference as "Father." For Jewish members of the clergy, the title is "Rabbi." Protestant members of the clergy are called "The Reverend."

g. *Generally, refer to adults by last name only on second references.* Soft news features can be exceptions; they may refer to adults by first name only. Clergy and national leaders should have a title before their last name on second reference.

h. *Generally, refer to children by first name only on second references.*

i. *Generally do not use middle initials, names, and Jr. or Sr.* unless you're trying to distinguish a common name. For example, when William Kennedy Smith was tried (and acquitted) on sexual assault charges in the early 1990s, reporters always used his middle name. Doing so distinguished him from the thousands of other William Smiths and served to remind the audience that he's related to the famous Kennedy family, which is why the case received national attention. It's also acceptable to use a middle name, initial, or Jr. or Sr. if it's an integral part of the name. Examples are former FBI Director J. Edgar Hoover, President John F. Kennedy, and John F. Kennedy, Jr.

Age

a. *Avoid using a person's age unless it's relevant, satisfies curiosity, or distinguishes.* For example, age would be "relevant" in a story about a lady beating up a robber if the lady is 85 years old and the robber is 30. Giving the age of a young child who managed to call 9-1-1 when his house caught fire would "satisfy the curiosity" of audience members who wonder *how* young he is. Giving a person's age can also serve to "distinguish" between people with common names.

b. *When using age, make it conversational.* Years ago, the rule was always to put age before a person's name, as in "The victim was identified as 28-year old Heather Murphy." However, there's a new trend, particularly at news networks. It's more conversational to say "The victim was identified as Heather Murphy, who was 28 years old." You can also choose to work the age into the story another way, such as "Jane Roxford refused to open the door. At age 67. . . she'd learned to be suspicious when strangers approached after dark."

Pronouncers

a. Use **pronouncers** for words written in television or radio news stories that may be mispronounced. Pronouncers are phonetic spellings broken down into syllables, telling an anchor or reporter reading the script aloud how to pronounce the word(s). Here's a pronouncer for Loxahatchee: (lox-uh-HATCH'-ee).

b. Enclose pronouncers with parentheses.

c. Separate syllables in a pronouncer with dashes.

d. Indicate which syllable of the pronouncer has the accent by capitalizing that syllable only and/or putting an apostrophe after it.

e. Radio pronouncers should be written next to the word itself.

f. Where television pronouncers are placed depends on the preference of the anchor or reporter who will be reading the story aloud. They can appear next to the word *or* on the left-hand side of the script.

Appendix B

Internet News Style Guide

Overall

Make sure your headline, photo, and short story work together clearly. If there's a mug shot [photograph of a person], be sure the subject is identified in the headline or short story.

Short Story Tease on Index (Primary) Page

These should be short, ideally about twenty-five words.

Teases

In general, try to keep a consistent tense within a story.

   a. *In features,* use the present tense for attributions (that is, he says, she notes, he adds). A feature story can be written with "said" in past tense if the action requires.
   b. *In news stories,* use the past tense (that is, he said, he noted, he added).

Story Length

News stories should be about 500 words. Features can be longer.

Translating Broadcast Scripts

   a. Often key information in the broadcast version is reported by use of the videotape or in the fonts or chyrons. When translating a broadcast story for the Web, watch the video to make sure you're not missing crucial information. Add any such information to the Web version.

b. Try to avoid using language such as "Madonna appears on *The Early Show*," which sounds too much like a broadcast script. It's better to say something such as "Madonna shares her parenting advice with *The Early Show*."

Punctuation

a. *Do not use the serial comma.* That means there is no comma before the "and" in the following: "I am having ice cream, cake and frozen yogurt on my birthday."

b. *Write in complete sentences as much as possible.*

c. *Punctuate run-on sentences within quotes.*

d. *Put periods after complete sentences in captions, but no period if it's a fragment.*

e. *Italicize a comma or a period if it's next to an italicized word.*

Quotes

a. *Inside articles, quoted matter should not be altered.* Words within the quote marks should remain exactly how the speaker said it, except for dialects, such as use of "gonna" and "gotta," which should always be "cleaned up" to "going to" and "got to." Other questions of dialect inside quotes should be handled on a case-by-case basis.

b. *The producer of a piece should replay any video attached to be sure that the corresponding quotes match the sound bites in the video.* Close captioning and scripts are **not** reliable sources.

c. *There's no need to capitalize the first letter of the job description of a person quoted* (i.e., coal miner Joe Jones) unless that title is usually capitalized (i.e., President Bush).

d. *Use bold face for all quotes.*

Word Usage

a. *Acronyms:* If an acronym is four or more letters, capitalize the first letter and lower case the rest.

b. *Names:* Children under age 18 should be referred to by their first names on second reference. Adults should be called by their last names on second reference. The only exception is for celebrities known by one name only (i.e., Madonna or Cher). When there's more than one family member in a story, use first and last names for *both* people on second reference to avoid confusion. Better yet, "write around it" when possible to avoid the scenario in the first place.

c. *Black Americans are to be referred to as "blacks."* African American is acceptable on second reference. Please note, however, there can be a difference between "blacks" and "African Americans"; not all blacks are African Americans.

Dates

a. *Always use the day of the week,* not "today" or "yesterday."
b. *The style for writing a date is* (note the comma afterward): "Nov. 5, 1999," or "Nov. 1997."
c. *Spell out the month when used alone.*

Time

Spell "a.m." and "p.m." in lower case letters with periods. Use "ET/PT" when referring to the times of a broadcast. Avoid a time reference in the short story.

Dateline

Spell out the city and then use a comma and the name of the state all spelled out.

Web-Specific Terms

- Online: one word, no hyphen
- Offline: one word, no hyphen
- Email: one word, no hyphen
- Logon: one word as an adjective
- Home page: two words
- Voice mail: two words
- Web site: two words
- 'Net is the appropriate way to abbreviate the "Internet." Both 'Net and Internet are capitalized.

Headlines and Subheadlines (Subheads)

a. Capitalize the first letter of headlines at the top of the story and subheads at the top. If a headline appears within the story's text, such as for a book title, capitalize only the initials of major words, but not article or prepositions less than four letters.
b. Typical headline style involves a subject and verb combination. It's more powerful if the headline and the subheads all work together as one unit. The main headline should have a subject and a verb, and the subheads should play off of that. Either the subheads should include another subject with a verb or should assume the same subject, but carry a different verb.
c. Headlines can also be label style, just describing a "thing" with no verb. Often, these are playful.

Captions

a. Captions should accompany all photos.

b. No caption is needed for illustrations or graphics.

c. A short sentence (one, two, or three lines) gets a period. Sentence fragments get no period at the end. Avoid using words such as "file photo" or indicating from which broadcast a snapshot was pulled unless this somehow figures into the news.

d. If you're stuck, experiment with this style: "Jim Jones: hard at work."

Links

a. *Do not link to a Web site at every proper name in the story,* only when it's relevant and useful for the reader.

b. *Do not link to any competitor's news site.*

c. *Be wary of linking to advocacy or partisan political sites.* Be sure they're relevant to the context of your story. Find an additional site with another viewpoint.

d. *When adding a link, use your discretion if it should appear on the first reference* (remember that may drive the reader away from your story to another Web site) or as a note at the bottom of the story. (For example, For more information on parents who skydive, read "Those Who Dared.")

e. *If you have a lot of suggestions at the bottom of the story for related stories and sites, use a horizontal line to set them off* or a box to highlight selections.

f. *If mentioning another Web site, it's ideal to give the name and the URL if they are different.* Write the URL in all lower case type.

Glossary

Active wording: Preferred wording (as opposed to *passive*) that has a subject acting upon, rather than being acted upon. For example, *The pitcher caught the ball* is active. *The ball was caught by the pitcher* is passive.

Actuality: In radio, a bit of audio from an interview, segment of a speech, or other "sound."

Ad-libbing: The practice of an anchor or reporter delivering news extemporaneously without reading from a script. Often employed in live situations.

Advancing the story: The practice of adding new, unique elements; moving it further along by reporting the next step in the process; providing a more updated version of the story or focusing on a related angle.

Archive video (also called *file video*):   In television, videotape shot for a past story, but kept on file for possible use in other stories.

Attribution: The practice of telling the source when including controversial or disputed information or opinions in a story. Also used to add credibility to information in a story.

B-roll: Videotaped pictures that go along with a television news story. Also called *cover video*.

Beat: An area of interest.

Beat calls (also called *beat checks*):   Regular contacts with area law enforcement and rescue agencies to find out if any news is happening.

Boomerang lead: A lead that throws basic information to the story and then repeats and expands on it in the body of the script.

Breaking lead: A lead used in breaking news stories that are still developing, even as they're being written.

Broadcast news diffusion: The concept of broadcast and Internet news traveling from one person to another by means other than the originating medium.

Camel squeezing: Condensing an extraordinary number of details into a short, crisp broadcast style script that's easy to listen to by omitting or condensing unnecessary repetition, wording, and details.

Cause and effect or **completed circle:**   The concept of including in a story *how and why* an event happened, as well as the impact or result.

Completed circle: See "Cause and effect."

Cover video: See "B-roll."

Day Rule: The theory that knowledge in three basic areas—context, philosophical foundation, and critical thinking—can equip people to carry out moral reasoning.

Defamation: Intentionally reporting something false and harmful about an ordinary person. Truth is always an absolute defense in defamation cases.

Enterprising a story: Refers to finding something original to report; a story not simply done from a press conference or a news release.

Feed: See "News feed."

Field elements: Components of a story gathered in the field, including bites and standups.

File video: See "Archive video."

Font (also called Chyron):   In television, on-screen words indicating the location where video was shot or a sound bite's name and title/organization.

Futures file: A comprehensive file or calendar of future events that may warrant news coverage.

Graphics: In television or on the Internet, a wide range of visual images other than videotape, including a graph, chart, list, still photograph, or other visual image. Among other things, graphics can reflect facts, figures, poll results, numbers, a page of a document with certain words highlighted, or written quotes. Writers can determine the content of graphics, and then a graphic artist typically designs them and builds them into the story.

Incue: In television or radio, the first few words of a sound bite, designated by "IN."

Internet: The international network of computer systems.

Invasion of privacy: Publicizing private affairs that are of no legitimate public concern resulting in suffering, shame, or humiliation.

L2W: The recommended practice of Localizing a news story for a particular audience and including Where and What in the lead sentence.

Lead: The first sentence in a broadcast or Internet news story.

Lead-in: The anchor's introduction to a reporter's live shot or prerecorded package.

Libel: The form of defamation that traditionally applies to print, but also may apply to broadcast material.

Line timing: The process of determining the length of a script by counting approximately four seconds per line of script.

Linking lead: A lead that connects two stories in a newscast or provides a transition to make one story flow smoothly and logically to the next.

Live: Not prerecorded; taking place in real time.

Live shot: A reporter's on-location report; *not* prerecorded.

Logging: See "Transcribing."

Long-form stories: A broad range of news stories and features, such as those lasting more than two minutes on television or radio; investigative and expanded reports on the Internet.

Media bias: The concept that journalists unfairly shape coverage to advance their own particular viewpoints.

Milieu Factor: The way in which your environment or surroundings can help you capture the essence of an event you're reporting.

Narration: The sentences in a package script that the reporter reads aloud; also referred to as *track*.

Natural sound (sometimes abbreviated as **"Natsound"** or **"Nats"**):   In radio or television, the naturally occurring sound on a given story that can be heard softly underneath the anchor or reporter's voice *or* can be "brought up full" for several seconds without the anchor or reporter's voice being heard.

News feed: In television and radio, the distribution of news material via satellite from a network to its affiliate subscribers.

News releases: Information provided to reporters by groups or organizations attempting to shed the most positive light on their group, organization, or issue.

News value: The importance and relevance assigned to a particular story. Influenced by factors such as proximity, timeliness, significance, and the medium.

Non-anti-co-semi rule: A broadcast style rule stating that words beginning with the prefixes "non," "anti," "co," or "semi" should be hyphenated.

One-on-ones: Interviews conducted by you, alone, rather than by a group of reporters in a news conference setting.

Online: The term used to indicate you're actively reading, surfing, or otherwise using the Internet.

Outcue: The last few words of an actuality or wrap or sound bite, designated by "OUT."

Package: In television, reporter's prerecorded story.

Payola: The unethical practice of taking anything of value from people who want to influence what's being reported.

Plagiarism: The unethical act of copying someone else's writings or ideas and passing them off as your own work.

Printcast: The style of writing on the Internet; a combination of print and broadcast writing with some original elements.

P.R.O.B.E.:   Five principles for conducting effective interviews: Prepare, Relax, Opportunity, Boldness, Example.

Pronouncers: Phonetic spellings of words broken down into syllables, instructing an anchor or reporter reading the script aloud how to pronounce the word(s).

Public figure: Anyone who is famous, infamous, or has assumed roles of special prominence because of who they are or what they've done.

Reader: Anchor copy with no video.

Run time: Total length of a sound bite, designated by "RUNS."

Rundown: The entire newscast organized and timed on paper.

Script signals: The road signs of radio and television scripts that tell what's ahead, including the outcue and time or length/duration of an actuality or wrap.

Sense of suspense: A writing technique that's best used in features to create and maintain a level of viewer interest throughout the story.

Short-form stories: A broad range of news stories and features typically found in daily news reports. They generally range in length from twenty seconds (:20) to several minutes.

Sit-down interviews: Formal interviews (even if they're not actually "seated") that are arranged, or set up, in advance.

Slander: The form of defamation that traditionally applies to spoken word, including broadcast reports.

Softy lead: A lead appropriate for feature (soft news) stories.

Sound bite or **SOT:**   A selected piece of an interview with a person

Source: A provider of information.

Sourcery: The practice of obtaining information from various reliable sources.

Standard outcue: A reporter's last few words in a taped or live wrap; usually includes the reporter's name, location (city), and the radio station's call letters (identity).

Standup: The part of a package in which the reporter appears on camera in the field.

Surprise endings: A writing technique best used in feature writing that withholds some key facts until the end of the story.

Transcribing: The process of listening to recordings of interviews and typing up what was said word for word. The resulting transcriptions or logs should include a time code (a running code displayed on the viewing machine) and the length of potential sound bites. Some people also call this process **logging.**

Screening: In television, the process of watching available b-roll (cover video) before writing a story to determine exactly what pictures can be used. When screening, it's helpful to make a log marking useful natural sound and interesting shots.

Umbrella lead: A form of linking lead that introduces the first of several related stories.

Vaughan-Attkisson Model of Broadcast News Diffusion: A diagram illustrating how pure information is filtered and shaped before it is received and diffused by listeners and viewers.

VO-SOT or **VO-BITE:**   Television anchor copy with video and a sound bite.

Wire services: Companies that provide a continuous stream of news and information to subscribing newsrooms.

Word fat: Unnecessary jargon or needlessly lengthy words and phrases. Concise wording is preferred.

World Wide Web: The user-friendly part of the Internet where people spend most of their time.

Wrap: In radio an entire self-contained story that's introduced by the anchor and prerecorded or delivered live by a reporter; may contain actualities.

Writing to graphics: In television or Internet writing, effectively using visual images other than videotape, such as charts and graphs, to reflect ideas such as facts and figures.

Writing to natural sound: The concept of integrating into a radio or television story various natural sound full breaks.

Writing to video: The television news concept of having an idea for videotape that can be used to go along with every sentence in a story.

Index